Constantin von der Groeben

Transnational Conflicts and International Law

AF138695

Kölner Schriften zum Friedenssicherungsrecht
Cologne Studies on International Peace and Security Law
Études colognaises sur le droit de la paix et de la sécurité internationales

Herausgegeben von/Edited by/Éditées par
Claus Kreß

Band/Volume 3

Constantin von der Groeben

Transnational Conflicts and International Law

INSTITUTE FOR
INTERNATIONAL PEACE
AND SECURITY LAW

Diese Arbeit wurde von der Rechtswissenschaftlichen Fakultät der
Universität zu Köln im Jahre 2013 als Dissertation angenommen.
Referent: Prof. Dr. Claus Kreß LL.M. (Cambridge)
Korreferent: Prof. Dr. Kempen
Tag der mündlichen Prüfung: 17.12.2013

Bibliografische Information der Deutschen Nationalbibliothek

Die Deutsche Nationalbibliothek verzeichnet diese Publikation in der Deutschen Nationalbibliografie; detaillierte bibliografische Daten sind im Internet über http://dnb.dnb.de abrufbar.

Bibliographic information published by the Deutsche Nationalbibliothek

The Deutsche Nationalbibliothek lists this publication in the Deutsche Nationalbibliografie; detailed
bibliographic data are available in the Internet at http://dnb.dnb.de.

Information bibliographique de la Deutsche Nationalbibliothek

La Deutsche Nationalbibliothek a répertorié cette publication dans la Deutsche
Nationalbibliografie; les données bibliographiques détaillées peuvent être consultées
sur Internet à l'adresse http://dnb.dnb.de.

ISSN: 2195-5719 · ISBN: 978-3-7357-5925-2 (Hardcover), 978-3-7357-5926-9 (Paperback)
Alle Rechte vorbehalten.

© 2014 Institute for International Peace and Security Law, Universität zu Köln,
Albertus-Magnus-Platz, D-50923 Köln; Internet: http://www.iipsl-cologne.com.

Herstellung durch BoD – Books on Demand, Norderstedt.

Gedruckt auf säurefreiem Papier.

To my parents, my brother and my sister in deep love and gratitude

Preface

This book is based on my PhD dissertation written at the University of Cologne and generously sponsored by the German Academic Foundation (Studienstiftung des deutschen Volkes).

First and foremost, I would like to thank Professor Claus Kreß. I could not have asked for a better supervisor. Whether in Cologne at his institute or during my studies and research in New York or Bogotá, I consistently relied on his support, feedback and advice. This work would have not been possible without his guidance. I would also like to thank Professor Bernhard Kempen for his time and thoughts as my second reviewer.

Many other individuals greatly contributed to both, my research and writing process. I am extremely grateful to my professors at NYU Law School, especially Ryan Goodman, Eyal Benvenisti and Tom Gerety for their thorough advice and comments. Next, I would like to sincerely thank Franco Ferrari for introducing and discussing my work at NYU's Academic Careers Program. I would also like to thank David Kretzmer and Georg Nolte for brainstorming and discussing and molding my work.

A special thank you goes to my support outside the world of academia. I would have not ventured into writing a Ph.D. without the encouragement and support of both, Azadeh Sharifi and Robert Kilian. I am deeply grateful to both of them for convincing and supporting me in this challenge which has brought me so much joy and intellectual stimulation. While at NYU I also relied on the support of many friends, among them Rahela Khorakiwala and Filippo Fontanelli. I owe thanks to my friend Carlos Arevalo in particular for inviting me to Bogotá and expanding my horizons to another country as well as a different perspective on transnational conflicts. This was truly a wonderful experience.

My deepest thanks go to my family. My parents, my brother and my sister have been an immense support and source of encouragement throughout.

Finally, I wish to thank Shireen Saxena, who helped me carry the work across the finish line. She was the best proofreader I could have asked for and by now likely knows my work better than myself. She is an incredible source of wisdom, inspiration and encouragement.

Berlin, July 2014

Constantin von der Groeben

Contents (Summary)

Contents

List of Abbreviations

ACHR	American Convention on Human Rights
AP I	Protocol Additional to the Geneva Conventions of 12 August 1949, and relating to the Protection of Victims of International Armed Conflicts (Protocol I), 8 June 1977
AP II	Protocol Additional to the Geneva Conventions of 12 August 1949, and relating to the Protection of Victims of Non-International Armed Conflicts (Protocol II), 8 June 1977
CIL	Customary International Law
ECHR	European Convention on Human Rights
FARC	Fuerzas Aramadas Revolucionarias de Colombia (Revolutionary Armed Forces of Colombia)
GC	Geneva Conventions
IAC	International Armed Conflict
ICCPR	International Covenant on Civil and Political Rights
ICESCR	International Covenant on Economic, Social and Cultural Rights
ICJ	International Court of Justice
ICRC	International Committee of the Red Cross
ICTR	International Criminal Tribunal for Rwanda
ICTY	International Criminal Tribunal for the former Yugoslavia
IHL	International Humanitarian Law
IHRL	International Human Rights Law
IRA	Irish Republican Army
NIAC	Non-International Armed Conflict
PKK	Partiya Karkeren Kurdistan (Kurdish Workers' Party)
PoW	Prisoner of War
RoE	Rules of Engagement
UN	United Nations

A. Introduction

"We must define the nature and scope of this struggle, or else it will define us."[1]

I. Background

In today's post-September 11th world, the relevance and importance of state struggles with violent non-state armed groups is ever increasing, as these multi-faceted conflicts permeate throughout the globe. The United States continues to fight members of Al Qaeda and several other terrorist groups, not only within the U.S., but also in foreign countries such as Yemen, Somalia, Afghanistan, Pakistan and Iraq.[2] Today, conflicts between states and non-state armed groups, in particular, are of significant international importance; this includes the Colombian operation against a FARC base in Ecuador,[3] Israel's fight against Hezbollah in Lebanon[4] or Hamas in Gaza,[5] and Turkish operations against the PKK in northern Iraq.[6] Even within Europe conflicts between states and non-state armed groups still take place as can be witnessed in Eastern Ukraine.[7] Furthermore, an international marine force remains actively engaged in an in-

---

[1] Barack Obama, *Remarks by the President at the National Defense University*, May 23, 2013, online available at http://www.whitehouse.gov/the-press-office/2013/05/23/remarks-president-national-defense-university (last visited May 24, 2013).

[2] *See, e.g.*, Walter Pincus, *U.S. Strike Kills Six in Al Qaeda*, Washington Post, Nov. 5, 2002, at A01; Erik Eckholm and David Johnston, *Qaeda Suspect, Sound Asleep at Trail's End, offers no Resistance*, N.Y. Times, Mar. 3, 2003; *Uzbek rebel "killed" in Pakistan*, BBC News, Oct. 2, 2009; *"Drone Attack" kills Taliban Wife*, BBC News, Aug. 5, 2009; *US bombs Islamist town in Somalia*, BBC News, Mar. 3, 2008; Jeffrey Gettleman and Eric Schmitt, *U.S. Kills Top Qaeda Militant in Southern Somalia*, N.Y. Times, Sep. 14, 2009.

[3] Jeremy McDermott, *FARC Aura of Invincibility Shattered*, BBC News, Mar. 1, 2008, http://news.bbc.co.uk/2/hi/americas/7273320.stm (last visited Jan. 21, 2011).

[4] For a good account of the conflict between Israel and Hezbollah in 2006 *see* Noam Lubell, *Extraterritorial Use of Force against Non-State Actors*, 250 *et seq.* (2010).

[5] Jodi Rudoren and Anne Barnard, *Israeli Military Invades Gaza*, N.Y. Times, July 17, 2014.

[6] Paul de Bendern, *Turkey Launches Major Land Offensive into N. Iraq*, Reuters, Feb. 22, 2008, http://uk.reuters.com/article/idUKL22614485._CH_.242020080222 (last visited Jan. 21, 2011); Peter Hilpold, *Die Kurden zwischen Irak und der Türkei*, in Krisenherde im Fokus des Völkerrechts, 73-97 (Thomas Giegerich and Alexander Proelß eds. 2010).

[7] The Ukraine Crisis Reaches a New Level, N.Y. Times, July 1, 2014.

creasing struggle with piracy in the Horn of Africa.[8] However, despite the afo-rementioned struggles, the 2001 terrorist attacks on New York City's World Trade Center remain of utmost importance. The terrorist attack served as the primary catalyst for the restructuring of world-views on conflicts between states and non-state armed groups.[9] In the past, conflicts generally occurred within a particular state, whereas modern conflicts now transcend individual nations' political systems and geographic borders.[10] The global nature of such conflicts is a cause for concern within the international community; it raises the question as to how international law addresses such global conflicts. Rules of international law that are applicable to such state border-transcending conflicts remain a debated issue. This book aims to contribute to the debate from an International Humanitarian Law and International Human Rights Law perspective.

II. Transnational Conflicts

In the following section, conflicts between states and non-state armed groups will be defined and categorized as transnational conflicts. The term transnational conflict has been used to reference conflicts that occur across state-borders, as opposed to conflicts between states.[11] The term *transnational* highlights that a conflict, although having occurred between a state and a non-state (i.e. private) actor, does not limit itself to the national arena, but rather occurs on the territory of two or more states. Thus, this book defines the term *transnational conflict* as any incidents of violence that, (1) is carried out between a state (henceforth: conflict state) and a non-state armed group that does not act on behalf of a state, and (2) that occurs across national borders and, as a result, affects another state (henceforth: territorial state).

According to the aforementioned definition, transnational conflicts encompass conflicts with various non-state armed groups. In fact, non-state armed groups differ in regard to their organization, their openness to violence and their political and religious agendas. While this book aims to present a broad perspective

---

[8] Sharon Otterman and Mark McDonald, *11 Pirates Seized by French Navy*, N.Y. Times, Apr. 15, 2009.

[9] Thomas Bruha and Matthias Bortfeld, *Terrorismus und Selbstverteidigung*, 49 Vereinte Nationen 161, 161 (2001).

[10] Thomas Bruha and Matthias Bortfeld, *Terrorismus und Selbstverteidigung*, 49 Vereinte Nationen 161, 161 (2001) (The authors speak of a third generation of terrorism).

[11] *See, e.g.,* Herfried Münkler, *The Wars of the 21th Century*, 85 International Review of the Red Cross 7, 20-21 (2003) (Münkler speaks of "transnational wars").

on non-state actors and their impact on the respective laws, transnational terror organizations, such as Al Qaeda, remain the primary focus.[12]

The conflict between the U.S. and Al Qaeda began far prior to the 9/11 terror attacks. Al Qaeda was originally formed in 1988 at the end of the conflict against the Soviet Union in Afghanistan, in order to support the struggle of oppressed Muslims worldwide.[13] Al Qaeda did not always oppose the U.S. Prior, Al Qaeda's goals, as stated in meeting minutes in August and September of 1988, were solely *"to lift the word of God, to make His religion victorious"*.[14] One decade later, on February 23rd, 1998, Al Qaeda issued a *Fatwa* against the United States in an Arabic newspaper published in London called *Al-Quds al-Arabi*. The *Fatwa* was co-signed by Osama Bin Laden, Ayman al-Zawahiri and other Islamist leaders, and reads as follows,

> "(t)o kill Americans and their allies, both civil and military, is an individual duty of every Muslim who is able, in any country where this is possible, until the Aqsa Mosque and the Haram Mosque are freed from their grip and until their armies, shattered and broken-winged, depart from all the lands of Islam, incapable of threatening any Muslim".[15]

The conflict between the U.S. and Al Qaeda was brought to broader public attention due to the 1998 U.S. embassy bombings in Tanzania and Kenya and, ultimately, because of the 9/11 attacks. The U.S. response to these attacks was the launch of the global war on terrorism and the invasion of Afghanistan, which ultimately lead to the end of the Taliban regime in late 2001. Numerous attacks lead by Al Qaeda have followed since, although it is difficult to determine which terrorist attacks the organization was actually responsible for.

---

[12] For background on this particular conflict *see* Lawrence Wright, *The Looming Tower: Al-Qaeda and the Road to 9/11* (2007 Vintage Books Edition); Marc Sageman, *Understanding Terror Networks* (2004); Peter Bergen, *The Longest War: The Enduring Conflict between America and al-Qaeda* (2011).

[13] *See* Uppsala Conflict Data Base at http://www.ucdp.uu.se/gpdatabase/gpcountry.php?id=164andregionSelect=3-Northern_Americas# (last visited May 28, 2012); Jörg Föh, *Die Bekämpfung des internationalen Terrorismus nach dem 11. September 2001*, 52 (2011).

[14] Peter Bergen, *The Longest War*, 18 (2011); *United States v. Enaam Arnaout*, No. 02-CR-892, Government's Evidentiary Proffer Supporting the Admissibility of Co-Conspirator Statements, (North District of Illinois, filed Jan. 6, 2003) online available at http://news.findlaw.com/wsj/docs/bif/usarnaout10603prof.odf (last visited May 29, 2013).

[15] For the text of the Fatwa *see* http://web.archive.org/web/20060422210853/http://www.ict.org.il/articles/fatwah.htm (last visited Feb. 19, 2012); Bernard Lewis, *License to Kill*, Foreign Affairs, 14-19 (1998); Lawrence Wright, *The Looming Tower: Al-Qaeda and the Road to 9/11*, 294 *et seq.* (2007 Vintage Books Edition).

While Al Qaeda continues to exist even post Osama bin Laden's assassination in May 2010, it remains relatively dormant ever since. Moreover, it has been weakened and is limited in its operations.[16] The conflict between the U.S. and Al Qaeda triggered the recent debate on international law as applied to transnational conflicts. This book analyzes various approaches to this debate, which range from applying International Humanitarian Law (IHL) to developing a new legal regime within IHL, to applying a transnational law enforcement regime, based on International Human Rights Law (IHRL).[17]

III. Structure of the Analysis

The international law which is primarily relevant to transnational conflicts will be introduced in chapter B. Chapter C analyzes the applicability of IHL to transnational conflicts. Chapter D discusses an alternative law enforcement approach based on IHRL. Subsequently, chapter E addresses prospects of international law regulating transnational conflicts, with a discussion and comparison of the IHL approach and the law enforcement approach. In conclusion, chapter F puts forth a recommendation for an integrated approach between IHL and an IHRL-based transnational law enforcement regime. This book evaluates existing legal regimes, their applicability to transnational conflicts, and possible approaches to overcome the divide between armed conflict and law enforcement regimes. It aims to contribute to current views as well as further the understanding of legal challenges raised by the phenomenon of transnational conflicts.

---

[16] Peter Bergen, *The Longest War*, xvii (2011) ("Though it survives intact and dangerous, al-Qaeda is hemmed in, weakened and limited in its operations. Its ability to force a decisive change in America's Middle East policy is close to zero, even though it remains capable of dealing lethal blows around the world"); *contra* Leah Farrall, *How Al Qaeda Works*, 90 Foreign Affairs 128-138 (2011) (Farrall argues that the central al Qaeda organization has to be assessed and comprehended in context with its subsidiary branches and franchises).

[17] For a general overview *see* Sylvain Vité, *Typology of Armed Conflicts in International Law: Legal Concepts and Actual Situations* 91 International Review of the Red Cross 69, 92-3 (2009).

B. Relevant International Law

IHL and IHRL are particularly pertinent as regards the regulation of conflicts and will both be addressed throughout this work. The following two sections serve as a brief introduction to both sets of law.

I. International Humanitarian Law

IHL, also known as the *Laws of Armed Conflict* or *jus in bello,* regulates permissible means and methods applied during the conduct of armed force.[1] IHL must be distinguished from *jus ad bellum* (or *jus contra bellum),* which pertains to the circumstances under which a state may resort to the use of force against another state.[2] The goal of IHL is not the preservation of peace, but rather the regulation of any armed conflict once it has begun. IHL regulates the way in which armed conflicts are carried out, including existing humanitarian concerns, most importantly the protection of civilians.[3]

1. Dichotomy of International Humanitarian Law

IHL is applied to armed conflicts and distinguishes between *International Armed Conflicts* (IACs) and *Non-International Armed Conflicts* (NIACs). While IACs are understood as conflicts which *"arise between two or more of the High Contracting Parties",*[4] a NIAC is an *"armed conflict not of an international character occurring in the territory of one of the High Contracting Parties".*[5] Therefore, NIACs encompass all forms of conflicts between forces of one particular state and one or several other non-state actors.

The full body of IHL primarily addresses IACs, whereas NIACs are solely addressed in Art. 3 of the Geneva Conventions (GC) and The Additional Protocol II to the Geneva Conventions (AP II). The rules corresponding to each of the aforementioned conflict types form two distinct legal regimes within IHL: the

---

[1] Matthias Herdegen, *Völkerrecht*, 403 (2013).

[2] Matthias Herdegen, *Völkerrecht*, 403 (2013).

[3] Matthias Herdegen, *Völkerrecht*, 403 (2013).

[4] Art. 2 GC.

[5] Art. 3 GC; *cf.* Hans-Peter Gasser & Nils Melzer, *Humanitäres Völkerrecht*, 64-5 (2012); International Law Association, *Final Report on the Meaning of Armed Conflict in International Law*, 8 (2010).

laws of IACs and the laws of NIACs. While the dichotomy of IACs and NIACs has been repeatedly criticized and questioned,[6] it continues to characterize the *lex lata* accepted by all states worldwide.[7] The differences between the two legal regimes of IACs and NIACs make it imperative to accurately assess the exact type of an occurring armed conflict. The applicable law directly depends on whether or not a conflict is an IAC or a NIAC. In a recently published report, the International Law Association suggests that IACs and NIACs share the common criterion of armed conflict, in which a common conflict threshold must be met.[8] This point of view, however, is misleading:[9] While the term *armed conflict* emphasizes that IHL applies only to violent situations, the threshold of violence that must be met to distinguish between an IAC or NIAC differs significantly. There is no common threshold of violence for IACs and NIACs.[10]

---

[6] ICTY, *Prosecutor v. Tadic*, Case No. IT-94-1-I, Decision on Defence Motion for Interlocutory Appeal on Jurisdiction, ¶ 96-7 (Oct. 2, 1995); Christopher Greenwood, *International Law and the 'War against Terrorism'*, 78 International Affairs, 301 (2002); James G. Stewart, *Towards a Single Definition of Armed Conflict in International Humanitarian Law: A Critique of Internationalized Armed Conflicts*, 85 International Review of the Red Cross, 313-350 (2003); Frits Kalshoven, *International Armed Conflict: Legal Qualification and IHL as Lex Specialis*, in International Humanitarian Law and Other Legal Regimes: Interplay in Situations of Violence 63, 72 *et seq.* (International Institute of Humanitarian Law ed. 2003); Roy S. Schöndorf, *Extra-State Armed Conflicts: Is there a Need for a New Legal Regime?*, 37 New York University Journal of Law and Politics 1, 2 (2004); Noelle Quénivet, *The Application of International Humanitarian Law to Situations of a (Counter-)Terrorist Nature,* in International Humanitarian Law and the 21st Century's Conflicts 25, 58 (Roberta Arnold and Pierre-Antoine Hildebrand eds. 2005); Hans-Peter Gasser & Nils Melzer, *Humanitäres Völkerrecht,* 65-6 (2012); Dieter Fleck, *The Law of Non-International Armed Conflict,* in The Handbook of International Humanitarian Law, ¶ 1202 (Dieter Fleck ed. 2008); Lars Mammen, *Völkerrechtliche Stellung von internationalen Terrororganisationen,* 278-9 (2008); Emily Crawford, *The Treatment of Combatants and Insurgents under the law of Armed Conflict,* 153 *et seq.* 2010; Ingrid Detter, *The Law of War,* 49 (2000).

[7] Hans-Peter Gasser & Nils Melzer, *Humanitäres Völkerrecht,* 66 (2012); Noelle Quénivet, *The Application of International Humanitarian Law to Situations of a (Counter-) Terrorist Nature,* in International Humanitarian Law and the 21st Century's Conflicts 25, 59 (Roberta Arnold and Pierre-Antoine Hildebrand eds. 2005).

[8] International Law Association, *Final Report on the Meaning of Armed Conflict in International Law*, 2 passim (2010).

[9] Marko Milanovic & Vidan Hadzi-Vidanovic, *A Taxonomy of Armed Conflict*, in Research Handbook of International Conflict and Security Law 256, 272 (Nigel White & Christian Henderson, eds. 2013).

[10] Marko Milanovic & Vidan Hadzi-Vidanovic, *A Taxonomy of Armed Conflict,* in Research Handbook of International Conflict and Security Law 256, 272 *et seq.* (Nigel White & Christian Henderson, eds. 2013).

In an IAC, no minimum threshold of violence must be met.[11] Any use of force by a state against another state is sufficient for the application of IHL[12] as the relationship between any two states is generally not characterized by the use of force. If one state should resort to force at any point, the gravity and exceptionality of the use of force would require the application of international law. Further proof would not be necessary. In such cases, it is the IAC legal regime that

---

[11] Recently it has been claimed that for an IAC to exist a conflict between States has to meet a certain threshold of violence, *see* Mary Ellen O'Connell, *Defining Armed Conflict,* 13 Journal of Conflict and Security Law 393 (2009); Christopher Greenwood, *Scope of Application of Humanitarian Law,* in The Handbook of International Humanitarian Law, 48 (Dieter Fleck ed. 2008); International Law Association, *Final Report on the Meaning of Armed Conflict in International Law,* 2 (2010) ("The violence must be organized and intense – even between sovereign states – before the otherwise prevailing peacetime rules are suspended"). On this discussion *see* Jann K. Kleffner, *Scope of Application of International Humanitarian Law,* in The Handbook of International Humanitarian Law, 44 *et seq.* (Dieter Fleck ed. 2013).

[12] Jean S. Pictet, *Commentary on the Geneva Convention for the Amelioration of the Condition of the Wounded and Sick in Armed Forces in the Field,* 32 (1952) ("It makes no difference how long the conflict lasts, or how much slaughter takes place"); Dietrich Schindler, *The Different Types of Armed Conflicts according to the Geneva Conventions and Protocols,* 163 Recueil des Cours de l'Academie de Droit International de la Haye 117, 131 (1979) ("The existence of an armed conflict within the meaning of Article 2 common to the Conventions can always be assumed when parts of the armed forces of two States clash with each other. Even a minor frontier incident is sufficient. Any kind of use of arms between two States brings the Conventions into effect."); Knut Ipsen, *Zum Begriff des "internationalen bewaffneten Konflikts",* in Recht im Dienst des Friedens FS für Eberhard Menzel 405, 419 (Jost Delbrück et al. eds. 1975); Claus Kreß, *Gewaltverbot und Selbstverteidigungsrecht nach der Satzung der Vereinten Nationen bei staatlicher Verwicklung in Gewaltakte Privater,* 193 (1995); Knut Ipsen, Eberhard Menzel and Volker Epping, *Völkerrecht,* 1272 ¶ 14 (2004); Friederike Bredt, *Anwendbarkeit der humanitären Völkerrechts im Israel-Palästina-Konflikt,* 266 *et seq.* (2009); International Committee of the Red Cross, *Violence and the Use of Force,* 30 (January 2008) available at http://www.icrc.org/Web/Eng/siteeng0.nsf/htmlall/p0943/$File/ICRC_002_0943.PDF (last visited Aug. 9, 2010) ("[...] no minimum level of intensity, military organization or control over territory is required for an international armed conflict to be recognized as such."); International Committee of the Red Cross, *How is the Term "Armed Conflict" Defined in International Humanitarian Law?* 5 (Mar. 2008), available at http://www.icrc.org/web/eng/siteeng0.nsf/htmlall/armed-conflict-article-170308/$file/Opinion-paper-armed-conflict.pdf (last visited Aug. 9, 2010) ("International armed conflicts exist whenever there is resort to armed force between two or more States").

grants the protection of the sick, wounded, prisoners and civilians from the very onset of violence.[13]

In the event of a NIAC, a threshold of violence must be met in order to qualify a conflict as an *armed conflict*. In non-international conflicts, in which only one state party is involved, a threshold of violence is required to separate a NIAC from any other form of inner-state violence below the NIAC level. Occasionally, isolated and sporadic acts of violence may occur within a certain state, but these do not automatically trigger the application of the laws of NIAC.[14] The state's sovereignty must always be respected.

2. Internationalized Non-International Armed Conflict

The umbrella term *internationalized non-international armed conflict*[15] is frequently used in reference to all non-international armed conflicts in which a second state is involved. The second state may be an ally of the conflict state or of the non-state party.[16] Internationalized non-international armed conflicts are not a legal category but rather are used as a descriptor. There is no independent legal regime of internationalized non-international armed conflicts within IHL. The legal treatment of internationalized non-international armed conflicts is therefore disputed.[17] Some authors argue that in any instance involving external

---

[13] Knut Ipsen, Eberhard Menzel and Volker Epping, *Völkerrecht*, 1224 (2004); Friederike Bredt, *Anwendbarkeit des humanitären Völkerrechts im Israel-Palästina-Konflikt*, 267 (2009).

[14] International Committee of the Red Cross, *Violence and the Use of Force*, 26 (Jan. 2008) online available at http://www.icrc.org/Web/Eng/siteeng0.nsf/htmlall/p0943 /$File/ICRC_002_0943.PDF (last visited Aug. 9, 2010) ("[...] a level of intensity exceeding that of isolated and sporadic acts of violence").

[15] International Committee of the Red Cross, *Violence and the Use of Force*, 33 *et seq.* (Jan. 2008) online available at http://www.icrc.org/Web/Eng/siteeng0.nsf/htmlall/ p0943/$File/ICRC_002_0943.PDF (last visited Aug. 9, 2010).

[16] Hans-Peter Gasser, *Internationalized Non-International Armed Conflicts: Case Studies of Afghanistan, Kampuchea and Lebanon*, 33 American University Law Review, 145 (1983); Hans-Peter Gasser & Nils Melzer, *Humanitäres Völkerrecht*, 72-3 (2012); Martin Hess, *Die Anwendbarkeit des humanitären Völkerrechts, insbesondere in gemischten Konflikten*, 143 *et seq.* (1985); Stefan Oeter, *Terrorismus und Menschenrechte*, 40 Archiv des Völkerrechts 422, 439 (2002); Ingrid Detter, *The Law of War*, 46 *et seq.* (2000); Lars Mammen, *Völkerrechtliche Stellung von internationalen Terrororganisationen*, 177 (2008).

[17] *See comprehensively* on this controversy David Zechmeister, *Die Erosion des humanitären Völkerrechts in den bewaffneten Konflikten der Gegenwart*, 109 *et seq.* (2007);

intervention by a state, the conflict should be characterized as an IAC, regardless of whether the state intervenes on the side of the conflict state or the non-state party.[18] This position is driven by the intention to apply the more comprehensive laws of IAC to internationalized non-international armed conflicts. However, the aforementioned view must be rebutted, as a conflict that involves non-state actors can, *de lege lata,* not be characterized as an IAC so long as non-state actors do not act on behalf of a state.[19]

According to the *"Theory of Pairings"*, *"Idea of Differentiation"* and the German *"Komponententheorie"*, a reference to the respective opposing parties involved in a conflict must be made in order to categorize the situation and determine the applicable law.[20] The analysis may result in four different relationships, each of which corresponds to a different legal regime:[21] (1) the relationship between the conflict state and the non-state party, that qualifies as a NIAC and is regulated by the applicable laws of NIAC, (2) the relationship between the non-state party and a second state that intervenes on behalf of the conflict-state, in which case the laws of NIAC must also be applied, (3) the relationship between the conflict state and a second state that intervenes on behalf of the non-state actor, which must be seen as an IAC and thereby regulated by the laws of IAC, and (4) the relationship between two states that intervene on opposing sides, which would also result in an IAC and thereby regulated by the laws of IAC. The *Theory of Pairings* should be approved as it provides a more accurate view and allows for all situations to be qualified correctly under the existing International Humanitarian Law. As a result, IACs and NIACs may coexist depending on the parties involved in international non-international armed con-

---

Lars Mammen, *Völkerrechtliche Stellung von internationalen Terrororganisationen,* 177 (2008).

[18] Stefan Oeter, *Terrorismus und Menschenrechte,* 40 Archiv des Völkerrechts 422, 439 (2002); Hans-Peter Gasser & Nils Melzer, *Humanitäres Völkerrecht,* 72-3 (2012); David Zechmeister, *Die Erosion des humanitären Völkerrechts in den bewaffneten Konflikten der Gegenwart,* 113 *et seq.* (2007) (using the term "modifizierte Komponententheorie").

[19] Martin Hess, *Die Anwendbarkeit des humanitären Völkerrechts, insbesondere in gemischten Konflikten,* 159 (1985).

[20] Martin Hess, *Die Anwendbarkeit des humanitären Völkerrechts, insbesondere in gemischten Konflikten,* 159 and 152 (1985); ICJ, *Military and Paramilitary Activities in and against Nicaragua* (Nicar. v. U.S.), 1986 ICJ 14, ¶ 219 (June 27); Lindsay Moir, *The Law of Internal Armed Conflict,* 47 (2002).

[21] International Committee of the Red Cross, *Violence and the Use of Force,* 33 (Jan. 2008) online available at http://www.icrc.org/Web/Eng/siteeng0.nsf/htmlall /p0943/$File/ICRC_002_0943.PDF (last visited Aug. 9, 2010).

flicts.[22] Internationalized non-international armed conflicts are therefore often and perhaps more accurately described as *mixed conflicts*.[23]

II. International Human Rights Law

IHRL, although often regarded as an entity, is not a separate body of norms. *Brownlie* correctly states,

> "human rights problems occur in specific legal contexts. The issues may arise in domestic law, or within the framework of a standard-setting convention or within general international law".[24]

Throughout this book, IHRL is referenced in order to encompass a number of international treaties, which can be divided into global and regional human rights treaties. Global treaties are accessible to all states, while regional treaties are only accessible to the states of that specific region.

The most important global human rights treaties[25] are the two international covenants from 1966: the *International Covenant on Civil and Political Rights* (ICCPR) and the *International Covenant on Economic, Social and Cultural Rights* (ICESCR). The Universal Declaration of Human Rights from 1948, while also an important human rights document, is not a treaty legally binding for UN member states. Rather, it is a declaration adopted by the UN General Assembly.[26] However, some of the rights stated in the Universal Declaration of Human Rights are directly binding for states, as they have achieved Customary International Law (CIL) status.[27] The regional human rights treaties are the *European Convention on Human Rights* (ECHR) of 1950, the *American Convention on Human Rights* (ACHR) of 1969, the *African Charter on Human and*

---

[22] ICJ, *Military and Paramilitary Activities in and against Nicaragua* (Nicar. v. U.S.), 1986 ICJ 14, ¶ 219 (June 27); Yoram Dinstein, *The Conduct of Hostilities under the Law of International Armed Conflict*, 14 *et seq.* (2004).

[23] Martin Hess, *Die Anwendbarkeit des humanitären Völkerrechts, insbesondere in gemischten Konflikten*, 143 *et seq.* (1985); Michael Bothe, *Friedenssicherung und Kriegsrecht, in Völkerrecht* 589, 666 *et seq.* (Wolfgang Vitzthum and Michael Bothe eds., 2004).

[24] Brownlie, *International Law*, 554 (7th ed. 2008).

[25] For a comprehensive list *see* Matthias Herdegen, *Völkerrecht*, 361 *et seq.* (2013); Christopher Greenwood, *Historical Development and Legal Basis*, in The Handbook of International Humanitarian Law, ¶ 128 (Dieter Fleck ed. 2008).

[26] David Zechmeister, *Die Erosion des humanitären Völkerrechts in den bewaffneten Konflikten der Gegenwart*, 125 (2007).

[27] Knut Ipsen, Eberhard Menzel and Volker Epping, *Völkerrecht*, 786 ¶ 36 (2004); Matthias Herdegen, *Völkerrecht*, 356 (2013).

People's Rights of 1981 and the *Arab Charter on Human Rights* of 2008.[28] The legal norms encompassed by the aforementioned sources form a complex but at times confusing system of human rights law.

The exact legal framework applicable to a specific conflict situation is generally dependent on each state's membership to the global treaties, a specific regional human rights treaty, and CIL. In addition, the exact set of norms applicable to a law-enforcement regime is also dependent on the involved state's domestic law.

A key difference between IHL and IHRL is that the former is applicable only to armed conflicts whereas the latter is a general legal framework applicable whenever a state has jurisdiction. IHRL does not address warring parties, but rather regulates the relationship between states and individuals subject to the state's jurisdiction.[29] IHL binds states and limits their authorities to guarantee their citizen's basic rights and liberties. Consequently, only the state is bound by IHRL, as it is regarded as *"the ultimate guardian of its [a state's] population's welfare"*.[30] Non-state entities, such as non-state armed groups, are generally not bound by the rules of IHRL. *Henkin* and *Bothe* argue that well-established non-state groups are bound by customary human rights law.[31] Furthermore, *Bothe* states that human rights can be applied horizontally between two non-state entities and that non-state entities can be bound through criminal law, which protects human rights values.[32] Nevertheless, it is undeniable that non-state entities are not bound by law to the same extent as states, as IHRL is based on the principle of state responsibility.[33]

---

[28] The Charta has entered into force since its seventh ratification by the United Arab Emirates in March 2008.

[29] Michael Bothe, *The Status of Captured Fighters*, in The Right to Life 195, 199 (Christian Tomuschat, Evelyne Lagrange and Stefan Oeter, eds. 2010).

[30] Chris Jochnick, *Confronting the Impunity of Non-State Actors: New Fields for the Promotion of Human Rights*, 21 Human Rights Quarterly 56, 59 (1999).

[31] Louise Henkin, *Human Rights*, in Encyclopedia of Public International Law, Vol. 2, 886, 890 (1995); Michael Bothe, *The Status of Captured Fighters*, in The Right to Life 195, 199 (Christian Tomuschat, Evelyne Lagrange and Stefan Oeter, eds. 2010).

[32] Michael Bothe, *The Status of Captured Fighters*, in The Right to Life 195, 199 (Christian Tomuschat, Evelyne Lagrange and Stefan Oeter, eds. 2010).

[33] Chris Jochnick, *Confronting the Impunity of Non-State Actors: New Fields for the Promotion of Human Rights*, 21 Human Rights Quarterly 56, 58 (1999).

C. International Humanitarian Law

This chapter analyzes if and how transnational conflicts are regulated through IHL. Transnational conflicts cannot easily be categorized as IACs or NIACs. They do not qualify as IACs as they do not occur between two state parties, as per the requirement of Art. 2 GC. Additionally, they cannot be classified as NIACs as they are not limited solely to one state's territory, but rather cross the national border, thus exceeding the scope of Art. 3 GC, which requires that the conflict occur *"in the territory of one of the High Contracting Parties"*.[1]

The main issue with the classic method of categorizing conflicts into IACs or NIACs is that two criteria are used to distinguish conflicts in IHL, namely the conflict party and the geographical scope of the conflict.[2] If, for example, two state parties are confronted with each other, the conflict is an IAC, whereas the conflict is a NIAC if only one or no state parties participate. Simultaneously, it is imperative to define whether the conflict crosses state borders, in which case it would be considered an IAC, or takes place within the borders of one state, and therefore would be considered a NIAC. Generally, the application of this two-criteria-distinction does not cause problems, as conflicts that cross state borders usually occur between states. Conflicts that involve one or no state parties are normally restricted to the territory of a single state. Particular to transnational conflicts is that the hostilities involve territories of two or more states. However, they do not occur between the states whose territories are affected. Classifying the nature of the conflict based on the conflict parties rather than the geographical scope of the conflict yields differing results. As a result, characterizing transnational conflicts is particularly difficult. However, despite the aforementioned difficulties, *Greenwood* claims that, *"the existing legal framework is perfectly capable of accommodating the use of force against terrorist groups"*.[3] Similarly, the ICRC argues that each transnational conflict must be individually categorized by considering its particular context. The established IHL would then be

---

[1] Art. 3 GC.

[2] Andreas Paulus and Mindia Vashakmadze, *Asymmetrical War and the Notion of Armed Conflict – A Tentative Conceptualization*, 91 International Review of the Red Cross 95, 110 (2009) ("While IHL provides two sets of rules, there are three potential combinations of warring parties and territory: a conflict may be a classic international armed conflict between states, a non-international conflict between a state and one or more non-state groups and, lastly, a 'transnational' conflict between a state and a non-state group (or between non-state groups) on the territory of more than one state").

[3] Christopher Greenwood, *Essays on War in International Law*, 432 (2006).

able to provide adequate legal guidance on all conflicts that qualify as an armed conflict.[4]

The following section will examine *Greenwood's* and the ICRC's assumptions by analyzing the applicability of the laws of IAC (Section I) and the laws of NIAC to transnational conflicts (Section II). Subsequently, suggestions for a new IHL regime will be discussed (Section III).

I. International Armed Conflicts

The laws of IACs can be applied to transnational conflicts as a legal framework. The following section will analyze the categorization of transnational conflicts as IACs and examine the resulting legal consequences.

1. Transnational Conflicts as Conflicts between States

IACs are generally regarded as inter-state conflicts.[5] Art. 2 GC describes them as

> "cases of declared war or of any other armed conflict which may arise between two or more of the High Contracting Parties".

Although the term *state* is not explicitly mentioned, it is evident that only states can be High Contracting Parties and that an IAC can only occur between

---

[4] International Committee of the Red Cross, *International Humanitarian Law and the Challenges of Contemporary Armed Conflict* 26 (2003), online available at http:/www.icrc.org/Web/eng/siteeng0.nsf/htmlall/5XRDCC/$File/IHLcontemp_armedco nflicts_FINAL_ANG.pdf (last visited Aug. 6, 2010) ("In the ICRC's view this body of law continues, on the whole, to adequately deal with today's conflict environment"); International Committee of the Red Cross, *International Humanitarian Law and the Challenges of Contemporary Armed Conflicts*, 89 IRRC 726 (Sep. 2007) ("To sum up, each situation of organized armed violence must be examined in the ‚specific context in which it takes place and must be legally qualified as armed conflict, or not, based on the factual circumstances").

[5] Knut Ipsen, Eberhard Menzel and Volker Epping, *Völkerrecht*, 1227 (2004) ("Das Merkmal 'international' weist ein bewaffneter Konflikt [...] stets dann auf, wenn Waffengewalt zwischen Staaten angewendet wird"); International Committee of the Red Cross, *How is the Term "Armed Conflict" Defined in International Humanitarian Law?* (2008), online available at http://www.icrc.org/web/eng/siteeng0.nsf/htmlall/armed-conflict-article-170308/$file/Opinion-paper-armed-conflict.pdf (last visited Apr. 6, 2009); International Committee of the Red Cross, *Interpretive Guidance on the Notion of Direct Participation in Hostilities under International Humanitarian Law*, 24 (2009).

states. A conflict that occurs between states and non-state actors can therefore not be classified as an IAC. Simultaneously, however, a non-state actor may, under specific circumstances, act on behalf of another state. In such instances, the hostile action of the non-state actor can be attributed to that other state. The non-state actor will then be regarded as a *de-facto* organ of that other state.[6] The other state then becomes a party in the armed conflict, which would then turn the conflict into a state versus state conflict, i.e. an IAC. Therefore, the key question lies in whether the act of a non-state actor can be attributed to a state.

a) Attributability of Non-State Actors' Actions to a State

The circumstances under which an action of a person or a group is attributable to a state continue to be debated.[7] The following remarks serve as a brief overview of the existing debate. In general, attributability requires sufficient state control over the respective person or group.[8] The amount of required control remains controversial. The ICJ requires *"effective control"*[9] whereas the ICTY requires *"overall control"*[10] to prove sufficient involvement of a state in the activities of non-state actors.

The ICJ assumes that the non-state actor's dependence on the state requires a high degree of control, such that the non-state actor may be regarded as a state

---

[6] Antonio Cassese, *International Law*, 247-9 (2005) ("These [de facto State organs] are individuals who, although they do not have the formal status and rank of a State officials, in fact act on behalf of a State").

[7] Antonio Cassese, *International Law*, 248 (2005) (Cassese sees three relevant case groups, when individuals can be regarded de facto State organs: "They can be regarded so [de facto State organ] when they (i) are under instructions from a State, or (ii) are under the overall control of a State, or (iii) in fact behave as State officials". But this is far from being generally accepted).

[8] For an overview over the competing positions and the status of the dispute *see* Noelle Quénivet, *The Application of International Humanitarian Law to Situations of a (Counter-)Terrorist Nature*, in International Humanitarian Law and the 21st Century's Conflicts 25, 54 *et seq.* (Roberta Arnold and Pierre-Antoine Hildebrand eds. 2005); International Law Commission, *Draft Articles on Responsibility of States for Internationally Wrongful Acts*, with Commentaries, Art. 8, commentary (4) and (5) (2001).

[9] ICJ, *Military and Paramilitary Activities in and against Nicaragua* (Nicar. v. U.S.), 1986 ICJ 14, ¶ 115 (June 27); ICJ, *Application of the Convention on the Prevention and Punishment of the Crime of Genocide* (Bosn. and Herz. v. Serb. and Mont.), ICJ GL No 91, ¶ 396 *et seq.* (Feb. 26, 2007).

[10] ICTY, *Prosecutor v. Tadic*, Case No. IT-94-1-A, Appeal Judgment, ¶ 88 *et seq.* and ¶ 131 (July 15, 1999).

organ *de facto*.[11] The relationship of dependence and control exists when the state exercises effective control, which requires that the state has *"directed or enforced the perpetration of the acts"*.[12] In this case, the state must have influence on the non-state actor throughout the actual execution of operations. The financing, organizing, training, equipping of non-state actors, and planning of an operation, are not sufficient to yield effective control.[13] As a result, the requirement of effective control establishes a high threshold for attributability.

The ICTY argues that the high general threshold posed by the ICJ is incorrect.[14] The ICTY states that the ICJ threshold deviates from the principle of the rules of state responsibility,[15] and is also contrary to state practice as well as judicial practice.[16] The ICTY's approach is to differentiate between cases of involvement by militarily organized groups, and individuals and groups without clear organizational structure.[17] The ICTY specifically argues that the ICJ's

---

[11] ICJ, *Military and Paramilitary Activities in and against Nicaragua* (Nicar. v. U.S.), 1986 ICJ 14, ¶ 109 (June 27) ("What the Court has to determine at this point is whether or not the relationship of the contras to the United States Government was so much one of dependence on the one side and control on the other that it would be right to equate the contras, for legal purposes, with an organ of the United States Government, or as acting on behalf of that Government"); ICJ, *Application of the Convention on the Prevention and Punishment of the Crime of Genocide* (Bosn. and Herz. v. Serb. and Mont.), ICJ GL No 91, ¶ 397 (Feb. 26, 2007) ("The answer to the latter question [whether those persons should be equated with State organs de facto, even though not enjoying that status under internal law] depends, as previously explained, on whether those persons were in a relationship of such complete dependence on the State that they cannot be considered otherwise than as organs of the State, so that all their actions performed in such capacity would be attributable to the State for purposes of international responsibility").

[12] ICJ, *Military and Paramilitary Activities in and against Nicaragua* (Nicar. v. U.S.), 1986 ICJ 14, ¶ 115 (June 27).

[13] ICJ, *Military and Paramilitary Activities in and against Nicaragua* (Nicar. v. U.S.), 1986 ICJ 14, ¶ 115 (June 27).

[14] ICTY, *Prosecutor v. Tadic*, Case No. IT-94-1-A, Appeal Judgment, ¶ 115 *et seq.* and ¶ 117 (July 15, 1999) ("The degree of control may, however, vary according to the factual circumstances of each case. The Appeals Chamber fails to see why in each and every circumstance international law should require a high threshold for the test of control. Rather, various situations may be distinguished"); *cf.* Kai Ambos, *Bestätigung der deutschen Strafgewalt für "Kriegsverbrechen" in Bosnien-Herzegowina*, 20 Neue Zeitschrift für Strafrecht, 71 (2000).

[15] ICTY, *Prosecutor v. Tadic*, Case No. IT-94-1-A, Appeal Judgment, ¶ 116 *et seq.* (July 15, 1999).

[16] ICTY, *Prosecutor v. Tadic*, Case No. IT-94-1-A, Appeal Judgment, ¶ 124 *et seq.* (July 15, 1999).

[17] ICTY, *Prosecutor v. Tadic*, Case No. IT-94-1-A, Appeal Judgment, ¶ 137 (July 15, 1999).

requirement of effective control is too high, and perhaps unnecessary, for militarily organized groups. In cases involving militarily organized groups, *overall* control, rather than *effective* control, suffices. A state's involvement in planning operations, even if not directly in its actual execution, is sufficient to have overall control over a militarily organized group. Hence, overall control does not require control over all actions at all times. Therefore, the threshold of overall control is not as high as that for effective control.[18] However, in cases of single persons or groups without a clear organizational structure, the ICTY does apply the ICJ's standard of effective control.[19]

While both the ICTY's and ICJ's approaches on overall and effective control are argued to be imprecise and requiring of furthering clarification,[20] the German Federal Court of Justice [*Bundesgerichtshof*] has elected to follow that of the ICTY.[21] Several arguments work in favor of the ICTY's approach. First, militarily organized groups have their own command structure, therefore making it sufficient to control this command structure to control the group, i.e. overall control. Second, a state cannot evade responsibility by claiming that it only exercised overall control and not effective control over a militarily organized group. Third, the ICTY approach takes into account that control by the state over unorganized groups cannot be inferred from overall control over a group's command structure. In such cases, it appears most appropriate to require effective control, i.e. control over every action performed by the unorganized non-state actor.

Recently, the ICJ has considered the inclusion of the overall control criterion,[22] but has rejected it due to issues related to state responsibility.[23] However,

---

[18] ICTY, *Prosecutor v. Tadic*, Case No. IT-94-1-A, Appeal Judgment, ¶ 137 (July 15, 1999) ("The control required by international law may be deemed to exist when a State (or, in the context of an armed conflict, the Party to the conflict) has a role in organising, coordinating or planning the military actions of the military group, in addition to financing, training and equipping or providing operational support to that group").

[19] ICTY, *Prosecutor v. Tadic*, Case No. IT-94-1-A, Appeal Judgment, ¶ 137 (July 15, 1999) ("[...] it is necessary to ascertain whether specific instructions concerning the commission of that particular act had been issued by that State to the individual or group in question [...]").

[20] Lars Mammen, *Völkerrechtliche Stellung von internationalen Terrororganisationen*, 173 (2008).

[21] *See* Bundesgerichtshof in Strafsachen [German Federal Court of Justice], 3 StR 372/00, ¶ 4a) aa) [BGHSt 2730] (The Bundesgerichtshof has followed the ICTY test).

[22] ICJ, *Application of the Convention on the Prevention and Punishment of the Crime of Genocide* (Bosn. and Herz. v. Serb. and Mont.), ICJ GL No 91, ¶ 402 *et seq.* (Feb. 26, 2007).

the ICJ has also opined that the ICTY threshold of overall control may be appropriate to assess the internationality of a conflict within *jus in bello*.[24] Further justifications are not provided. The ICJ may assume that attributability in IHL follows its own distinct criteria. It is plausible that the ICJ applies different criteria to determine the involvement of a state in an armed conflict and to assess a state's responsibility for specific actions committed by non-state actors on the state's behalf.[25] Ultimately, an in-depth understanding of the context and situation in question is essential in determining which approach is most appropriate.

b) States Fighting alongside Non-State Actors

It is argued that the participation of a state's military units alongside terrorists or non-state actors ultimately leads to an IAC, irrespective of the attributability of the non-state actors' actions to the state.[26] Adherents of this position argue that, when fighting against a common enemy, it is not feasible to distinguish between the state and the non-state units.[27] However, this approach lacks legal

---

[23] ICJ, *Application of the Convention on the Prevention and Punishment of the Crime of Genocide* (Bosn. and Herz. v. Serb. and Mont.), ICJ GL No 91, ¶ 403 (Feb. 26, 2007).

[24] ICJ, *Application of the Convention on the Prevention and Punishment of the Crime of Genocide* (Bosn. and Herz. v. Serb. and Mont.), ICJ GL No 91, ¶ 404 (Feb. 26, 2007).

[25] ICJ, *Application of the Convention on the Prevention and Punishment of the Crime of Genocide* (Bosn. and Herz. v. Serb. and Mont.), ICJ GL No 91, ¶ 405 (Feb. 26, 2007) ("It should first be observed that logic does not require the same test to be adopted in resolving the two issues, which are very different in nature: the degree and nature of a State's involvement in an armed conflict on another State's territory which is required for the conflict to be characterized as international, can very well, and without logical inconsistency, differ from the degree and nature of involvement required to give rise to that State's responsibility for a specific act committed in the course of the conflict").

[26] Lars Mammen, *Völkerrechtliche Stellung von internationalen Terrororganisationen*, 174 (2008); Thomas Bruha, *Gewaltverbot und humanitäres Völkerrecht nach dem 11. September 2001*, 40 Archiv des Völkerrechts 383, 414 *et seq.* (2002) ("Ob die Widerstand leistende [staatliche] Partei mit den Terroristen gemeinsame Sache macht [...] ist für die Frage des Vorliegens eines internationalen bewaffneten Konflikts unerheblich.[...] Terrorismusbekämpfung und Gewaltanwendung gegen ein anerkanntes Völkerrechtssubjekt lassen sich in solchen Konstellationen nicht mehr trennen"); Stefan Oeter, *Terrorismus und Menschenrechte*, 40 Archiv des Völkerrechts 422, 439 *et seq.* (2002); Dapo Akande, *Classification of Armed Conflicts: Relevant Legal Concepts*, in International Law and the Classification of Conflits 32, 70 *et seq.* (Elizabeth Wilmshurst, ed. 2012).

[27] Dapo Akande, *Classification of Armed Conflicts: Relevant Legal Concepts*, in International Law and the Classification of Conflits 32, 75 (Elizabeth Wilmshurst, ed. 2012) ("[...] the conflict with the non-state group will be so bound up with the international

foundation. While IAC rules apply to both state parties involved, the same rules do not apply to the non-state actors, assuming a sufficient connection to a state party does not exist. However, if the state were to adopt the actions of the non-state group, IAC rules would be applied.[28] Parallel acting of the state and non-state actors is not sufficient to convert non-state armed groups in to *de-facto* agents of the state. In conclusion, legal attributability of the actions of non-state actors to a state is an essential requirement to apply IAC rules to non-state actors.

c) The War on Terror as a Conflict between States

The following section addresses attributability of specific actions of non-state groups during transnational conflicts and the application of IAC rules. In the case of the conflict between the U.S. and Al Qaeda, for example, the possibility that Al Qaeda's actions are attributable to Afghanistan must be considered. Until at least December 2001, a stabilized de-facto regime was established by the Taliban on Afghan territory.[29] Hence, the Taliban regime was considered a party in an IAC.[30] Therefore, the conflict between U.S. forces and the Taliban qualified as an IAC. Al Qaeda members operating under the control of the Taliban and *"integrated within the organizational structure of the Taliban forces"*

---

armed conflict between the two States that it will be impossible to separate the two conflicts").

[28] International Law Commission, *Draft Articles on Responsibility of States for Internationally Wrongful Acts, with Commentaries*, Art. 11 (2001) ("Conduct which is not attributable to a State under the preceding articles shall nevertheless be considered an act of that State under international law if and to the extent that the State acknowledges and adopts the conduct in question as its own").

[29] After December 2001 with the ousting of the Taliban out of power and the installation of a new Afghan government, the Taliban lost their status as de-facto-Regime thus the IAC between them and the U.S. ended and turned into a NIAC between the new Afghan government forces and the Taliban with the U.S. and allied forces fighting alongside the Afghan government.

[30] On the notion of de-facto regime *see* Jochen Frowein, *Das de-facto-Regime im Völkerrecht. Eine Untersuchung zur Rechtsstellung "nichtanerkannter Staaten" und ähnlicher Gebilde*, 34 *et seq.* (1968); Dietrich Schindler, *The Different Types of Armed Conflicts according to the Geneva Conventions and Protocols*, 163 Recueil des Cours de l'Academie de Droit International de la Haye 117, 129 (1979) ("If a de facto regime declares its accession to the Geneva Conventions it should be considered a contracting party, irrespective of whether it is generally recognized as a State or not").
On the status of the Taliban *see* Christian Schaller, *Humanitäres Völkerrecht und nichtstaatliche Gewaltakteure*, 16-7 (Dec. 2007); Jörg Föh, *Die Bekämpfung des internationalen Terrorismus nach dem 11. September 2001*, 157-9 (2011).

served as *de-facto* agents of the Taliban.[31] The question lies in whether these Al Qaeda fighters were ever truly agents of the Taliban. While Al Qaeda members may, at times, have fought alongside the Taliban, current evidence suggests the Taliban did not have sufficient control (effective or overall) over Al Qaeda members.[32] Over the course of Bin Laden's stay in Afghanistan, his relationship with the Taliban and their leader Mullah Omar was ambiguous; the nature of the partnership was neither harmonic nor one of subordination.[33] In conclusion, the argument that the Al Qaeda was part of the IAC during the first period of the U.S. invasion in Afghanistan until the fall of the Taliban regime is unconvincing.

Even if Al Qaeda fought as *de-facto* agents of the Taliban, the IAC would have occurred between the U.S. and the Taliban, and not the U.S. and Al Qaeda. Hence, even in the most prominent transnational conflict, IAC rules would not have been applied to Al Qaeda.

2. Non-State Actors as Party to International Armed Conflicts

If a non-state actor's actions cannot be attributed to a state, the corresponding conflict falls outside the scope of IACs, as defined in Art. 2 GC. Regardless, a number of new approaches have been developed to apply the laws of IACs to transnational conflicts. According to these novel approaches, non-state actors can be party to an IAC, irrespective of their allegiance to a state. These approaches will be discussed in the following sections.

a) A New Form of International Armed Conflict

On September 20, 2001, former U.S. President George W. Bush declared the *War on Terror*. The Bush administration argued that the U.S. conflict with Al Qaeda was a new form of international armed conflict, not governed by the Geneva Conventions.[34] *Bush* stated,

---

[31] Noam Lubell, *Extraterritorial Use of Force Against Non-State Actors*, 98 (2010).

[32] Christian Schaller, *Humanitäres Völkerrecht und nichtstaatliche Gewaltakteure*, 18, (Stiftung Wissenschaft und Politik Studie 2007).

[33] Lawrence Wright, *The Looming Tower: Al-Qaeda and the Road to 9/11*, 325 *et seq.* (2007 Vintage Books Edition).

[34] George W. Bush, *Memorandum for the Vice President: Humane Treatment of Al Qaeda and the Taliban Detainees* (Feb. 7, 2002); John Yoo and Robert J. Delahunty, *Memorandum for William J. Haynes II*, 12 (Jan. 09, 2002); *cf.* Marko Milanovic, *Lesson for Human Rights and Humanitarian Law in the War on Terror: comparing Hamdan and*

"[This war] begins with Al Qaeda, but it does not end there. It will not end until every terrorist group of global reach has been found, stopped and defeated."[35]

What initially sounded like political rhetoric ultimately reflected a legal claim.[36] In response to 9/11, the U.S. resorted to means justifiable only within an armed conflict under IHL.[37] The military operations in Afghanistan were regarded as part of one single international armed conflict between the U.S. and Al Qaeda,[38] and potentially of global nature.[39] However, because Al Qaeda was not a state party, the conflict was not an IAC as per Art. 2 GC. Hence, it was argued that the conflict was an IAC *sui generis*, situated outside the scope of the Geneva Conventions and governed by customary international law.[40] The precise content of this customary international law was not addressed by the U.S.

---

the Israeli Targeted Killings, 89 International Review of the Red Cross 373, 376 *et seq.* (June 2007).

[35] George W. Bush, *Address to a Joint Session of Congress and the American People* (Sep 20, 2001), online available at http://georgewbush-whitehouse.archives.gov/news/releases/2001/09/20010920-8.html (last visited Aug. 9, 2010).

[36] *See* U.S. Memos regarding the treatment of captured Al Qaeda and Taliban members – so called Torture Memos, online available at http://lawofwar.org/torture_memos_analysis.htm; For an overview over the development of the U.S. position towards the application of the Geneva Conventions *cf.* Lori Hosni, *The ABCs of the Geneva Conventions and Their Applicability to Modern Warfare*, 14 New England Journal of International and Comparative Law 135, 155 *et seq.* (2007); Marco Sassòli, *Transnational Armed Groups and International Humanitarian Law*, Occasional Paper Series, Program on Humanitarian Policy and Conflict Research, 5 (Harvard University Winter 2006) online available at http://www.hpcrresearch.org/pdfs/OccasionalPaper6.pdf.
For a critical assessment of the U.S. position *see* Joan Fitzpatrick, *Speaking Law to Power: The War Against Terrorism and Human Rights*, 14 European Journal of International Law 241, 248 *et seq.* (2003); Jordan J. Paust, *War and Enemy Status after 9/11: Attacks on the Laws of War*, 28 Yale Journal of International Law 325, 326 *et seq.* (2003).

[37] Mary Ellen O'Connell, *Defining Armed Conflict*, 13 Journal for Conflict and Security Law 393, 394 (2009) ("[...] it became apparent that the United States was claiming rights available to a state only during a de jure armed conflict afflicting all parts of the globe").

[38] George W. Bush, *Memorandum for the Vice President: Humane Treatment of Al Qaeda and the Taliban Detainees*, ¶ 2a (Feb. 7, 2002) ("[...] our conflict with Al Qaeda in Afghanistan or elsewhere throughout the world [...]").

[39] George W. Bush, *Memorandum for the Vice President: Humane Treatment of Al Qaeda and the Taliban Detainees*, ¶ 2c (Feb. 7, 2002) ("[...] the relevant conflicts [with al Qaeda and with the Taliban] are international in scope [...]").

[40] John Yoo and Robert J. Delahunty, *Memorandum for William J. Haynes II*, 12 (Jan. 9, 2002); Jay Bybee, *Application of Treaties and Laws to al Qaeda and Taliban Detainees*, 5 *et seq.* (Jan. 22, 2002).

administration. Thus, the U.S. profited from establishing a grey area of law in which it was bound by unclear rules and general principles.

The U.S. asserted that the Geneva Conventions did not cover armed conflicts in an exhaustive manner.[41] The Martens Clause was used in support of this position.[42] The Martens Clause enables the application of rules not yet incorporated into a formal treaty as customary international law.[43] Furthermore, the purpose of the Martens Clause is to extend protection beyond that of strict treaty law. However, the Bush administration used the Martens Clause to reduce levels of protection. A CIL category of IAC was created by the administration in an attempt to circumvent the applicability of the Geneva Conventions' treaty law, ultimately reversing the original purpose of the Martens Clause.[44] This can only be described as a deliberate attempt to create a legal lacuna or a *"legal black hole"*[45] in order to free the state actor from any legal constraints while asserting power.

Contrary to the opinions of the Bush administration, the Geneva Conventions cover all armed conflicts.[46] Therefore, the Geneva Conventions must be applied

---

[41] George W. Bush, *Memorandum for the Vice President: Humane Treatment of Al Qaeda and the Taliban Detainees*, ¶ 1 (Feb. 7, 2002) ("Our Nation recognizes that this new paradigm – ushered in not by us, but by terrorists – requires new thinking in the law of war, but thinking that nevertheless be consistent with the principles of Geneva"); *Hamdan v. Rumsfeld*, Government Brief on the Merits, available at http://www.hamdanvrumsfeld.com/HamdanSGmeritsbrief.pdf (last visited Jan. 26, 2011), 26 ("If an armed conflict, therefore, does not fall within the Convention, the Convention simply does not regulate it").

[42] *Hamdan v. Rumsfeld*, Government Brief on the Merits, available at http://www.hamdanvrumsfeld.com/HamdanSGmeritsbrief.pdf (last visited Jan. 26, 2011), 26 n.5.

[43] Theodor Meron, *The Martens Clause, Principles of Humanity, and Dictates of Public Conscience*, 94 American Journal of International Law 78, 79-80 and 87 *et seq.* (2000).

[44] *See* Marko Milanovic, *Lesson for Human Rights and Humanitarian Law in the War on Terror: comparing Hamdan and the Israeli Targeted Killings Case*, 89 International Review of the Red Cross 373, 377 (June 2007) ("Here we have the first example of the Martens Clause being cited by a government for purposes which are everything but humanitarian").

[45] *See* Claimants' Complaint in Royal Court of Justice, Court of Appeal (Civil Division) *Abbasi v. Secretary of State for Foreign and Commonwealth Affairs*, No: C/2002/0617 A, 0617 B (Judgment), ¶ 22 ((Nov. 6, 2002); Lars Mammen, *Völkerrechtliche Stellung von internationalen Terrororganisationen*, 218 (2008).

[46] International Committee of the Red Cross, *How is the Term "Armed Conflict" Defined in International Humanitarian Law?* 1 (2008) online available at

whenever violence crosses the threshold of an armed conflict. Furthermore, there can be no IAC outside the Geneva Conventions. Any attempt to subsume transnational conflicts under the term IAC must accommodate the Geneva Conventions' understanding and scope of the term, rather than arguing for an IAC regime beyond the conventions. Consequently, the US Supreme Court rejected the Bush administration's approach in its *Hamdan-Judgment*.[47] The U.S. administration then abandoned their original position and applied Art. 3 GC to detainees suspected of being Al Qaeda members.[48]

b) Non-State Actors and Possible Legal Subjectivity

Mammen suggests broadening the range of entities which qualify as IAC parties.[49] He asserts that not only states, but all international legal subjects including those with just partial legal subjectivity, should qualify as a party to an IAC.[50] He argues further that even a terrorist organization can, under certain circumstances, be a holder of international legal rights and duties, thereby making the organization a partial legal subject of the international legal order and an IAC party.[51] *Mammen's* argument is based on the assumption that legal subjectivity, in any form, is sufficient to qualify as a party in an armed conflict.

aa) Legal Subjects as Parties to an International Armed Conflict

Mammen does not adequately explain the assumption that legal subjectivity is sufficient to qualify as a party in an armed conflict. The sole argument presented

---

http://www.icrc.org/web/eng/siteeng0.nsf/htmlall/armed-conflict-article-170308/$file/ Opinion-paper-armed-conflict.pdf (last visited Aug. 9, 2010).

[47] *Hamdan vs. Rumsfeld*, 548 U.S. 557, 628 *et seq.* (2006) ("The latter kind of conflict [non-international] is distinguishable from the conflict described in Common Article 2 chiefly because it does not involve a clash between nations (whether signatories or not)").

[48] George W. Bush, *Executive Order 13440: Interpretation of the Geneva Conventions Common Article 3 as Applied to a Program of Detention and Interrogation Operated by the Central Intelligence Agency*, (July 20, 2007) available at http://edocket.access.gpo. gov/2007/pdf/07-3656.pdf (last visited Aug. 9, 2010).

[49] Lars Mammen, *Völkerrechtliche Stellung von internationalen Terrororganisationen* (2008).

[50] Lars Mammen, *Völkerrechtliche Stellung von internationalen Terrororganisationen*, 279 (2008).

[51] Lars Mammen, *Völkerrechtliche Stellung von internationalen Terrororganisationen*, 238 *et seq.* (2008).

35

is a quotation from a German textbook,[52] which states, *"Die Anwendung von Waffengewalt muss einer Konfliktpartei als Völkerrechtssubjekt zurechenbar sein."* (The application of the use of force must be attributed to a party to the conflict as an international legal subject).[53] While this statement suggests that any party to an IAC must be a legal subject, it does not imply that any legal subject is eligible as a party.[54] The following section examines this argument in further detail.

The assertion that every international legal subject, and not just states (as genuine international legal subjects), can be parties to an IAC is based on an interpretation of the Geneva Convention which focuses on the humanitarian object and purpose of the law *(raison d'être)*. According to this interpretation, a broad application of the Conventions is necessary.[55] However, this interpretation of IHL is contentious.

According to Art. 31 of the Vienna Convention of the Laws of Treaties (VCLT), the literal and systematic interpretations are of equal importance as the object and purpose of the law. Additionally, in accordance with Art. 32 VCLT, the historic interpretation may be resorted to as a subsidiary means. In 1985, *Hess* stated these rules of interpretations clearly suggest that only states, as High-Contracting Parties, can be parties to an IAC.[56] The question ultimately lies in which interpretation is correct.

---

[52] Lars Mammen, *Völkerrechtliche Stellung von internationalen Terrororganisationen*, 279 (2008).

[53] Knut Ipsen, Eberhard Menzel and Volker Epping, *Völkerrecht*, 1224 (2004).

[54] That the author of the quotation does in fact share Mammen's interpretation follows only from another source: Knut Ipsen, *Zum Begriff des "internationalen bewaffneten Konflikts"*, in Recht im Dienst des Friedens FS für Eberhard Menzel 405, 407 *et seq.* (Jost Delbrück et al. eds. 1975).

[55] Henri Meyrowitz, *The Law of War in the Vietnamese Conflict*, in The Vietnam War and International Law 516, 537 (Richard A. Falk ed., 1969); Georges Abi-Saab, *Wars of National Liberation in the Geneva Conventions and Protocols*, 165 Recueil des Cours de l'Academie de Droit International de la Haye 353, 401 (1979) ("The Geneva Conventions being humanitarian, law-making treaties par excellence, their object and purpose commend the widest possible application"); Martin Hess, *Die Anwendbarkeit des humanitären Völkerrechts, insbesondere in gemischten Konflikten*, 22 (1985); Antonio Cassese, *International Law*, 420 (2005) ("[…] the object and purpose of international humanitarian law impose that in case of doubt the protection deriving from this body of law be as extensive as possible, and it is indisputable that the protection accorded by the rules on international conflicts is much broader than that relating to internal conflicts […]").

[56] Martin Hess, *Die Anwendbarkeit des humanitären Völkerrechts, insbesondere in gemischten Konflikten*, 17 *et seq.* (1985).

The adherents of the broader purpose-oriented interpretation pinpoint cases in which IHL accepts non-state actors as parties to IACs. Four cases can be identified: 1) a situation referred to as the recognition of non-state actors as belligerents,[57] 2) the participation of UN armed forces,[58] 3) Art. 1.4 AP I, which refers to the armed forces of a people fighting for the right to self-determination and, 4) stabilized de-facto regimes,[59] entities that have achieved effective political authority over a country without being recognized as the legitimate government.[60] All four cases demonstrate that IACs are not exclusively inter-state armed conflicts.[61] The aforementioned four cases are, however, only exceptions. Hence, no analogy can be drawn for the purpose of transnational conflicts.

Paulus and *Vashakmadze's* analysis of state practice demonstrates that states do not accept non-state actors as parties of an IAC.[62] Hence, under the *lege lata* the interpretation of IHL, that non-state actors cannot be parties to IACs, prevails. The above-mentioned cases in which non-state actors may qualify as parties to an IAC remain exceptions to the rule. There are, however, reasons to change the law as per suggestions set forth by *Mammen*, in addition to adding another exception to the existing four. His assertion that partial international

---

[57] Eibe H. Riedel, *Recognitino of Belligenrency*, in Encyclopedia of Public International Law, Vol. 4, 47-50 (2000).

[58] Christopher Greenwood, *Scope of Application of Humanitarian Law*, in The Handbook of International Humanitarian Law, 51 *et seq.* (Dieter Fleck ed. 2008).

[59] Jochen Frowein, *Das de-facto-Regime im Völkerrecht. Eine Untersuchung zur Rechtsstellung „nichtanerkannter Staaten" und ähnlicher Gebilde*, 34 *et seq.* (1968); Dietrich Schindler, *The Different Types of Armed Conflicts according to the Geneva Conventions and Protocols*, 163 Recueil des Cours de l'Academie de Droit International de la Haye 117, 129 (1979) ("If a de facto régime declares its accession to the Geneva Conventions it should be considered a contracting party, irrespective of whether it is generally recognized as a State or not"); Christian Schaller, *Humanitäres Völkerrecht und nichtstaatliche Gewaltakteure*, 16-7, (Stiftung Wissenschaft und Politik Studie, 2007).

[60] Matthias Herdegen, *Völkerrecht*, 104 (2013).

[61] Henri Meyrowitz, *The Law of War in the Vietnamese Conflict*, in The Vietnam War and International Law 516, 533 (Richard A. Falk ed., 1969); Aldo Virgilio Lombardi, *Bürgerkrieg und Völkerrecht*, 356-7 (1976); Martin Hess, *Die Anwendbarkeit des humanitären Völkerrechts, insbesondere in gemischten Konflikten*, 39 (1985); James G. Stewart, *Towards a Single Definition of Armed Conflict in International Humanitarian Law: A Critique of Internationalized Armed Conflicts*, 85 International Review of the Red Cross 313, 319 (2003).

[62] Andreas Paulus and Mindia Vashakmadze, *Asymmetrical War and the Notion of Armed Conflict – A Tentative Conceptualization*, 91 International Review of the Red Cross 95, 112 (2009) ("[...] there is no consistent state practice or opinio juris to support such an assertion [that the concept of international armed conflict under customary international law might cover non-state entities").

legal subjectivity is sufficient to recognize an entity as party to an IAC begs the question as to under which conditions an entity acquires partial legal subjectivity and how exactly this is legally conceptualized.

bb) Terror Organizations as (Partial) Legal Subjects

In his work, *Mammen* identifies a parallel between terror organizations and insurgents. He states that his idea of conflict classification derives from the concept of recognition of insurgency.[63] According to this concept, insurgents may be granted partial legal subjectivity.[64] *Mammen* suggests applying a similar concept of recognition with the consequence that, at least temporarily, the transnational conflict between states and terror organizations can be legalized (*Verrechtlichung*) through the laws of IACs.[65]

Mammen argues further that a terror organization must fulfill three requirements to be a recognizable entity. It must (1) have an external link, (2) be a permanent and effective organization and, (3) have a substantial impact on the international level.[66] The first criterion, the external link, demonstrates that the terror organization is not a domestic phenomenon that can be attributed to a state, but rather one that operates as a transnational terror network.[67] *Mammen* argues that an external link is required for the applicability of international law. The criterion of the external link is met when the terrorist attack is performed in a different state, has its origin in that state, or purposefully chooses individuals from that state as its target.[68]

---

[63] Lars Mammen, *Völkerrechtliche Stellung von internationalen Terrororganisationen*, 183 (2008). Generally on the concept *see* Eibe H. Riedel, *Recognitino of Insurgency*, in Encyclopedia of Public International Law, Vol. 4, 54-6 (2000).

[64] Michael Bothe, *Streitkräfte internationaler Organisationen*, 103 (Heymann 1968) ("Deshalb entspricht es der Notordnungsfunktion kriegsrechtlicher Regeln, wenn Aufständische zum Zwecke der Anwendung von Kriegsrecht als (partiell) völkerrechtsfähig angesehen werden").

[65] Lars Mammen, *Völkerrechtliche Stellung von internationalen Terrororganisationen*, 183 (2008).

[66] Lars Mammen, *Völkerrechtliche Stellung von internationalen Terrororganisationen*, 240 (2008) ("Der terroristische Verband muss folgenden Kriterien gerecht werden: grenzüberschreitender Bezug ('External Link'), gewisse organisatorische Dauerhaftigkeit und Effektivität, signifikante Wirkungsintensität auf internationaler Ebene").

[67] Lars Mammen, *Völkerrechtliche Stellung von internationalen Terrororganisationen*, 240 (2008).

[68] Lars Mammen, *Völkerrechtliche Stellung von internationalen Terrororganisationen*, 240 (2008) ("Mit Blick auf die von einer transnationalen Terrororganisation verübte Gewalt bedeutet es, dass ein grenzüberschreitender Bezug immer vorliegt, wenn sie ihren

The second criterion requires the terror organization to be a permanent and effective organization. This requires that it have a command structure as well as consist of various cells in different states. Both would enable the terror organization to perform several attacks over a given period of time in multiple states.[69] Effective control over a specific territory is not required.[70]

The third and perhaps most important criterion requires the terror organization to have substantial impact on an international level. Therefore, the violence would have to cross a specific threshold of significance for the terror organization to be considered a subject of international norms.[71] *Mammen* does not elaborate on how high this threshold is, but rather states that the threshold cannot be assessed in abstract. Furthermore, he argues the threshold depends on the specific norm applied to the terror organization.[72] The amount of violence should be comparable to the amount required for a state's act of aggression under Art. 51 UN Charter.

Even if a terrorist organization were to meet all three criteria, *Mammen's* reference to the recognition of insurgency is unconvincing for two reasons. First, the recognition of insurgency was relevant to internal armed conflicts, without them being turned into IACs.[73] This raises the question as to why *Mammen* draws a parallel between an insurgent and a terrorist without addressing the

---

Anschlag in einem anderen Staat ausübt, aus einem anderen Staat stammt oder zielgerichtet Personen aus einem anderen Land als Objekte eines terroristischen Angriffs auswählt").

[69] Lars Mammen, *Völkerrechtliche Stellung von internationalen Terrororganisationen,* 241 (2008) ("Eine Terrororganisation, die über eine eigene Kommandostruktur verfügt und sich aus verschiedenen Zellen in unterschiedlichen Staaten zusammensetzt, sodass sie über einen gewissen Zeitraum hinweg mehrere Anschläge in verschiedenen Staaten durchführen kann, ist als politisch wie militärisch gefestigte Größe anzusehen").

[70] Lars Mammen, *Völkerrechtliche Stellung von internationalen Terrororganisationen,* 241 (2008) ("Der Effektivitätsstatus ist unabhängig von der territorialen Verfestigung der Terrorgruppe zu verstehen").

[71] Lars Mammen, *Völkerrechtliche Stellung von internationalen Terrororganisationen,* 241 (2008)1 ("Eine Terrororganisation gelangt nur in den Anwendungsbereich der völkerrechtlichen Normen, falls die durch sie verübte Gewalt eine 'Erheblichkeitsschwelle' überschritten hat").

[72] Lars Mammen, *Völkerrechtliche Stellung von internationalen Terrororganisationen,* 241 (2008) ("Wie hoch diese [Erheblichkeitsschwelle] im Einzelnen liegt, kann nicht pauschal bestimmt werden, sondern hängt von der jeweils betrachteten Norm ab").

[73] Eibe H. Riedel, *Recognitino of Insurgency,* in Encyclopedia of Public International Law, Vol. 4, 54 (2000) ("it [recognition of insurgency] may be necessitated by the existence of an internal armed conflict which has lasted for some time, and in which the insurgents have achieved a measure of success and control part of the territory of a State").

possible applicability of the laws of NIACs. It is possible that *Mammen* may have either confused the recognition of insurgency with the recognition of belligerency, or considered the two interchangeable.[74] Additionally, he considers the laws of NIACs as rudimentary, and ultimately leaving far too many legal loopholes. However, *Mammen* does not apply all IACs rules to the participants in the conflict either. Rather he suggests the application of an asymmetrical combatant status. This also creates legal uncertainties and loopholes. Second, a reference to the recognition of insurgency would require the recognition of terrorists as legal subjects by the state. It is highly unlikely that this will ever take effect. The U.S. is currently far from recognizing Al Qaeda as a legal subject. *Mammen* claims that, other than the recognition of insurgency, his approach does not require states to recognize the terrorist group as a legal entity.[75] He asserts that a terror organization gains legal subjectivity through an *implicit recognition*, due to the applicability of rights and duties under international law. *Mammen* also asserts that the implicit recognition of the terrorist organization takes place through organs of the UN, when terrorism is qualified as a threat to peace, or states that apply international norms, such as Art. 51 UN Charter and IHL rules, to terrorist groups.[76] This assertion is unconvincing as the qualification of terrorism as a threat to peace does not automatically imply that terrorists are recognized as legal subjects. Additionally, the fact that states resort to Art. 51 UN Charter, the right to self-defense against terrorists, does not automatically mean that they recognize the terrorists as parties to an IAC. Therefore, *Mammen's* suggestion of an implicit recognition lacks legal ground and requires further supportive evidence.

Mammen's approach is a position de *lege ferenda* that presents a novel set of criteria to determine when exactly a terror organization should gain legal subjectivity, but fails to be properly legally conceptualized. The reference to the legal concept of the recognition of insurgency is not convincing. It is rather surprising that *Mammen* does not consider applying his criteria within an NIAC model. Instead, he rejects the NIAC approach entirely, with the argument that conflicts

---

[74] Rejecting a distinction between recognition of belligenrency and recognition of insurgency, *see* Daniel Patrick O'Connell, *International Law*, Vol. 1, 151-2 (2nd ed., 1970) ("At this point insurgency is assimilated to belligerency, and the supposed distinction has vanished").

[75] Lars Mammen, *Völkerrechtliche Stellung von internationalen Terrororganisationen*, 252 (2008) ("Auch ist die Anerkennung von terroristischen Verbänden als Völkerrechtssubjekte nicht mit derjenigen von Aufständischen als kriegführende Partei im herkömmlichen Sinne gleichzusetzen").

[76] Lars Mammen, *Völkerrechtliche Stellung von internationalen Terrororganisationen*, 253-4 (2008).

with terror organizations are not just internal armed conflicts, and that only minimal conflict rules apply during NIACs.[77] However, as will be further explained, IHL is increasingly applied to the laws of NIAC, and not only to internal conflicts.

Mammen's claim that a higher standard of human rights law is provided by applying the law of IACs[78] is incorrect, as he does not correctly distinguish between the laws of IHL and IHRL. *Mammen* overlooks the possible consequence that, by applying IAC laws, the application of IHRL may subsequently be overruled.[79] Thus, by applying the laws of IACs, the protection granted through human rights law would not be ensured and improved, but instead possibly diminished or reduced. *Mammen's* approach of applying the laws of IACs to conflicts between states and terror organizations must therefore be refuted.

c) A Focus on the Cross-Border Nature of the Conflict

The approach arguing *de lege lata* for the application of IAC laws to transnational conflicts operates on the assumption that an *international* conflict is not necessarily an *inter-state* conflict.[80] The term *international* is claimed to refer

---

[77] Lars Mammen, *Völkerrechtliche Stellung von internationalen Terrororganisationen*, 181 (2008) ("Es erscheint geradezu paradox, die weltweit geführte Auseinandersetzung mit einer grenzüberschreitend agierenden Terrororganisation als einen nicht-internationalen Konflikt zu qualifizieren. In diesen Konflikten gilt nur ein Minimalmaß der konfliktrechtlichen Vorschriften, da der staatliche Souveränitätsanspruch der umfassenden Anwendung der völkerrechtlichen Normen entgegen steht").

[78] Lars Mammen, *Völkerrechtliche Stellung von internationalen Terrororganisationen*, 253 (2008) ("Hier geht es vor allem um die Gewährleistung grundlegender Menschenrechte für alle an den Auseinandersetzungen mit Terrorgruppen beteiligten ud von terroristischer Gewalt betroffenen Parteien. Erst ihre Anerkennung ermöglicht die Anwendung der Regeln des Völkerrechts – insbesondere des humanitären Völkerrechts").

[79] Christopher Greenwood, *Scope of Application of Humanitarian Law*, in The Handbook of International Humanitarian Law, 75 (Dieter Fleck ed. 2008) ("The IJC has repeatedly stated that international human rights law refers to internatinal humanitarian law as lex specialis which informs the content of human rights norms in areas to which both are applicable").

[80] For this general assumption *see* Henri Meyrowitz, *The Law of War in the Vietnamese Conflict,* in *The Vietnam War and International Law* 516, 533 (Richard A. Falk ed., 1969); Remigiusz Bierzanek, *Quelques remarques sur l'applicabilité du droit international humanitaire des conflits armés aux conflits internes internationalisés,* in Etudes et essais sur le droit international humanitaire et sur les principes de la Croix-Rouge. En l'honneur de Jean Pictet. Genève 281, 284 (Christophe Swinarski and Jean Pictet, eds., Nijhoff Publ. 1984) ("[L]e conflit international n'est pas synonyme de conflit interétatique; de plus, le droit de la guerre ne présuppose pas, pour toutes ses règles, que les

only to the cross-border nature of the respective conflicts. This would no longer require two states to be parties in an IAC. As long as fighting occurs on the territory of two states, only one state and a non-state actor may be involved. This occurred in 2006 during the conflict between Israel and Hezbollah, which took place on Israeli and Lebanese territory and was therefore characterized as an international armed conflict.[81]

The Supreme Court of Israel's view, which states that the border-crossing nature of an IAC is the decisive element and not the parties to the conflict, is evident in the *Targeted Killings Case*.[82] The Israeli Supreme Court explicitly stated,

> "an armed conflict of international character [is] [...] one that crosses the borders of a state – whether or not the place in which the armed conflict occurs is subject to belligerent occupation".[83]

This judgment raises the question as to whether all cross-border conflicts qualify as international armed conflicts.

The wording of Art. 2 GC can be interpreted as not requiring that hostilities occur between two states, but rather that they occur on their actual territory. Art. 2.2 GC states that,

> "the Convention shall also apply to all cases of partial or total occupation of the territory of a High Contracting Party, even if the said occupation meets with no armed resistance".[84]

Even without hostilities between two affected states, a conflict may qualify as an IAC.[85] Art. 2.2 GC captures a conflict involving two adversary states, even if

---

collectivités belligérantes doivent être des Etats"); James G. Stewart, *Towards a Single Definition of Armed Conflict in International Humanitarian Law: A Critique of Internationalized Armed Conflicts*, 85 International Review of the Red Cross 313, 319 (2003).

[81] *See* Gerd Hankel, *Das Tötungsverbot im Krieg*, 30 (2011).

[82] Supreme Court of Israel, HCJ 769/02 *Public Committee against Torture in Israel v. Israel* ¶ 18 (Dec. 13, 2006) ("[...] armed conflict of international character – in other words, one that crosses the borders of the state [...]") online available at http://elyon1.court.gov.il/Files_ENG/02/690/007/A34/02007690.A34.pdf (last visited Aug. 9, 2010).

[83] Supreme Court of Israel, HCJ 769/02 *Public Committee against Torture in Israel v. Israel* ¶ 18 (Dec. 13, 2006).

[84] Art. 2.2 GC.

[85] Jean S. Pictet, *Commentary on the Geneva Convention for the Amelioration of the Condition of the Wounded and Sick in Armed Forces in the Field*, 23 (1952) ("Any difference arising between two States and leading to the intervention of members of the armed forces is an armed conflict within the meaning of Article 2 ...It makes no difference how long the conflict lasts, or how much slaughter takes place, or how numerous are the participating forces; it suffices for the armed forces of one Power to have captured

one evades actual combat. It does not, however, capture a conflict between a state and a non-state party where hostilities occur on the territory of the state and another neutral state. *De lege lata*, in addition to its geographical scope, the nature of the conflict parties determines whether the conflict is an IAC.[86] Therefore, the notion that *international* conflict exclusively implies *cross-border* does not reflect the historical and *lege lata* understanding of the legal term at hand.

Furthermore, three arguments speak against a new reading of Art. 2 GC *de lege ferenda*. First, it is questionable whether one should let the rather coincidental geographical scope of a conflict determine which rules are applicable.[87] Second, the extent to which the conflict must be border-crossing remains unanswered. Relying solely on the transnationality of a conflict, without further specification, does not establish a clear criterion. Whether a single transnational act of violence across borders is sufficient to apply an IAC remains unclear. For example, the conflict between Colombian authorities and the FARC became transnational as Colombian armed forces conducted an operation outside Colombia, ultimately killing the FARC commander Raúl Reyes.[88] However, this single cross-border operation is not sufficient to change the entire nature of the conflict. Third, a new understanding of Art. 2 GC raises methodological problems with regard to the dichotomy of IHL: Distinguishing between IACs and NIACs on the basis of geographical scope alone presupposes that the existence of an armed conflict can be determined irrespective of whether it is international or non-international. This fails to consider the logic of the dichotomy of IHL, as no overarching term for armed conflict exists for both NIACs and IACs.[89] Hence, one cannot determine the nature of a conflict as an armed conflict and then determine the geographical scope to classify the conflict as an IAC or NIAC.

In conclusion, the Israeli's conceptualization satisfies neither *de lege lata*, nor *de lege ferenda*.

---

adversaries falling within the scope of Article 4. Even if there has been no fighting, the fact that persons covered by the Convention are detained is sufficient for its application").

[86] Liesbeth Zegveld, *Accountability of Armed Opposition Groups in International Law*, 136 (2003).

[87] Andreas Paulus and Mindia Vashakmadze, *Asymmetrical war and the notion of armed conflict – a tentative conceptualization*, 91 International Review of the Red Cross 95, 112 (2009) ("Yet the geographical element should not determine whether a conflict is qualified as international [...]").

[88] *Venezuela Condemn's Colombia over Rebel's Death*, N.Y. Times, Mar. 2, 2008 online available at http://www.nytimes.com/2008/03/02/world/americas/02iht-bogota.5. 10628446.html?_r=1 (last visited July 9, 2012); Simon Romero, *Files Suggest Venezuela Bid to Aid Colombia Rebels*, N.Y. Times, Mar. 30, 2008.

[89] Lindsay Moir, *The Law of Internal Armed Conflict*, 33-4 (2002).

3. Consequences of Applying the Laws of International Armed Conflicts

When assessing the application of IAC laws to transnational conflicts, one must consider not only the limits of proper legal conceptualization, but also the practical consequences. IACs are subject to a comprehensive set of rules, which provide the greatest possible amount of legal certainty within IHL to all participants. However, the recognition of transnational conflicts as IACs leads to a multitude of complications and difficulties. Two of them, the determination of the legal status of the members of the non-state armed groups and the protection of civilians, will be examined in the following sections.

a) The Legal Status of the Non-State Party

Determining the legal status of the members of the non-state groups, and thereby assessing whether a new one is required, is of utmost importance. The law of IACs distinguishes between combatants and civilians.[90] Generally, only combatants may be targeted and killed during an IAC. Additionally, only they are permitted to participate directly in the hostilities.[91] Combatants become prisoners of war (PoW) upon capture and can then be detained until the end of the hostilities.[92] During the time of their detention, they are protected by the third Geneva Convention. Civilians are generally protected from attacks and can only be targeted under Art. 51.3 AP I (which reflects Customary International Law), *"if and for such time"* as they take a *"direct part in hostilities"*.[93] As a result of having acted illegally, these civilians are not granted PoW status, but fall under the provisions of GC IV instead.[94]

Art. 1 of the Hague Regulations Respecting the Customs of War on Land (HLWR), Art. 4A GC III and Art. 43.2 AP I address criteria to qualify as a combatant. According to these provisions, combatants are members of the armed forces of a party to a conflict, as well as militias, if they meet certain requirements (see Art. 1 HLCW and Art. 4A GC III). If the laws of IAC are applied to a conflict that involves non-state actors as a party, the legal status of the armed forces of the non-state party comes in to question. A formal membership does

---

[90] Knut Ipsen, *Combatants and Non-Combatants*, in The Handbook of Internatoinal Humanitarian Law, 80 (Dieter Fleck ed. 2013) ("The primary status under international law of persons in an international armed conflict will be one of the two categories of persons: 'combatants and civilians'").

[91] Art. 43.2 AP I.

[92] Art. 44.1 AP II.

[93] Art. 51.3 AP I.

[94] Hans-Peter Gasser & Nils Melzer, *Humanitäres Völkerrecht*, 91-3 (2012).

not exist, as in the case for states. All approaches to classifying transnational conflicts as IACs between a state and a non-state actor mostly, if not exclusively, address the possible legal status of members of the non-state armed groups and present alternative solutions.

aa) Unlawful Combatants

At the start of the Afghanistan operations, the Bush administration stated that the Geneva Conventions were not applicable to the conflict with Al Qaeda. As a result, a *new paradigm* was proposed which rendered the current provisions of the Geneva Conventions in the U.S.-Al Qaeda conflict *obsolete*.[95] There was then no need to justify why Al Qaeda members were not real combatants (and ergo not PoWs after being captured) as the combatant category did not exist under the "new paradigm".[96] The Bush administration's view was subsequently overruled by the US Supreme Court's decision in *Hamdan v. Rumsfeld*, which held that Art. 3 GC of the Geneva Conventions was applicable as a minimum standard. As a response, the term *unlawful combatants* was applied to Al Qaeda fighters who were similarly treated as Taliban members.[97] Consequently, Al Qaeda members were not qualified as civilians. Members were also not granted the protection of the fourth Geneva Convention due to their constant participation, and because they did not fulfill the requirements of Art. 4 A GC III and Art. 1 Hague Regulations on Land Warfare.

---

[95] Memorandum from Alberto R. Gonzales for the President, *Decision Re Application of the Geneva Conventions on Prisoners of War to the Conflict with Al-Qaeda and the Taliban* (Jan. 25, 2002) online available at http://www.hereinreality.com/alberto_gonzales_torture_memo.html (last visited Jan. 26, 2011) ("In my judgment, this new paradigm renders obsolete Geneva's strict limitations on questioning of enemy prisoners and renders quaint some of its provisions requiring that captured enemy be afforded such things as commissary privileges, scrip (i.e., advances of monthly pay), athletic uniforms, and scientific instruments"); George W. Bush, *Memorandum for the Vice President: Humane Treatment of Al Qaeda and the Taliban Detainees* (Feb. 7, 2002); John Yoo and Robert J. Delahunty, *Memorandum for William J. Haynes II*, 12 (Jan. 09, 2002); *cf.* other U.S. Memos regarding the treatment of captured Al Qaeda and Taliban members – so called Torture Memos, online available at http://lawofwar.org/torture_memos_analysis.htm (last visited Jan. 26, 2011).

[96] *See* George W. Bush, *Memorandum for the Vice President: Humane Treatment of Al Qaeda and the Taliban Detainees*, ¶ 2a (Feb. 7, 2002).

[97] George W. Bush, *Executive Order 13440: Interpretation of the Geneva Conventions Common Article 3 as Applied to a Program of Detention and Interrogation Operated by the Central Intelligence Agency*, section 1 a) (July 20, 2007) available at http://edocket.access.gpo.gov/2007/pdf/07-3656.pdf (last visited Aug. 9, 2010).

Similar to the Taliban, Al Qaeda members were generally seen as combatants with the restriction that they were not granted the privileged status of PoWs. Members did not clearly distinguish themselves from the civilian population, often did not carry their arms openly, or abide by the rules of IHL.[98] However, treating Al Qaeda members the same way as Taliban fighters is contradictory. While the conflict with the Taliban was characterized as an IAC, the conflict with Al Qaeda was qualified as a NIAC. Within the laws of NIACs, combatant status, and hence *unlawful* combatants, does not exist.[99]

In sum, the term *unlawful combatants* has been used by the Bush administration to circumvent both the protection of the fourth Geneva Convention (as the persons are *combatants*) and the third Geneva Convention (as the persons are *unlawful*) in order to create a legal black hole. This contradicts the principle of the Geneva Conventions, according to which the legal status of all persons, involved or affected by an armed conflict, is regulated.[100] If an individual were to fall outside the categories of combatants or civilians, the conventions provide a minimum level of protection according to Art. 45.3 AP I and Art. 75 AP I.

The approach of the Bush administration must be interpreted as an attempt to create a new status of persons without legal protection. Accordingly, unlawful combatants would effectively be considered outlaws, and thus entirely dependent on the mercy of their enemy state. This approach must be refuted.

---

[98] George W. Bush, *Memorandum for the Vice President: Humane Treatment of Al Qaeda and the Taliban Detainees*, ¶ 2d (Feb. 7, 2002) ("[…] I determine that the Taliban detainees are unlawful combatants and, therefore, do not qualify as prisoners of war under Article 4 of Geneva."); Office of the Press Secretary, Statement by the Press Secretary on the Geneva Convention (May 7, 2003) ("Under Article 4 of the Geneva Convention, however, Taliban detainees are not entitled to POW status"), online available at http://georgewbush-whitehouse.archives.gov/news/releases/2003/05/20030507-18.html (last visited Aug. 10, 2010).

[99] Knut Dörmann, *The Legal Situation of "Unlawful/Unprivileged Combatants"*, 85 International Review of the Red Cross 45, 47 *et seq.* (Mar. 2003); Jelena Pejic, *"Unlawful/Enemy Combatants": Interpretations and Consequences*, in International Law and Armed Conflict 335 (Michael Schmitt and Jelena Pejic eds., 2007).

[100] Jelena Pejic, *"Unlawful/Enemy Combatants": Interpretations and Consequences*, in International Law and Armed Conflict 335, 342 (Michael Schmitt and Jelena Pejic eds., 2007) ("The view that there is an 'intermediate' category of persons who are neither combatants nor civilians and are therefore outside humanitarian law coverage is not borne out by the language of the relevant treaty texts. This position can also be questioned from the perspective of the logic and spirit that underlie the rules").

bb) Civilians Taking Direct Part in the Hostilities

According to the Supreme Court of Israel, members of terrorist groups qualify as a subcategory of civilians.[101] The court argues that, by not fulfilling the requirements outlined in Art. 4 A GC III and Art. 1 of the Hague Regulations, the combatant status is forfeited. As a result, these persons can only qualify as civilians, and therefore would be protected by the fourth Geneva Convention.[102]

Art. 50.1 AP I, which has achieved the status of Customary International Law,[103] states:

> "A civilian is any person who does not belong to one of the categories of persons referred to in Article 4 A (1), (2), (3) and (6) of the Third Convention and in Article 43 of this Protocol. In case of doubt whether a person is a civilian, that person shall be considered to be a civilian."[104]

As civilian members of non-state groups are prima facie not legitimate targets of military operations, they can only be attacked according to Art. 51.3 AP I, while they take a *"direct part in hostilities"*.[105] As a result, the authority to attack a participating civilian is further restricted compared to the authority to attack a regular combatant. If members of the non-state groups are treated as civilians taking direct part in hostilities, they will ultimately, and unjustifiably, benefit from a higher level of protection from attacks than ordinary combatants. This does not adequately capture the nature of non-state group members. These persons are not just civilians who sporadically participate in the conflict, but rather irregular forces that simply do not fulfill the requirements of Art. 4 A.2 GC III. Members of non-state groups must be treated as armed forces, or at least part of the armed forces, according to Art. 43.1 AP I, even if they do not meet

---

[101] Supreme Court of Israel, HCJ 769/02 *Public Committee against Torture in Israel v. Israel*, ¶ 28 (Dec. 13, 2006); Supreme Court of Israel, HCJ 6659/06 *A and B vs. State of Israel*, ¶ 12 (June 11, 2008); Knut Dörmann, *The Legal Situation of "Unlawful/Unprivileged Combatants"*, 85 International Review of the Red Cross 45, 46 *et seq.* (Mar. 2003); Jelena Pejic, *"Unlawful/Enemy Combatants": Interpretations and Consequences,* in International Law and Armed Conflict 335, 338 (Michael Schmitt and Jelena Pejic eds., 2007); Ryan Goodman, *The Detention of Civilians in Armed Conflicts*, 103 American Journal of International Law 48, 51 (2009).

[102] Knut Dörmann, *The Legal Situation of "Unlawful/Unprivileged Combatants"*, 85 International Review of the Red Cross 45, 73. (2003).

[103] Jean-Marie Henckaerts and Louise Doswald-Beck, *Customary International Humanitarian Law*, Rule 5 (2005).

[104] Art. 50.1 AP I.

[105] Art. 51.3 AP I.

the requirements of Art. 4 A.2 GC III.[106] Fulfilling these requirements allows persons to benefit from combatant-privilege and PoW status, however, as the ICRC has pointed out, these requirements *"are not constitutive elements of the armed forces of a party to a conflict"*.[107] Members of non-state groups must also be distinguished from offensive civilians who take direct part in hostilities for a specific amount of time. If this were not the case, members of non-state groups would benefit from a higher level of protection than combatants of the state. They would then profit from their disregard for Art. 4 A.2 GC III as well as from their own wrongdoing. This would contradict the logic of the principle of distinction.[108] In conclusion, members of non-state groups should not be categorized as civilians who take direct part in hostilities.

cc) Asymmetric Combatants

Mammen argues for a new *asymmetric combatant status*, which falls between civilian and combatant status,[109] to describe the structural imbalance between the high number of duties and the limited number of a terrorist's rights. The suggested status is described as a *vorverlagerte* (anticipated) version of the combatant status of Art. 4 A GC III.[110] Methodologically, this is the teleological reduc-

---

[106] International Committee of the Red Cross, *Interpretive Guidance on the Notion of Direct Participation in Hostilities under International Humanitarian Law*, 22 (2009) ("Thus, while members of irregular armed forces failing to fulfill the four requirements may not be entitled to combatant privilege and prisoner-of-war status after capture, it does not follow that any such person must necessarily be excluded from the category of armed forces and regarded as a civilian for the purposes of the conduct of hostilities").

[107] International Committee of the Red Cross, *Interpretive Guidance on the Notion of Direct Participation in Hostilities under International Humanitarian Law*, 22 (2009) ("Strictly speaking, however, these requirements [Art. 4A (2) GK III] constitute conditions for the post-capture entitlement of irregular armed forces to combatant privilege and prisoner-of-war status and are not constitutive elements of the armed forces of a party to a conflict").

[108] International Committee of the Red Cross, *Interpretive Guidance on the Notion of Direct Participation in Hostilities under International Humanitarian Law*, 22 (2009) ("[...] it would contradict the logic of the principle of distinction to place irregular armed forces under the more protective legal regime afforded to the civilian population merely because they fail to distinguish themselves from that population, to carry their arms openly, or to conduct their operations in accordance with the laws and customs of war").

[109] Lars Mammen, *Völkerrechtliche Stellung von internationalen Terrororganisationen*, 282 et seq. (2008).

[110] Lars Mammen, *Völkerrechtliche Stellung von internationalen Terrororganisationen*, 283 (2008) ("[Eine] vorverlagerte Stufe des Kombattantenstatus nach Art. 4 A III. Genfer Konvention [...]").

tion of the Geneva Conventions. Its provisions are applied to a limited extent due to the special characteristics of terror organizations.[111] Asymmetric combatants may be targeted as normal combatants, however, they do not have the right to participate in hostilities. As a result, if detained, they are not granted combatant immunity from criminal prosecution.[112] Consequently, this creates an imbalance between combatants of the state party and combatants of the non-state group. The only reason to describe the members of the non-state groups as combatants is to affirm they can legally be targeted. An asymmetric combatant can be detained for the entire duration of a conflict.[113] The asymmetric combatant has a right to basic humanitarian protection, in accordance with Art. 3 GC,[114] which applies to all detainees in IHL.[115]

Mammen's approach uniquely divides the norms of the GC III into those based on human rights values, which grant basic standards in the treatment of conflict parties such as Art. 12-16 GC III,[116] and those specifically for PoWs, which express IHL principles and do not contain general human rights values. Only the first set of provisions is applicable to asymmetric combatants. The second set of provisions, those specifically for PoWs, are the more privileged rights reserved for the *real* combatants.[117] Aside from impending criminal prosecution, asymmetric combatants face alternative detention conditions and are not entitled to all GC III provisions. The asymmetric combatant lacks the privilege to fight without threat of criminal prosecution and is not granted full PoW status. Individuals who do not abide by the combatants' rules (mainly to carry arms openly and distinguish themselves from the civilian population) do not deserve the privileges of the combatant status. The question then lies in what occurs when terrorists or other non-state actors (*Mammen* claims the asymmetric com-

---

[111] Lars Mammen, *Völkerrechtliche Stellung von internationalen Terrororganisationen*, 282 (2008).

[112] Lars Mammen, *Völkerrechtliche Stellung von internationalen Terrororganisationen*, 287 (2008).

[113] Lars Mammen, *Völkerrechtliche Stellung von internationalen Terrororganisationen*, 287 (2008).

[114] Lars Mammen, *Völkerrechtliche Stellung von internationalen Terrororganisationen*, 285 et seq. (2008).

[115] Lars Mammen, *Völkerrechtliche Stellung von internationalen Terrororganisationen*, 285 (2008).

[116] Lars Mammen, *Völkerrechtliche Stellung von internationalen Terrororganisationen*, 286 (2008).

[117] Lars Mammen, *Völkerrechtliche Stellung von internationalen Terrororganisationen*, 285 (2008).

batant status would be relevant not only for terrorists)[118] abide by the rules of IHL. *Mammen* does not address whether asymmetric combatants should be granted full combatant status in the event they abide by the rules of IHL, however two approaches are plausible.

On the one hand, one could assume that states do not grant non-state actors regular combatant status, even when they abide by the rules of Art. 4 A GC III. As a result, members of non-state groups would not be given the right to participate in the conflict, irrespective of their actual behavior during the conflict. This would eliminate every incentive for the non-state party to abide by IHL and contradict the compliance mechanisms of the laws of IACs, which are based on reciprocity and mutual respect for the laws of war. One must be aware that the purpose of IHL is not to keep certain actors away from the battlefield, but rather to regulate their conduct. On the other hand, if asymmetric combatants, who abide by Art. 4 A 2 GC III, were allowed to participate in conflicts, the asymmetric combatant status would be in accordance with the IAC framework. Non-state actors could be criminally prosecuted for their participation in the conflict only in the event of violating Art. 4 A 2 GC III. The advantage lies in that reciprocity between the two parties is preserved to a greater extent and that the non-state party may subsequently be incentivized to abide by Art. 4 A 2 GC III. However, this understanding of asymmetric combatants faces two central problems.

First, the effectiveness of IHL suffers when many non-state actors, and terrorists in particular, are unwilling to abide by the law. In fact, non-compliance is part of their strategy. The non-state actors use illegal methods of fighting in order to outweigh the military superiority of the state party.[119] By breaching IHL, they persistently gain military advantage. From a purely legal point of view, IHL remains binding to the state, even in the event that the non-state actor does not abide by the law (the *tu quoque* argument has no relevance for justifying breaches of IHL).[120] Eventually, however, the state party may also disregard IHL, as its expectation of reciprocal respect is not met. Ultimately, IHL may not be followed by either party.

Second, states are likely to deny non-state actors asymmetrical combatant status. States will most likely prosecute non-state actors for their participation in

---

[118] Lars Mammen, *Völkerrechtliche Stellung von internationalen Terrororganisationen*, 284-5 (2008).

[119] This is what Münkler calls the "attractiveness of asymmetry" which has to be prevented if a legal regulation of armed conflicts shall be achieved, *see* Herfried Münkler, *Der Wandel des Krieges*, 60 *et seq.* (2006).

[120] Hans-Peter Gasser & Nils Melzer, *Humanitäres Völkerrecht*, 24 (2012).

hostilities, even if they have abided by the rules of IACs, particularly Art. 4 A GC III. This is due to states' view that transnational conflicts are not conflicts between two equally legitimate conflict parties. Instead, transnational conflicts are, if qualified as armed conflicts, considered to be just wars fought against illegitimate non-state parties who are merely criminals.[121]

In conclusion, the status of non-state actors is inadequately regulated by the existing IAC laws. However, a new concept of asymmetric combatant status may serve as a starting point for a development *de lege ferenda*. This requires that the asymmetric combatants be recognized as full combatants if they abide by IHL, particularly Art. 4 A GC III. The concept of asymmetric combatants is more appropriate than the approaches set forth by the Bush-Administration, or the Israeli Supreme Court. Whether the concept of asymmetric combatants will gain relevance depends on the future conduct of the conflict parties. Unfortunately, however, it is highly questionable if non-state actors abide by IAC rules at all. Considering the unpredictability of the non-state actors' behavior, it is equally questionable whether a state would recognize asymmetric combatant status. After all, asymmetric combatant status would require states to accept that they cannot criminally prosecute non-state actors, so long as the non-state actors abide by IAC rules.

b) Protection of Civilians

This section analyzes the consequences of applying an IAC approach to the protection of civilians in transnational conflicts. During an IAC between states, civilians are involved in both conflict parties. However, during a transnational conflict between a state and a non-state group, civilians are found only on the side of the state party. This anomaly must be factored into the analysis. In addition, the protection of civilians in the territorial state from which the non-state group may operate must be addressed.

The conflict state's civilians are not protected from acts by their own state.[122] IHL was not initially designed to impose restrictions on a state towards its own

---

[121] *Cf.* Hans-Georg Dederer, *Krieg gegen Terror*, 59 Juristen Zeitung 421, 426 Fn. 73, (2004).

[122] Art. 4.1 GC IV ("Persons protected by the Convention are those who, at a given moment and in any manner whatsoever, find themselves, in case of a conflict or occupation, in the hands of a Party to the conflict or Occupying Power of which they are not nationals"); David Kretzmer, *Rethinking the Application of IHL in Non-International Armed Conflicts*, 42 Israel Law Review 8, 12 (2009) ("[...] Article 4 of the Fourth Geneva Convention excludes from the definition of 'protected persons' nationals of the Party in

citizens.[123] Under GC IV, civilians of the conflict state are therefore only protected from attacks by the non-state actors. However, the non-state party may simply not abide by GC IV. While some non-state actors, such as guerilla groups, who depend on civilian support may have incentive to spare civilians from violence, others, including terrorists, base their strategic concept on terrorizing the civilian population.[124] As a result, there is little hope that terrorists would refrain from attacks against the civilian population, although they may be held accountable for any violation of GC IV,[125] war crimes in particular.

The protection of the territorial state's citizens is even more difficult to determine. Transnational conflicts expose citizens of the territorial state to violence from both the conflict state and non-state actors. This occurred in the case of Lebanese citizens harmed when Israel fought Hezbollah on Lebanese territory. The question is whether these citizens are also protected under GC IV. The occurrence of transnational conflicts was not initially considered by those who drafted the GCs. Civilians originally referred to citizens of a conflict party and not citizens of a neutral state. However, Art. 4.1 GC IV does not specify that civilians must be citizens of a conflict party, hence, GC IV can be applied to citizens of the territorial state as well.[126] This has a double effect. On the one hand, GC IV imposes constraints on states. On the other hand, GC IV also grants the state party certain rights vis-à-vis the civilian population, including the right to detain civilians under specified circumstances.[127] Generally, a state has no authority over citizens of another state. During a traditional IAC, civilians are

---

whose hands they find themselves, as well as nationals of a State that is not bound by the Convention").

[123] Jean S. Pictet, *Commentary on the Geneva Convention (IV) Relative to the Protection of Civilian Persons in Times of War*, 46 (1958) ("The definition has been put in a negative form; as it is intended to cover anyone who is 'not' a national of the Party to the conflict or Occupying Power in whose hands he is. The Convention thus remains faithful to a recognized principle of international law: it does not interfere in a State's relations with its own nationals"); David Kretzmer, *Rethinking the Application of IHL in Non-International Armed Conflicts*, 42 Israel Law Review 8, 12 (2009) ("Traditional laws of war did not address the relationship between a belligerent State and its own forces or civilians; under the prevailing concepts this relationship was not conceived as a matter of concern for international law").

[124] Lars Mammen, *Völkerrechtliche Stellung von internationalen Terrororganisationen*, 70 (2008).

[125] On the accountability of the non-state armed group *see* Liesbeth Zegveld, *Accountability of Armed Opposition Groups in International Law* (2003).

[126] If the direct application of GC IV is rejected the Convention can at least be applied by analogy.

[127] *See* Art. 5, 42, 78 GC IV.

essentially obligated to tolerate and endure the opposing party's coercive measures as a result of their own state being involved in the armed conflict. Civilians themselves are likely to participate in the general war effort.[128] During a transnational conflict, the conflict state fighting non-state actors cannot claim rights over the territorial state's civilian population as the territorial state does not participate as a party in the transnational conflict. As a result, the conflict states need not be granted authority to wield power over the territorial state's citizens. Therefore, only prohibitive provisions of GC IV intended to protect civilians should be applied, and not permissive provisions that allow the state to take coercive measures against civilians. Limiting the conflict state's authority is justified. However, obliging the territorial state's citizens to tolerate and endure the conflict state's coercive measures is unnecessary.

Even when GC IV is applied, civilians are not protected from being victims of a lawful attack on a combatant in the heat of the battle, an example being the case of Afghanistan. The UN Assistance Mission in Afghanistan (UNAMA) counted 440 Afghan civilian deaths by pro-governmental forces in 2010.[129] Even if one were to assume that the Afghan civilian population would be protected through GC IV, many of these deaths would be deemed lawful as per IHL. The Kunduz Air-Strike is a particularly striking example. NATO forces bombed a gas truck killing up to 150 people, many of whom were civilians.[130] The *Generalbundesanwalt* [German Federal Prosecutor General], who investigated the

---

[128] The general war effort has to be distinguished carefully from a direct participation in hostilities, *see* Yves Sandoz, Christophe Swinarski and Bruno Zimmermann (eds.), *Commentary on the Additional Protocols of 8 June 1997 to the Geneva Conventions of 12 August 1949*, 619 (1987) ("There should be a clear distinction between direct participation in hostilities and participation in the war effort. The latter is often required from the population as a whole to various degrees. Without such a distinction the efforts made to reaffirm and develop international humanitarian law could become meaningless. In fact, in modern conflicts, many activities of the nation contribute to the conduct of hostilities, directly or indirectly; even the morale of the population plays a role in this context").

[129] United Nations Assistance Mission in Afghanistan, *Annual Report 2010 – Protection of Civilians in Armed Conflict*, 2009, 21 (Mar. 2011) online available at http://www.google.de/url?sa=tandrct=jandq=AFGHANISTAN+-+ANNUAL+REPORT+ON+PROTECTION+OF+CIVILIANS+IN+ARMED+CONFLICT%2C+2009andsource=webandcd=3andved=0CEIQFjACandurl=http%3A%2F%2Funama.unmissions.org%2FPortals%2FUNAMA%2Fhuman%2520rights%2FMarch%2520PoC%2520Annual%2520Report%2520Final.pdfandei=7Y5XT8rPN8WeOrvLjIcNandusg=AFQjCNFREDrw_RIBK2qAyeGY-W-EQQt1Jw (last visited Mar. 7, 2012).

[130] *See* Constantin von der Groeben, *Criminal Responsibility of German Soldiers in Afghanistan: The Case of Colonel Klein*, 11 German Law Journal No 5, 469-492 (2010).

case against the officer in command and a sergeant, dropped investigations due to what he believed was no violation of IHL.[131]

4. Conclusion

De lege lata the laws of IACs are applicable only when non-state actors are attributable to a state. As previously mentioned, the threshold for attribution is high and cannot be met when non-state armed groups do no more than use the territorial state's territory as a base for operations, perhaps even without the knowledge of the territorial state.

Attributing Al Qaeda's actions to the Taliban (as Afghanistan's *de-facto-*regime until the end of 2001) remains highly controversial. Current evidence suggests that Al Qaeda only fought alongside the Taliban and was not actually controlled by or integrated into the Taliban forces. If the non-state actors act on their own behalf rather than being attributed to a state, IAC rules do not apply *de lege lata* to the transnational conflict. Therefore, three *de lege ferenda* propositions for a new, broader understanding of IAC have been addressed in this book: the Bush administration's approach, the Israeli Supreme Court's approach and *Mammen's* approach.

The Bush administration's original approach must be rejected, as it was no more than an attempt to create a legal *lacuna*. Additionally, no further practice in IHL would support this approach.

The proposition of the Israeli Supreme Court, which interprets Art. 2 GC as no longer requiring the participation of two states, but instead simple cross-border violence, must also be rejected. The geographical scope of a conflict alone is too vague a criterion to determine IACs. The Israeli Supreme Court's view fails to acknowledge the importance of the nature of the warring parties for the characterization of the conflict. Additionally, it fails to develop an appropriate legal status for the non-state group's members. Qualifying these members as civilians who directly participate in the conflict does not accurately capture events on the ground.

Mammen's approach of applying IAC laws to transnational conflicts is more appropriate as he suggests granting non-state actors limited legal subjectivity

---

[131] Einstellungsvermerk des Generalbundesanwalts [Memorandum of the Federal Prosecutor General], 3 BJs 6/10-4 (April 16, 2010), online available at www.generalbundesanwalt.de/docs/einstellungsvermerk20100416offen.pdf (last visited Mar. 7, 2012) (In fact the Federal Prosecutor General qualified the conflict as a NIAC, but the applicable german criminal law provision, Art. 11 Abs. 1 Nr.3 VStGB, that implements IHL is applicable during both IAC and NIAC.).

and their own party status to an IAC. However, this too would require an entirely new reading of the treaty. The conceptual weakness of this approach lies in the requirement of some form of recognition of the non-state actor by the international community. This is to occur if and only when non-state actors convey the expectation that they will abide by the law to some extent. This, however, is highly unlikely in the context of terror organizations.

Conceptual weaknesses aside, the presented approaches raise the issue of consequences that follow an application of IAC laws. The *lege lata* of IACs is insufficient for the legal qualification of members of non-state armed groups. Therefore, if the rules of IACs are to be applied to transnational conflicts, further clarification and the development of a new legal category would be necessary. This, however, is problematic due to the refusal of non-state armed groups to abide by IHL.

The problem with applying the law of IACs to transnational conflicts is the tension between the intrinsic asymmetry of transnational conflicts and the symmetry of IACs.[132] In addition, when considering the protection of civilians, one must distinguish between the conflict state's and the territorial state's citizens. As previously mentioned, the protection of the conflict state's citizens is granted through GC IV. Similarly, the application of GC IV can be applied in order to protect citizens of the territorial state, given that authority over the territorial state's citizens, granted by GC IV, is limited.

In conclusion, the laws of IACs are inapplicable to transnational conflicts *de lege lata*. Additionally, the *lege ferenda* approaches are conceptually inaccurate. The practical problems that result from their applicability, particularly with respect to the status of the members of non-state armed groups, strongly caution against the introduction of a new understanding of international armed conflict. The IAC laws should be applied only to non-state armed groups that accept being bound by the same laws.

---

[132] Toni Pfanner, *Asymmetrical Warfare from the Perspective of Humanitarian Law and Humanitarian Action*, 87 International Review of the Red Cross 149, 173 (Mar. 2005) ("International humanitarian law should not be overstretched. It cannot be extended to situations other than those it is intended to cover without giving wrong directives. This is particularly relevant for the fight against international terrorism, which despite many warlike aspects does not necessarily amount to an 'armed conflict' in the current sense of the law of war"); Robin Geiß, *Asymmetric Conflict Structures*, 864 International Review of the Red Cross 775, 777 (2006) ("It [the analysis of asymmetric conflict structures] has nonetheless revealed some aspects that caution against any premature over-extension of IHL's scope of application to cover asymmetric constellations akin to subordinative patterns of law enforcement, which therefore lack the minimum degree of symmetry required for the fundamental principles of IHL to be applicable").

II. Non-International Armed Conflicts

The second possible categorization of transnational conflicts within the current dichotomy of IHL is that of a NIAC. The following section will first analyze the determinants for the existence of NIACs, with special respect to transnational conflicts. Subsequently, the consequences of applying NIAC laws to transnational conflicts will be addressed.

1. Transnational Conflicts and the Determining Criteria of NIACs

There is no clear definition of NIACs.[133] As a result, distinguishing NIACs from incidents of violence that do not amount to armed conflicts is particularly challenging.[134] The main legal source, Art. 3 GC, addresses only an

"armed conflict not of an international character occurring in the territory of one of the High Contracting Parties [...]".

In order to analyze the criteria for categorizing a conflict as an NIAC, additional legal sources must be consulted. These include all other provisions of the Geneva Conventions, as well as their Additional Protocol II, the commentary of the Geneva Conventions by *Jean Pictet*, the important *Tadic-Decision* by the ICTY and the ICC-Statute.[135] Even the aforementioned sources form just a small selection of the materials available to determine a NIAC. However, it is these sources and the criteria following from them that are constantly cited when categorizing a NIAC.[136]

---

[133] Jelena Pejic, *Terrorist Acts and Groups: A Role for International Law?* 75 British Yearbook of International Law, 71, 86 (2004); Marco Sassòli, *Transnational Armed Groups and International Humanitarian Law*, Occasional Paper Series, Program on Humanitarian Policy and Conflict Research, 6 (Harvard University Winter 2006) online available at http://www.hpcrresearch.org/pdfs/OccasionalPaper6.pdf.

[134] *See* Georges Abi-Saab, *Non-International Armed Conflicts*, in International Dimensions of Humanitarian Law 217, 237 *et seq.* (UNESCO ed. 1988); Steven R. Ratner and Jason S. Abrams, *Accountability for Human Rights Atrocities in International Law*, 96 (2001) ("The level of conflict necessary to trigger these protections [of Art. 3] has been a source of uncertainty and contention since the Conventions' drafting").

[135] For an overview over these sources *see* Knut Dörmann and Louise Doswald-Beck, *Elements of War Crimes under the Rome Statute of the International Criminal Court*, 384 *et seq.* (2004).

[136] *See* Dieter Fleck, *The Law of Non-International Armed Conflict*, in The Handbook of International Humanitarian Law, 593 *et seq.* (Dieter Fleck ed. 2013);
For a list of relevant factors *see* Marco Sassòli, *Transnational Armed Groups and International Humanitarian Law*, Occasional Paper Series, Program on Humanitarian Policy

The two core criteria following from above mentioned sources are the degree of organization of the party and the amount of violence during the conflict.[137] In addition, as a third element, the geographical scope of the conflict is crucial.[138] Transnational conflicts pose difficulties with respect to all three criteria. Firstly, wether non-state actors fulfill the requirements to qualify as a party to NIACs is often questionable. Second, it is doubtful whether the degree of violence in transnational conflicts, which is often rather sporadic and low in intensity, is sufficient to reach the armed conflict threshold. Finally, fitting transnational conflicts into a regime that was designed for internal conflicts is inherently problematic. Each of these three criteria, the conflict parties, the threshold of violence, and, the geographical scope, will be addressed in the following sections.

a) Parties to a Non-International Armed Conflict

Whether, and under which circumstances, non-state armed groups can be parties to NIACs is addressed in this section. While IACs require the participation of two states, NIACs require the participation of only one state, if at all. This raises the question as to whether this implies that every non-state actor and every

---

and Conflict Research, 6 (Harvard University Winter 2006) online available at http://www.hpcrresearch.org/pdfs/OccasionalPaper6.pdf;

For a slightly diverging list of factors *see* Roberta Arnold, *The ICC as a New Instrument for Repressing Terrorism*, 116 (2004) (Arnold makes strong reference to Martin Hess, *Die Anwendbarkeit des humanitären Völkerrechts, insbesondere in gemischten Konflikten*, 97 *et seq.* (1985)).

[137] ICTR, *The Prosecutor vs. Jean-Paul Akayesu*, Case No. ICTR-96-4-T, Trial Judgment, ¶ 620 (Sep. 02, 1998); International Law Association, *Final Report on the Meaning of Armed Conflict in International Law*, 2 passim (2010); Jelena Pejic, *Terrorist Acts and Groups: A Role for International Law?* 75 British Yearbook of International Law, 71, 86 (2004); René Provost, *International Human Rights and Humanitarian Law*, 267 (2004); Dieter Fleck, *Non-International Armed Conflict: Legal Qualifications and Parties to the Conflict*, in International Humanitarian Law and other Legal Regimes: Interplay in Situations of Violence 27, 28 (International Institute of Humanitarian Law ed. 2003); Magne Frostad, *Jus in Bello after September 11*, 2001 at 42 (2005); Heike Spieker, *The International Criminal Court and Non-International Armed Conflicts*, 13 Leiden Journal of International Law 395, 408 (2000); Lars Mammen, *Völkerrechtliche Stellung von internationalen Terrororganisationen*, 169 (2008); Sylvain Vité, *Typology of Armed Conflicts in International Humanitarian Law: Legal Concepts and Actual Situations*, 91 International Review of the Red Cross, 69, 76 (2009); Sandesh Sivakumaran, *The Law of Non-International Armed Conflict*, 164 *et seq.* (2012).

[138] Sylvain Vité, *Typology of Armed Conflicts in International Humanitarian Law: Legal Concepts and Actual Situations*, 91 International Review of the Red Cross, 69, 78 (2009).

loose assembly of individuals can be party to a NIAC.[139] The traditional understanding of the laws of NIACs suggests this is not the case. The general consensus and common practice is that the armed group must fulfill certain minimum
requirements to be classified as a party to a NIAC.[140] The difficulty lies in defining and specifying these minimum requirements.

aa) Organized Armed Groups

In his commentary on Art. 3 GC, *Pictet* presents a number of situations in
which a conflict may qualify as a NIAC.

"(1) That the Party in revolt against the de jure Government possesses an organized
military force, an authority responsible for its acts, acting within a determinate territory
and having the means of respecting and ensuring respect for the Convention.

(2) That the legal Government is obliged to have recourse to the regular military forces
against insurgents organized as military and in possession of a part of the national territory.

(3) (a) That the de jure Government has recognized the insurgents as belligerents; or

(b) that it has claimed for itself the rights of a belligerent; or

(c) that it has accorded the insurgents recognition as belligerents for the purposes only
of the present Convention; or

(d) that the dispute has been admitted to the agenda of the Security Council or the General Assembly of the United Nations as being at threat to international peace, a breach
of the peace, or an act of aggression.

(4) (a) That the insurgents have an organisation purporting to have the characteristics
of a State.

(b) That the insurgent civil authority exercises de facto authority over persons within a
determinate territory.

(c) That the armed forces act under the direction of the organized civil authority and
are prepared to observe the ordinary laws of war.

---

[139] *See* Jean S. Pictet, *Commentary on the Geneva Convention for the Amelioration of
the Condition of the Wounded and Sick in Armed Forces in the Field*, 49 (1952) ("[...] if
a handful of individuals were to rise in rebellion against a State and attack a police station, would that suffice to bring into being an armed conflict within the meaning of the
Article [Art. 3 GK]?").
[140] Liesbeth Zegveld, *Accountability of Armed Opposition Groups in International
Law*, 140 (2003); Lindsay Moir, *The Law of Internal Armed Conflict*, 36 (2002).

(d) That the insurgent civil authority agrees to be bound by the provisions of the Convention." [141]

The above-mentioned situations set high standards for the non-state armed groups to qualify as parties to a NIAC. However, this list is not exhaustive.[142] *Pictet* stated Art. 3 GC should be applied as broadly as possible.[143]

Similarly, the AP II suggests that,

> "organized armed groups which, under responsible command, exercise such control over a part of its territory as to enable them to carry out sustained and concerted military operations and to implement this Protocol".[144]

Paust and *Mammen* argue that this high threshold applies to all NIACs.[145] However, the AP II threshold goes beyond what it required for an Art. 3 GC conflict. As a result, the field of application for AP II is narrower and more restricted than that of Art. 3 GC.[146] Furthermore, NIACs, within the definition outlined in Art. 3 GC, do not have to meet the threshold of AP II. Parties to an Art. 3 conflict are not required to exercise control over a certain territory.[147]

---

[141] Jean S. Pictet, *Commentary on the Geneva Convention for the Amelioration of the Condition of the Wounded and Sick in Armed Forces in the Field*, 49 (1952).

[142] Jean S. Pictet, *Commentary on the Geneva Convention for the Amelioration of the Condition of the Wounded and Sick in Armed Forces in the Field*, 50 (1952).

[143] Jean S. Pictet, *Commentary on the Geneva Convention for the Amelioration of the Condition of the Wounded and Sick in Armed Forces in the Field*, 50 (1952).

[144] Art. 1.1 AP II.

[145] Jordan J. Paust, *There Is No Need to Revise the Laws of War in Light of September 11th*, The American Society of International Law Task Force on Terrorism, 2 (2002); Lars Mammen, *Völkerrechtliche Stellung von internationalen Terrororganisationen*, 176 (2008).

[146] Christopher Greenwood, *Scope of Application of Humanitarian Law*, in The Handbook of International Humanitarian Law, 55 (Dieter Fleck ed. 2008); Michael Bothe, Karl J. Partsch and Waldemar A. Solf, *New Rules for Victims of Armed Conflicts*, 623 (1982).

[147] *E.g.,* Inter-American Commission on Human Rights, *Juan Carlos Abella v. Argentina* [Tablada] Case 11.137, Report No. 55/97, OEA/Ser.L/V/II.98, doc. 6 rev. ¶ 152 (1998); Dietrich Schindler, *The Different Types of Armed Conflicts according to the Geneva Conventions and Protocols*, 163 Recueil des Cours de l'Academie de Droit International de la Haye 117, 146 (1979); William A. Schabas, *Theoretical and International Framework: Punishment of Non-State Actors in Non-international Armed Conflicts*, 26 Fordham International Law Journal 907, 916 (2003); Gabor Rona, *Interesting Times for International Humanitarian Law: Challenges form the "War on Terror"*, 27/2 Fletcher Forum of World Affairs, 55, 60 (2003); Marco Sassòli, *Transnational Armed Groups and International Humanitarian Law*, Occasional Paper Series, Program on Humanitarian Policy and Conflict Research, 13 (Harvard University Winter 2006) online available at http://www.hpcrresearch.org/pdfs/OccasionalPaper6.pdf; Roberta Arnold, *The ICC as a New Instrument for Repressing Terrorism*, 117 (2004); *cf.* Claus Kreß, *Völkerstrafrecht*

In its *Tadic-Decision*, the ICTY used the formulation *"organized armed groups"*.[148] This same term was repeated in Art. 8 (2) (f) of the ICC-Statute, which requires a minimum degree of organization. The demand for a minimum level of organization of non-state actors is necessary to identify them as responsible for the violence and as addressees of international legal norms. An organizational structure which oversees a command structure is necessary to ensure that the non-state group can abide by international norms. Although Art. 3 GC does not require reciprocity, its foundation lies in the mutual respect for IHL. Hence, the ability to implement IHL provisions is crucial. The criterion of organization itself can be determined alongside various factors, which include *"the existence of headquarters, designated zones of operations, the ability to procure, transport and distribute arms"*.[149] The existence of a command structure, disciplinary rules and mechanisms, control of territory, ability to gain access to weapons and other military equipment, to recruit members and provide them with military training, to carry out military operations using tactics and strategy, and the ability of the group to speak with one voice are of critical importance.[150] The decisive element among these factors is the ability to implement the provisions of Art. 3 GC.[151] To qualify as an organized armed group, the non-state

---

der dritten Generation gegen transnationale Gewalt Privater?, in Die Macht und das Recht, 323, 363 *et seq.* (Gerd Hankel ed., 2008) (Kreß agrees in general but points to a lack of sufficient state practice).

[148] ICTY, *Prosecutor v. Tadic*, Case No. IT-94-1-I, Decision on Defence Motion for Interlocutory Appeal on Jurisdiction, ¶ 70 (Oct. 2, 1995).

[149] ICTY, *Prosecutor v. Farnir Limaj et. al.*, Case No. IT-03-66-T, Trial Judgement, ¶ 90 (Nov. 30, 1995).

[150] *See* ICTY, *Prosecutor v. Ramush Haradinaj et. a.,* Case No. IT-04-84-I, Trial Judgement, ¶ 64 (Apr. 3, 2008).

[151] Gerald. I. A. D. Draper, *The Geneva Conventions of 1949*, 114 Recueil des Cours de l'Academie de Droit International de la Haye 59, 90 *et seq.* (1965); Dietrich Schindler, *The Different Types of Armed Conflicts according to the Geneva Conventions and Protocols*, 163 Recueil des Cours de l'Academie de Droit International de la Haye 117, 147 (1979); Lindsay Moir, *The Law of Internal Armed Conflict*, 36 (2002); International Committee of the Red Cross, *International Humanitarian Law and the Challenges of Contemporary Armed Conflicts*, 18 *et seq.* (2003), online available at http://www.icrc.org/Web/eng/siteeng0.nsf/htmlall/5XRDCC/$File/IHLcontemp_armedco nflicts_FINAL_ANG.pdf (last visited Mar 02, 2009); Gabor Rona, *Interesting Times for International Humanitarian Law: Challenges form the "War on Terror"*, 27/2 Fletcher Forum of World Affairs, 55, 60 (2003); Helen Duffy, *The "War on Terror" and the Framework of International Law*, 222 (2005); Toni Pfanner, *Asymmetrical Warfare from the Perspective of Humanitarian Law and Humanitarian Actions*, 857 International Review of the Red Cross 149, 164 *et seq.* (2005); Marco Sassòli, *Transnational Armed Groups and International Humanitarian Law*, Occasional Paper Series, Program on Humanitarian Policy and Conflict Research, 14 (Harvard University Winter 2006) online

actor must provide for an organizational structure that allows it to implement the rules of NIACs among its men, which is decided on a case-by-case basis.[152] Recent practice suggests that the rejection of the non-state armed group to comply with IHL does not affect its ability to be a party to a NIAC.[153]

bb) Non-State Actors in Transnational Conflicts as Organized Armed Groups

This section will address the qualification of non-state actors in transnational conflicts as parties of a NIAC.

Externally determining whether a non-state armed group encompasses the required degree of organization and internal disciplinary structure is particularly difficult. Some long-existing groups, such as the FARC, are composed of such a structure. Groups such as Al Qaeda, however, do not show evidence of the same strict disciplinary structure. Additionally, far less insight into this particular organization is available.

Prior to and immediately after 9/11, Al Qaeda was sufficiently organized. The group was controlled by Osama Bin Laden and a command structure of his lieutenants, and contained a base and training camps in Afghanistan. With the destruction of most Al Qaeda camps in Afghanistan, and ultimately the death of Osama Bin Laden, the organization appears to have been shattered and no longer satisfies the party requirement of Art. 3 GC. Currently, Al Qaeda appears to be organized solely within independent cells working on their own behalf.[154] As a

---

available at http://www.hpcrresearch.org/pdfs/OccasionalPaper6.pdf; René Provost, *International Human Rights and Humanitarian Law*, 267 (2004); Claus Kreß, *Völkerstrafrecht der dritten Generation gegen transnationale Gewalt Privater?*, in Die Macht und das Recht 323, 363 *et seq.* (Gerd Hankel ed., 2008); Heiko F. Schmitz-Elvenich, *Targeted Killing*, 195-6 (2008).

[152] ICTY, *Prosecutor v. Farnir Limaj et. al.*, Case No. IT-03-66-T, Trial Judgement, ¶ 90 (Nov. 30, 1995).

[153] ICTY, *Prosecutor v. Boskoski et al.*, Case No. IT-04-82-T, Trial Judgement, ¶ 205 (Jul. 10, 2008); Claus Kreß, *Some Reflections on the International Legal Framework Governing Transnational Armed Conflicts*, 15 Journal of Conflict and Security Law 245, 259 (2010).

[154] Jochen Bittner, *Das weltweite Al-Qaida Netz*, Die Zeit (July 14, 2005) ("An die Stelle der alten, vertikal organisierten al-Qaida ist ein loses, horizontales Netzwerk aus Netzen getreten"), online availabe at http://www.zeit.de/2005/29/terrorismus_bittner (last visited June 4, 2012); Sylvain Vité, *Typology of Armed Conflicts in International Humanitarian Law: Legal Concepts and Actual Situations*, 91 International Review of the Red Cross 69, 93 (2009) ("Basically, Al Qaeda's way of operating probably excludes it from being defined as an armed group that could be classified as a party to a global non-international armed conflict. In accordance with the current state of intelligence, it

result, it lacks the organization structure necessary to qualify as a party to a NIAC.[155] One might even argue that Al Qaeda has turned into a terrorist social movement rather than an organized group.[156] To the contrary, the German *Generalbundesanwalt* [Federal Prosecutor General] has characterized the Taliban and its associates as a party to a NIAC.[157] The Taliban substantially differs from Al Qaeda in that they have a strong leader, Mullah Omar, and a hierarchical internal structure with military and political branches. While being heterogeneous, they are not organized in to clandestine cells, but instead are divided into regional branches linked to a central command that cooperate with each other.[158] Furthermore, evidence suggests that other non-state groups, such as Hezbollah and the PKK, may be party to a NIAC as they are located in a specific region, have a political branch, and are composed of an organizational structure to internally enforce rules.[159] The previously mentioned examples demonstrate that two challenges must be considered when determining the organization of a non-state group: the challenge in gaining sustainable information from inside the organiza-

---

appears, rather, to be a loosely connected, clandestine network of cells. These cells do not meet the organization criterion for the existence of a non-international armed conflict within the meaning of humanitarian law"); Jörg Föh, *Die Bekämpfung des internationalen Terrorismus nach dem 11. September 2001*, 52 (2011).

[155] Michael Bothe, *Friedenssicherung und Kriegsrecht*, in Völkerrecht 639, 738 (Wolfgang Graf Vitzthum ed. 2010) ("Ein bewaffneter Konflikt setzt konfliktfähige Parteien voraus (Staaten, bewaffnete Gruppe). Der 'Terror' ist dies nicht, ebensowenig Al Qaida").

[156] Marc Sageman, *Leaderless Jihaad*, 143 *et seq.* (2008).

[157] Einstellungsvermerk des Generalbundesanwalts [Memorandum of the Federal Prosecutor General], 3 BJs 6/10-4, Page 43 (Apr. 16, 2010), online available at www.generalbundesanwalt.de/docs/einstellungsvermerk20100416offen.pdf (last visited Mar. 7, 2012) ("[…] die aufständischen Taliban und die mit ihnen assoziierten Gruppen [sind] völkerrechtlich als Konfliktpartei zu qualifizieren, die mit ausreichenden strategischen, personellen, militärischen und propagandistischen Fähigkeiten und Kapazitäten ausgestattet ist, um die afghanische Regierung und die ISAF in einen bewaffneten Konflikt zu verwickeln, der seit Jahren besteht und sich zunehmende verstärkt").

[158] Citha D. Maaß, *Gespräche mit Taleban*, 14 SWP-Aktuell 1, 2 (Mar. 2009) "Als *afghanische Taleban* wird eine heterogene Koalition oppositioneller militanter Kräfte (OMK) unter Führung Mullah Omars bezeichnet", online available at http://www.swp-berlin.org/de/publikationen/produkt-detail/article/afghanistan_riskanter_politikwechsel.html (last visited June 2, 2012).

[159] Against a status under IHL for Hezbollah *see* Christian Tomuschat, *Der Sommerkrieg des Jahres 2006 im Nahen Osten*, 81 Friedenswarte (2006) 179, 185 ("Auch die Angehörigen der Hisbollah sind nicht vogelfrei, sie stehen zumindest unter dem Schutz der allgemeinen Menschenrechte, auch wenn sie nach humanitärem Recht keinen speziellen Status genießen, da sie allein auf eigene Faust handeln und nicht im Dienst des libanesischen Staates stehen").

tion, and the fact that the character of the organization must be regularly reassessed as a result of having potentially changed status.

To address the aforementioned challenges, one may dismiss the requirement of internal disciplinary structure, as well as the ability to internally enforce IHL rules, in order to be party to a NIAC. The group's ability to conduct massive violence may suffice to be regarded as a party to a NIAC. This particular approach has the advantage of legal clarity by lowering the threshold of the laws of NIACs. Rather than gaining insights into the group, an assessment of past and future inflicted violence may be all that is required.

The Supreme Court applied Art. 3 GC to the conflict between the U.S. and Al Qaeda, without further inquiry into the ability of Al Qaeda to be a party to a NIAC.[160] This view is supported by the UN Commission on Human Rights' statement[161] as well as a Security Council resolution,[162] which pertains to the conflicts in Somalia and Sierra Leone.[163] The ICC has recently interpreted the notion of *organized armed groups* as

> "[groups which] have the ability to plan and carry out military operations for a prolonged period of time".[164]

This allows for the application of Art. 3 GC to organizations able to conduct prolonged violence, irrespective of their ability to enforce IHL standards. However, the emphasis on *military* operation implies that some degree of organization is necessary. Similarly, *Arnold*, who appears to waive any organizational minimum requirement, states that, as soon as *"terrorist organizations engaged in subversive activities against a state"* overstep the threshold of armed conflicts, they are liable under Art. 8 (2) ICC-Statute.[165] Additionally, *Arnold* does not regard the organization of the party as a determining factor for armed con-

---

[160] *Hamdan vs. Rumsfeld*, 548 U.S. 557, 630 *et seq.* (2006).

[161] UN Commission on Human Rights, Res. 1998/59, *Assistance to Somalia in the Field of Human Rights*, ¶ 3, U.N. Doc. E/CN.4/RES/1998/59 (Apr. 17, 1998) ("Urges all parties in Somalia: to respect... international humanitarian law pertaining to internal armed conflict"); UN Commission on Human Rights, Res. 1999/1, *Situation of Human Rights in Sierra Leone*, ¶ 1 (Apr. 6, 1999) ("Appeals to all factions and forces in Sierra Leone to abide by applicable international humanitarian law").

[162] S.C. Res 814, ¶ 13, U.N. Doc. S/Res/814 (Mar. 26, 1993).

[163] It has to be acknowledged though, that both of these statements are political and bear limited legal significance, *see* Liesbeth Zegveld, *Accountability of Armed Opposition Groups in International Law*, 140 (2003).

[164] ICC, *Prosecutor v. Lubanga*, ICC-01/04-01/06-803, Decision on the Confirmation of Charges, ¶ 234 (Jan. 29, 2007).

[165] Roberta Arnold, *The ICC as a New Instrument for Repressing Terrorism*, 339 (2004).

flicts. Instead, she focuses solely on the amount of violence and consequently accepts the possibility that even *"loose civilian combatants"*[166] may be party to a conflict. The fundamental idea behind each approach is to make the application of the laws of NIACs dependent on the quality of threat posed by the organizations. Further requirements regarding internal structure are ignored, so long as the danger from these organizations is considered to be high enough to justify the application of IHL.[167]

The aforementioned approaches, each of which applies NIAC laws to various groups capable of inflicting massive damage to states, must be rejected. NIAC laws must not be applied to any instance of violence, as this would overgeneralize the scope of Art. 3 GC. This would in turn harm both IHL and IHRL.[168] In addition, it would be futile to apply IHL rules to an armed group without the capacity to abide by these rules. Only an organized group with an internal disciplinary structure and the ability to enforce rules within the group can possibly abide by IHL.

b) The Threshold of Violence

In order to qualify as a NIAC, a conflict must meet a specific threshold of violence to exclude plain banditry from the scope of humanitarian law.[169] This is further emphasized in AP II, which states,

"This Protocol shall not apply to situations of internal disturbances and tensions, such as riots, isolated and sporadic acts of violence and other acts of a similar nature, as not being armed conflicts."[170]

---

[166] Roberta Arnold, *The ICC as a New Instrument for Repressing Terrorism*, 201 (2004) (" [...] where the violence [...] reaches the level of a non-international conflict").

[167] Robin Geiß, *Armed Violence in Fragile States: Low-Intensity Conflicts, Spillover Conflicts, and Sporadic Law Enforcement Operations by Third States*, 873 International Review of the Red Cross 127, 137 (2009) (referring to that as the interchangeability of the criteria intensity of violence and organization of the party – determining the notion of armed conflict).

[168] Philip Alston, *Report of the Special Rapporteur on Extrajudicial, Summary or Arbitrary Executions*, ¶ 56, U.N. Doc. A/HRC/14/24/Add.6 (May 28, 2010) ("To expand the notion of non-international armed conflict to groups that are essentially drug cartels, criminal gangs or other groups that should be dealt with under the law enforcement framework would be to do deep damage to the IHL and human rights framework").

[169] Jean Pictet, *Commentary on the Geneva Convention relative to the Treatment of Prisoners of War*, 35 (1960).

[170] Art. 1.2 AP II.

The exclusion of isolated and sporadic acts of violence falls under CIL,[171] and can therefore be directly applied to Art. 3 GC conflicts.[172] Determining the amount of violence necessary to meet the threshold of NIAC is more difficult compared to IACs.[173] Occurrence of violence within a state is a common phenomenon. A state itself regularly applies violence through its police forces to maintain internal stability and security.[174] Therefore, a clear-cut distinction between *war* and *peace*, as can be found on the international level, does not exist in the internal sphere.

The ICTY has, in its *Tadic*-Judgment, coined the requirement of *protracted armed violence*.[175] This is primarily understood as encompassing two aspects of violence, intensity and duration.[176] Although both aspects are crucial, they can be referred to interchangeably. An overall assessment of either is decisive to sufficiently determine the amount of violence.[177] An intense fight, which may include military means, can therefore amount to an armed conflict, even if its duration is rather short.[178] Both criteria, intensity and duration, will be analyzed in the following sections.

---

[171] Magne Frostad, *Jus in Bello after September 11*, 2001, 42 (2005); Michael Bothe, Karl J. Partsch and Waldemar A. Solf, *New Rules for Victims of Armed Conflicts*, 624 *et seq.* (1982); Lindsay Moir, *The Law of Internal Armed Conflict*, 102 (2002).

[172] *Cf.* Roberta Arnold, *The ICC as a New Instrument for Repressing Terrorism*, 122 (2004).

[173] Lindsay Moir, *The Law of Internal Armed Conflict*, 31 (2002); Derek Jinks, *September 11 and the Laws of War*, 28 Yale Journal of International Law 1, 21 *et seq.* (2003).

[174] Lindsay Moir, *The Law of Internal Armed Conflict*, 34 (2002).

[175] ICTY, *Prosecutor v. Tadic*, Case No. IT-94-1-I, Decision on Defence Motion for Interlocutory Appeal on Jurisdiction, ¶ 70 (Oct. 2, 1995).

[176] Sylvain Vité, *Typology of Armed Conflicts in International Humanitarian Law: Legal Concepts and Actual Situations*, 91 International Review of the Red Cross, 69, 76-7 (2009).

[177] Sylvain Vité, *Typology of Armed Conflicts in International Humanitarian Law: Legal Concepts and Actual Situations*, 91 International Review of the Red Cross, 69, 77 (2009) ("[...] they [the assessment factors] are not conditions that need to exist concurrently").

[178] *Juan Carlos Abella v. Argentina* [Tablada] Case 11.137, Inter-American Commission on Human Rights, Report No. 55/97, OEA/Ser.L/V/II.98, doc. 6 rev. ¶ 152, 154-6 (1998) ("It is important to understand that the application of Common Article 3 does not require the existence of large-scale and generalized hostilities or a situation comparable to a civil war in which dissident armed groups exercise control over parts of national territory. [...] despite the brief duration, the violent clash between the attackers and members of the Argentine armed forces triggered application of the provisions of Common Article 3"); *critical* Liesbeth Zegveld, *Accountability of Armed Opposition Groups in Interna-*

aa) Intensity and Duration of the Conflict

Violence must reach a certain intensity to qualify as a NIAC.[179] However, the question lies in how exactly this intensity is determined. A clear definition of the *minimum intensity requirement*[180] does not exist. *Paust, Ratner* and *Abrams* suggest the conflict must consist of a form of insurgency, which reaches the dimensions of a *civil war.*[181] Both civil wars and conventional wars are similar, with the only difference being that civil wars are confined to the territory of one state and include only one state party.[182]

The U.S. Civil War and the Spanish Civil War are classic examples. Art. 3 GC was created for internal, but still warlike, situations.[183] Nevertheless, relying on the term civil war to assess whether a situation reaches the necessary threshold of violence is not sufficient.[184] The text of Art. 3 GC does not provide any indication of this rather narrow understanding.[185] This understanding does not derive from Art. 3 GC's genesis.[186] Furthermore, most conflicts would not meet the implied high threshold of violence. As a result, Art. 3 GC would be of little significance. Finally, diminishing NIACs to civil wars is inaccurate. Civil war is itself unclear in its definition as per international law and is often used to sum-

---

tional Law, 137 *et seq.* (2003) (seeing the position of the Inter-American Comission as deviation from the "protracted"-criterion of the ICTY).

[179] Hans-Georg Dederer, *Krieg gegen Terror*, 59 Juristen Zeitung 421, 425 (2004); Silja Vöneky, *Die Anwendbarkeit des humanitären Völkerrechts auf terroristische Akte und ihre Bekämpfung*, in Rechtsfragen der Terrorismusbekämpfung durch Streitkräfte, 149 (Dieter Fleck and Wolfgang S. Heinz eds. 2004); International Law Association, Final Report on the Meaning of Armed Conflict in International Law, 30 (2010).

[180] René Provost, *International Human Rights and Humanitarian Law*, 266 (2004).

[181] *See, e.g.*, Jordan J. Paust, *Addendum: War and Responses to Terrorism, ASIL Insights: Terrorist Attacks on the World Trade Center and the Perntagon* (Sep. 2001) available at http://www.asil.org/insights (arguing that Common Article 3 requires fighting a "war" against insurgents or belligerents); Steven R. Ratner and Jason S. Abrams, *Accountability for Human Rights Atrocities in International Law*, 95-7 (2001) (m.w.N. in Fn. 82).

[182] Lindsay Moir, *The Law of Internal Armed Conflict*, 17 (2002).

[183] Martin Hess, *Die Anwendbarkeit des humanitären Völkerrechts, insbesondere in gemischten Konflikten*, 97 (1985).

[184] Derek Jinks, *September 11 and the Laws of War*, 28 Yale Journal of International Law 1, 39-40 (2003); *Juan Carlos Abella v. Argentina* [Tablada] Case 11.137, Inter-American Commission on Human Rights, Report No. 55/97, OEA/Ser.L/V/II.98, doc. 6 rev. ¶ 152 (1998).

[185] Derek Jinks, *September 11 and the Laws of War*, 28 Yale Journal of International Law 1, 39 (2003).

[186] Derek Jinks, *September 11 and the Laws of War*, 28 Yale Journal of International Law 1, 39-40 (2003).

marize various non-international conflicts.[187] Therefore, the term civil war does not accurately capture the degree of violence required to cause a NIAC. Instead, the intensity must be determined by a number of factors.[188] In *Boskoski* the Trial Chamber of the ICTY lists the factors used by the ICTY to assess the intensity of the conflict:

"These [factors to assess the intensity of the conflict] include the seriousness of attacks and whether there has been an increase in armed clashes, the spread of clashes over territory and over a period of time, any increase in the number of government forces and mobilisation and the distribution of weapons among both parties to the conflict, as well as whether the conflict has attracted the attention of the United Nations Security Council, and whether any resolutions on the matter have been passed. Trial Chambers have also taken into account in this respect the number of civilians forced to flee from the combat zones; the type of weapons used, in particular the use of heavy weapons, and other military equipment, such as tanks and other heavy vehicles; the blocking or besieging of towns and the heavy shelling of these towns; the extent of destruction and the number of casualties caused by shelling or fighting; the quantity of troops and units deployed; existence and change of front lines between the parties; the occupation of territory, and towns and villages; the deployment of government forces to the crisis area; the closure of roads; cease fire orders and agreements, and the attempt of representatives from international organisations to broker and enforce cease fire agreements."[189]

This aforementioned list is essential when assessing each instance of violence on a case-by-case basis. Of particular importance are the number of casualties and the resort to military means. Similarly, the *Pictet*-Commentary on the GC highlights resorting to military means as one of the main criteria to identify a NIAC.[190]

The duration of violence is yet another aspect of the intensity of violence necessary to cross the NIAC threshold.[191] This temporal criterion is mentioned in

---

[187] Derek Jinks, *September 11 and the Laws of War*, 28 Yale Journal of International Law 1, 40 (2003).

[188] International Law Association, *Final Report on the Meaning of Armed Conflict in International Law*, 30 (2010).

[189] ICTY, *Prosecutor v. Boskoski et al.*, Case No. IT-04-82-T, Trial Judgement, ¶ 177 (Jul. 10, 2008) (footnotes omitted).

[190] Jean S. Pictet, *Commentary on the Geneva Convention for the Amelioration of the Condition of the Wounded and Sick in Armed Forces in the Field*, 49 *et seq.* (1952), *cf.* Hans-Peter Gasser & Nils Melzer, *Humanitäres Völkerrecht*, 68-9 (2012); Martin Hess, *Die Anwendbarkeit des humanitären Völkerrechts, insbesondere in gemischten Konflikten*, 97 (1985).

[191] Lindsay Moir, *The Law of Internal Armed Conflict*, 31 (2002) ("[...] the requirement that violence must be protracted hints that it must have reached a certain level of intensity, although expressed in terms of the duration rather than the scale of the vio-

Art. 1.1 AP II, which states that isolated and sporadic acts of violence do not suffice to reach the amount of violence necessary to categorize a NIAC. The ICTY built upon this with the introduction of the term *protracted armed violence* as its understanding of an armed conflict.[192] Recently, the term *protracted* was used in Art. 8(2) (f) of the ICC-Statute. The term *conflict* itself implies a chain of violence and an exchange of violent acts that together form the conflict. Therefore, a single act of violence cannot be regarded as an armed conflict.

bb) Intensity and Duration in Transnational Conflicts

With respect to the *intensity* criterion, previous evidence clearly indicates that most transnational conflicts meet the required threshold, particularly considering the number of casualties and resort to military means. Terrorist non-state actors, in particular, intentionally spread massive violence leading to a high number of deaths and wounded victims. More Americans died in the 9/11 attack than in all other attacks since 1968 combined.[193] To counter such attacks of massive violence, the state parties involved often rely on their armed forces, particularly when fighting non-state actors abroad. The intensity of violence on 9/11 led to then President George Bush's introduction of the war-paradigm to the fight against terrorism. The military response of the U.S. against Al Qaeda clearly indicates that this conflict has reached the intensity of violence necessary for a NIAC.

The *duration* of violence during transnational conflicts is far more difficult to assess. Generally, violence occurs sporadically and only occasionally results in protracted fighting. This ultimately gives rise to the question as to whether such conflicts should be treated as one single NIAC. This is particularly problematic when the non-state actor is a terrorist organization, such as Al Qaeda, that attempts to evade an open battle with ongoing fighting. Despite the absence of an open battle, some claimed that in the early days of the War on Terror, an armed conflict did in fact occur between the U.S. and Al Qaeda.[194] This particular

---

lence"); Noelle Quénivet, *The Application of International Humanitarian Law to Situations of a (Counter-)Terrorist Nature*, in International Humanitarian Law and the 21st Century's Conflicts 25, 33 *et seq.* (Roberta Arnold and Pierre-Antoine Hildebrand eds. 2005); International Law Association, *Final Report on the Meaning of Armed Conflict in International Law*, 30 (2010).

[192] ICTY, *Prosecutor v. Tadic*, Case No. IT-94-1-I, Decision on Defence Motion for Interlocutory Appeal on Jurisdiction, ¶ 70 (Oct. 2, 1995).

[193] Bruce Hoffmann, *Inside Terrorism*, 19 (2006).

[194] Curtis A. Bradley and Jack L Goldsmith, *The Constitutional Validity of Military Commissions*, 5 The Green Bag, 249, 256 *et seq.* (2002); Anne-Marie Slaughter and

claim was supported by legal advisers to the Bush administration[195] and was also endorsed by some scholars.[196] However, others, such as the ICRC, are reluctant to accept this assertion.[197]

Former conflicts with terror organizations, such as the RAF, ETA, and IRA, have never been regarded as armed conflicts.[198] Furthermore, the ICTY aimed to exclude terrorist activities from the concept of armed conflict when it introduced the notion of protracted armed violence.[199] *Sassòli* argues in favor of this statement. He argues that there is no ground to regard Al Qaeda differently from

---

William Burke-White, *An International Constitutional Moment*, 43 Harvard International Law Journal, 1, 8 (2002); Carsten Stahn, *International Law at a Crossroads?* 62 Zeitschrift für ausländisches öffentliches Recht und Völkerrecht, 184, 194 (2002); Derek Jinks, *September 11 and the Laws of War*, 28 Yale Journal of International Law 1-49 (2003).

[195] John Bellinger, *Legal Issues in the War on Terrorism*, 8 German Law Journal, 735, 737 (2007) ("[...] It is clear as a matter of international law, the United States and its allies were engaged in an armed conflict – not a police action – against Al Qaeda and the Taliban in Afghanistan [...]").

[196] Silja N. U. Vöneky, *The Fight against Terrorism and the Rules of International Law – Comment on Papers and Speeches of John B. Bellinger, Chief Legal Advisor to the United States State Department*, 8 German Law Journal, 747, 750 (2007).

[197] International Committee of the Red Cross – Official Statement, *When is a War not a War: The Proper Role of the Law of Armed Conflict in the "Global War on Terror"*, presentation given by Gabor Rona (Mar. 16, 2004); Jelena Pejic, *Terrorist Acts and Groups: A Role for International Law?* 75 British Yearbook of International Law, 71, 85-88 (2004); Marco Sassòli, *Terrorism and War*, 4 Journal of International Criminal Justice 959, 966 (2006); Frits Kalshoven, *International Armed Conflict: Legal Qualification and IHL as Lex Specialis*, in International Humanitarian Law and Other Legal Regimes: Interplay in Situations of Violence 63, 72 (International Institute of Humanitarian Law ed. 2003); Noelle Quénivet, *The Application of International Humanitarian Law to Situations of a (Counter-)Terrorist Nature*, in International Humanitarian Law and the 21st Century's Conflicts 25, 49 (Roberta Arnold and Pierre-Antoine Hildebrand eds. 2005).

[198] Roberta Arnold, *The ICC as a New Instrument for Repressing Terrorism*, 119 *et seq.* (2004) (on the RAF); Noelle Quénivet, *The Application of International Humanitarian Law to Situations of a (Counter-)Terrorist Nature*, in International Humanitarian Law and the 21st Century's Conflicts 25, 31 (Roberta Arnold and Pierre-Antoine Hildebrand eds. 2005) (on the ETA and IRA; Marco Sassòli, *Terrorism and War*, 4 Journal of International Criminal Justice 959, 966 (2006).

[199] ICTY, *Prosecutor v. Delalic et al.*, Case No. IT-96-21-T Trial Judgment, ¶ 184 (Nov. 16, 1998) ("In the latter situation [conflicts which are regarded as internal to a state], in order to distinguish from cases of civil unrest or terrorist activities, the emphasis is on the protracted extent of the armed violence and the extent of organisation of the parties involved"); *see also*, Claus Kreß, *Völkerstrafrecht der dritten Generation gegen transnationale Gewalt Privater?*, in Die Macht und das Recht, 323, 365 Fn. 129 (Gerd Hankel ed., 2008).

terror organizations such as RAF, ETA and IRA.[200] One must acknowledge, however, that the paradigms continue to change today and there is an overall trend towards low intensity wars in modern warfare.[201] In such conflicts, including the fight against terrorism, violence brews on a low level with only sporadic outbursts of violence. Despite this, violence can be protracted.

For single acts of violence, such as terrorist attacks, to qualify as protracted violence, one can draw on a concept of the *jus contra bellum*: the *accumulation of events doctrine*. This doctrine allows for a series of violent acts, which do not independently amount to an armed conflict, to be viewed conjunctively to amount to an armed conflict.[202] This doctrine can be applied to categorize a conflict in *jus in bello,* consequently interpreting a number of violent incidents as one single armed conflict, so long as involved parties remain consistent.

The accumulation of events doctrine can be applied to the conflict between the U.S. and Al Qaeda by considering the events prior to 9/11: the attacks on the U.S. embassies in Kenya and Tanzania in 1998, and the attack on the USS Cole in 2000.[203] However, the several acts must be attributable to one identifiable organized armed group. Linking various terrorist attacks performed by several actors with nothing but ideology in common is not permitted. There can be no NIACs against *global terrorism*.[204] If an organized group is identified and responsible, separate attacks over a given period of time may qualify as one

---

[200] Marco Sassòli, *Terrorism and War*, 4 Journal of International Criminal Justice 959, 966 (2006).

[201] *See generally* Herfried Münkler: *Der Wandel des Krieges* (2006); International Committee of the Red Cross – Official Statement, *The Relevance of International Humanitarian Law in Contemporary Armed Conflicts*, Intervention by Jakob Kellenberger (Sep. 19, 2004) online available at http://www.icrc.org/Web/eng/siteeng0. nsf/html/66EMA9 ("[...] low intensity of fighting and high intensity of suffering by civilian population [...]"); Robin Geiß, *Armed Violence in Fragile States: Low-Intensity Conflicts, Spillover Conflicts, and Sporadic Law Enforcement Operations by Third States*, 873 International Review of the Red Cross 127, 134 *et seq.* (2009).

[202] *See* Claus Kreß, *Gewaltverbot und Selbstverteidigungsrecht nach der Satzung der Vereinten Nationen bei staatlicher Verwicklung in Gewaltakte Privater*, 197 (1995); Rainer Grote, *Between Crime Prevention and the Laws of War*, in Terrorism as a Challenge for National and International Law: Security Versus Liberty? 951, 964 *et seq.* (Christian Walter ed., 2004); Christiane Wandscher, *Internationaler Terrorismus und Selbstverteidigungsrecht*, 170 (2006).

[203] Curtis A. Bradley and Jack L Goldsmith, *The Constitutional Validity of Military Commissions*, 5 The Green Bag, 249, 256 (2002); Carsten Stahn, *International Law at a Crossroads?* 62 Zeitschrift für ausländisches öffentliches Recht und Völkerrecht, 184, 194 (2002).

[204] Jelena Pejic, *Terrorist Acts and Groups: A Role for International Law?* 75 British Yearbook of International Law, 71, 86-7 (2004).

NIAC, as per the accumulation of events-doctrine. Until 2001, Al Qaeda quali-fied as a party to a NIAC. Hence, the conflict between Al Qaeda and the U.S. qualified as a NIAC as far as the intensity and duration of the conflict are con-cerned.

c) Geographical Scope of the Conflict

This section addresses whether NIACs are limited to internal conflicts, in which case this would *per se* exclude any transnational conflict from qualifying as a NIAC. Art. 3 GC refers to conflicts as

"occurring in the territory of one of the High Contracting Parties".

This has traditionally been understood as limiting the applicability of Art. 3 GC to internal conflicts. Hence, the terms *Non-International Armed Conflict* and *Internal Conflict* are often used synonymously.[205] Additionally, the *Pictet* com-ment uses the term *within* a *determinate* territory.[206] This was most likely meant to address *within* a *national* territory, a term used in a following passage. The ICTY is even more explicit in its *Tadic* decision, where the term *within a state* is used to reflect the traditional understanding of NIACs as internal conflicts.[207] However, internal conflicts in which violence occasionally crosses borders, also known as spill-over conflicts, fall under Art. 3 GC.[208] The Statute of the Interna-tional Criminal Tribunal for Rwanda (ICTR), for example, states,

---

[205] *See* Gerald. I. A. D. Draper, *The Geneva Conventions of 1949*, 114 Recueil des Cours de l'Academie de Droit International de la Haye 59, 82 *et seq.* (1965); Dietrich Schindler, *The Different Types of Armed Conflicts according to the Geneva Conventions and Protocols*, 163 Recueil des Cours de l'Academie de Droit International de la Haye 117, 147 (1979); *cf.* Lindsay Moir, *The Law of Internal Armed Conflict* (2002) (The title alone indicates that Moir thinks of non-international conflicts as internal conflicts").

[206] Jean S. Pictet, *Commentary on the Geneva Convention for the Amelioration of the Condition of the Wounded and Sick in Armed Forces in the Field*, 49 (1952).

[207] ICTY, *Prosecutor v. Tadic*, Case No. IT-94-1-I, Decision on Defence Motion for Interlocutory Appeal on Jurisdiction, ¶ 70 (Oct. 2, 1995) ("On the basis of the foregoing, we find that an armed conflict exists whenever there is a resort to armed force between States or protracted armed violence between governmental authorities and organized armed groups or between such groups within a State").

[208] *See* Liesbeth Zegveld, *Accountability of Armed Opposition Groups in International Law*, 136 (2003); Marco Sassòli, *Transnational Armed Groups and International Human-itarian Law*, Occasional Paper Series, Program on Humanitarian Policy and Conflict Research, 9 (Harvard University Winter 2006) online available at http://www.hpcrresearch.org/pdfs/OccasionalPaper6.pdf; Dieter Fleck, *The Law of Non-*

"The International Tribunal for Rwanda shall have the power to prosecute [...] Rwandan citizens responsible for such violations [of international humanitarian law] committed in the territory of neighboring States."[209]

This clarifies that the conflict may stretch or spill over into neighboring territories.

Transnational conflicts do not qualify as internal conflicts as the non-state group acts from outside the territory of the conflict state. Additionally, the conflict state responds by sending troops into the territorial state where the non-state actor's bases may be located. If Art. 3 GC is strictly applied to internal situations only, most transnational conflicts between states and non-state groups would fall out of Art. 3 GC's scope of application. Some transnational conflicts may qualify as spill-over conflicts, thus falling under Art. 3 GC. In some cases, the conflict state may be seen as intervening on behalf of the territorial state already involved in a NIAC with the same non-state group.[210] However, by and large, most transnational conflicts would not qualify as NIACs according to its traditional understanding. Due to the U.S.-Al Qaeda conflict's transnational character, the Bush administration did not qualify the conflict as a NIAC from the very beginning. Instead, the conflict was regarded as an international conflict outside the Geneva Conventions.[211] *Mammen* also rejects qualifying the corresponding conflict as a NIAC as it is not internal. Instead, he argues for the application of IAC laws.[212]

However, an even broader application of Art. 3 GC, which encompasses even non-internal transnational conflicts, is possible. *Jinks* proposes three core arguments in favor of a broader application.[213] First, *in the territory* does not neces-

---

International Armed Conflicts, in The Handbook of International Humanitarian Law, 582 (Dieter Fleck ed. 2013).

[209] Statute for the ICTR, Art. 1 and Art. 7.

[210] Stefan Oeter, *Terrorismus und Menschenrechte*, 40 Archiv des Völkerrechts 422, 439 (2002).

[211] George W. Bush, *Memorandum for the Vice President : Humane Treatment of Al Qaeda and the Taliban Detainees*, ¶ 2c (Feb. 7, 2002) ("I also accept the legal conclusion of the Department of Justice and determine that common Article 3 of Geneva does not apply to either al Qaeda or Taliban detainees, because [...] the relevant conflicts are international in scope and common Article 3 applies only to 'armed conflict not of an international character'").

[212] Lars Mammen, *Völkerrechtliche Stellung von internationalen Terrororganisationen*, 181 (2008) ("Es erscheint geradezu paradox, die weltweit geführte Auseinandersetzung mit einer grenzüberschreitend agierenden Terrororganisation als einen nicht-internationalen Konflikt zu qualifizieren").

[213] *See* Derek Jinks, *September 11 and the Laws of War*, 28 Yale Journal of International Law 1, 40-1 (2003).

sarily equate to *within the territory*. *In the territory* may simply be regarded as an affirmation of Art. 3 GC's exclusive applicability to states which are parties to the treaties.[214] The emphasis would lie less on *in the territory,* but rather on *High Contracting Party.*[215] Today, this function is almost redundant as 194 states are currently parties to the GCs,[216] although this was clearly not the case when the conventions were first signed in 1949. The wording of Art. 3 GC leaves room for a broader understanding. In his second argument, *Jinks* argues that if internal conflicts were made subject to international law through Art. 3 GC, *a fortiori* a conflict that goes beyond national borders would certainly be subject to the same.[217] The more a conflict affects the international community, the more necessary it is that its regulation is not left to the discretion of just one state. The third and final argument states that confining Art. 3 GC to purely internal conflicts would leave a gap in the regulation of conflicts through IHL.[218] If an IAC regime is understood as solely covering conflicts between states, con-

---

[214] Derek Jinks, *September 11 and the Laws of War*, 28 Yale Journal of International Law 1, 40-1 (2003); Marco Sassòli, *Transnational Armed Groups and International Humanitarian Law*, Occasional Paper Series, Program on Humanitarian Policy and Conflict Research, 9 (Harvard University Winter 2006) online available at http://www.hpcrresearch.org/pdfs/OccasionalPaper6.pdf; John Cerone, *Jurisdiction and Power: The Intersection of Human Rights Law and the Law of Non-International Armed Conflict in an Extraterritorial Context*, 40 Israel Law Review, 396, 405-408 (2007); Sylvain Vité, *Typology of Armed Conflicts in International Humanitarian Law: Legal Concepts and Actual Situations*, 91 International Review 73 of the Red Cross, 69, 89 *et seq.* (2009); *see also* Lindsay Moir, *The Law of Internal Armed Conflict*, 31 (2002) (sharing this view but at the same time confining NIACs to internal conflict, hence seeing two functions in this wording of Art. 3 GC).

[215] Sandesh Sivakumaran, *The Law of Non-International Armed Conflict*, 229 (2012).

[216] *See* numbers provided by the International Committee of the Red Cross (6.10.2008), online available at http://www.icrc.org/IHL.nsf/(SPF)/party_main_treaties/$File/IHL _and_other_related_Treaties.pdf.

[217] Derek Jinks, *September 11 and the Laws of War*, 28 Yale Journal of International Law 1, 41 (2003); Marco Sassòli, *Transnational Armed Groups and International Humanitarian Law*, Occasional Paper Series, Program on Humanitarian Policy and Conflict Research, 9 (Harvard University Winter 2006) online available at http://www.hpcrresearch.org/pdfs/OccasionalPaper6.pdf; Marty Lederman, *Top Ten Myths About Hamdan, Geneva and Interrogations*, Georgetown Law Faculty Blog, Myth No 4 (2006), online available at http://gulcfac.typepad.com/georgetown_university _law/2006/07/top_ten_myths_a_1.html.

[218] Derek Jinks, *September 11 and the Laws of War,* 28 Yale Journal of International Law 1, 40-1 (2003); Marco Sassòli, *Transnational Armed Groups and International Humanitarian Law*, Occasional Paper Series, Program on Humanitarian Policy and Conflict Research, 9 (Harvard University Winter 2006) online available at http://www.hpcrresearch.org/pdfs/OccasionalPaper6.pdf.

flicts between a state and a non-state group, which generally qualify as NIAC but are still border-crossing, would be unregulated by the Geneva Conventions. An armed conflict not regulated by the Geneva Conventions is, however, not acceptable. Those who regard transnational conflicts as armed conflicts, but do not want to apply IAC laws, must also apply Art. 3 GC to non-internal conflicts.

The aforementioned arguments render the criterion of geographic limitation to the territory of one state obsolete. The question remains as to whether this is merely a *lege ferenda* understanding of NIAC that has yet to gain prevalence, or if it can be considered *lege lata*. Evidence by the jurisprudence of both international and national courts support the latter.

The understanding of Art. 3 GC as a subsidiary regime to the IAC regime was first raised in the *Nicaragua-Case* of the ICJ Regulations of Art. 3 GC were applied as customary international law to all conflicts.[219] In the *Delalic*-Case, the ICTY stated,

> "The Trial Chamber's finding that the conflict in Bosnia and Herzegovina in 1992 was of an international nature does not, therefore, impact upon the application of Article 3."[220]

This reflects the understanding of Art. 3 GC as a norm, which is always applicable, even during non-*internal* conflicts.

The US Supreme Court explicitly applied Art. 3 GC to the conflict with Al Qaeda. This rendered the geographical limitation of Art. 3 GC obsolete and subsequently created a distinction between IACs and NIACs based solely on the parties to the conflict.[221] This view is supported by Art. 3 GC, which outlines *non-international* as opposed to *internal* conflicts.[222] The Bush administration abided by the Supreme Court's decision,[223] a position also adhered to by the

---

[219] ICJ, *Military and Paramilitary Activities in and against Nicaragua* (Nicar. V. U.S.), 1986 ICJ 14, ¶ 218 (June 27).

[220] ICTY, *Prosecutor v. Delalic et al.,* Case No. IT-96-21-T Trial Judgment, ¶ 314 (Nov. 16, 1998).

[221] *Hamdan vs. Rumsfeld*, 548 U.S. 557, 630 (2006) ("The latter kind of conflict [non-international] is distinguishable from the conflict described in Common Article 2 chiefly because it does not involve a clash between nations (whether signatories or not)").

[222] *Hamdan vs. Rumsfeld*, 548 U.S. 557, 630 (2006) ("[...] the phrase 'not of an international character' bears its literal meaning").

[223] George W. Bush, *Executive Order 13440: Interpretation of the Geneva Conventions Common Article 3 as Applied to a Program of Detention and Interrogation Operated by the Central Intelligence Agency*, sec. 3 (Jul. 20, 2007) ("I hereby determine that Common Article 3 shall apply to a program of detention and interrogation operated by the Central Intelligence Agency [...]"), online available at http://edocket.access.gpo.gov/2007/pdf/07-3656.pdf (last visited Aug. 9, 2010); Office of the Secretary of Defense, *Memorandum on*

Obama administration.[224] Further evidence on explicit state practice on the geographical dimension of NIACs is still missing.[225] However, there is no evidence of state-practice to the contrary.[226] In addition, most scholars have already endorsed the new understanding of NIACs as not necessarily being geographically limited to one state.[227] Even the ICRC has accepted that the geographical scope of a conflict must not determine the applicability of Art. 3 GC.[228]

---

the Application of Common Article 3 of the Geneva Convention to the Treatment of Detainees in the Department of Defense, (Jul. 07, 2006) online available at http://www.defense.gov/pubs/pdfs/DepSecDef%20memo%20on%20common%20article %203.pdf (last visited Sep. 8, 2010).

[224] Barak Obama, *Executive Order 13491: Ensuring Lawful Interrogations*, § 3(a) (Jan. 22, 2009); *Report of the United States of America Submitted to the U.N. High Commissioner for Human Rights in Conjunction with the Universal Periodic Review*, ¶ 84 (2010) online available at http://www.state.gov/documents/organization/146379.pdf (last visited Feb. 2, 2011); Eric Holder, United States Attorney General, Speech at Northwestern University School of Law (Mar. 5, 2012) online available at http://www.justice.gov/iso/opa/ag/speeches/2012/ag-speech-1203051.html (last visited May 29, 2013).

[225] *See* Claus Kreß, *Völkerstrafrecht der dritten Generation gegen transnationale Gewalt Privater?*, in Die Macht und das Recht, 323, 362 (Gerd Hankel ed., 2008) (being is very skeptical about an already sufficiently developed state practice).

[226] The then German Foreign Minister Guido Westerwelle qualified the situation in Afghanistan as armed conflict, based only on the intensity of the conflict and the military organization of the insurgents irrespective of the transnational character of the conflict. *See* Government Statement, 10 Feb. 2010 ("Die Intensität der mit Waffengewalt ausgetragenen Auseinandersetzung mit Aufständischen und deren militärischer Organisation führen uns zu der Bewertung, die Einsatzsituation von ISAF auch im Norden Afghanistans als bewaffneten Konflikt im Sinne des humanitären Völkerrechts zu qualifizieren"), available at http://www.auswaertiges-amt.de/DE/Infoservice/Presse/Reden/2010/100210-BM-BT-Afghanistan.html?nn=432726.

[227] Curtis A. Bradley and Jack L Goldsmith, *The Constitutional Validity of Military Commissions*, 5 The Green Bag, 249, 258 (2002); M. Cherif Bassiouni, *Legal Control of International Terrorism: A Policy-Oriented Assessment*, 43 Harvard International Law Journal 83, 99 (2002); Liesbeth Zegveld, *Accountability of Armed Opposition Groups in International Law*, 136 (2003); Derek Jinks, *September 11 and the Laws of War*, 28 Yale Journal of International Law 1, 38 *et seq.* (2003); Jelena Pejic, *Terrorist Acts and Groups: A Role for International Law?* 75 British Yearbook of International Law, 71, 85 (2004); Noelle Quénivet, *The Application of International Humanitarian Law to Situations of a (Counter-)Terrorist Nature*, in International Humanitarian Law and the 21st Century's Conflicts 25, 57 (Roberta Arnold and Pierre-Antoine Hildebrand eds. 2005); Marco Sassòli, *Transnational Armed Groups and International Humanitarian Law*, Occasional Paper Series, Program on Humanitarian Policy and Conflict Research, 8 (Harvard University Winter 2006) online available at http://www.hpcrresearch.org/pdfs/ OccasionalPaper6.pdf; Marco Sassòli, *Terrorism and War*, 4 Journal of International

With the U.S.'s increasing use of drones during the War on Terror, drone attacks on a terrorist outside the battlefield remain debated. Could U.S. forces attack a single member of Al Qaeda in Yemen while they were actually engaged in protracted hostilities against Al Qaeda in Afghanistan? According to the U.S. stance, U.S. forces would be permitted to do so.[229] However, according to the

---

Criminal Justice 959, 966 (2006); Claus Kreß, *Völkerstrafrecht der dritten Generation gegen transnationale Gewalt Privater?*, in Die Macht und das Recht, 323, 361 *et seq.* (Gerd Hankel ed., 2008); Andreas Paulus and Mindia Vashakmadze, *Asymmetrical War and the Notion of Armed Conflict – A Tentative Conceptualization*, 91 International Review of the Red Cross 95, 117 (2009); Philip Alston, *Report of the Special Rapporteur on Extrajudicial, Summary or Arbitrary Executions*, ¶ 52, U.N. Doc. A/HRC/14/24/Add.6 (May 28, 2010).

But see Marko Milanovic & Vidan Hadzi-Vidanovic, *A Taxonomy of Armed Conflict*, in Research Handbook of International Conflict and Security Law 256, 307 (Nigel White & Christian Henderson, eds. 2013) (rejecting the idea of a global NIAC: "Even under the framework that we have outlined above, which allows for various kinds of cross-border NIACs, the idea of a global NIAC makes sense only as an oxymoron. [...] the existing legal framework does not seem to allow for a construction as amorphous as a global NIAC."); Yoram Dinstein, *The Conduct of Hostilities under the Law of Interantional Armed Conflict*, 56 (2010) ("[...] from the vantage point of international law [...] a non-international armed conflict cannot possibly assume global dimensions").

[228] Jelena Pejic, *Terrorist Acts and Groups: A Role for International Law?* 75 British Yearbook of International Law, 71, 86 (2004).

[229] *See* John O. Brennan, Assistant to the President for Homeland Security and Counterterrorism, *Remarks at the Program on Law and Security, Harvard Law School: "Strengehting Our Security by Adhering to Our Values and Laws"* (Sept. 16, 2011) ("The United States does not view our authority to use military force against al-Qa'ida as being restricted solely to 'hot' battlefields like Afghanistan") online available at http://www.whitehouse.gov/the-press-office/2011/09/16/remarks-john-o-brennan-streng thening-our-security-adhering-our-values-an (last visited Aug. 22, 2013); Department of Justice White Paper, *Lawfulness of a Lethal Operation Directed Against a U.S. Citizen Who is a Senior Operational Leader of Al-Qaida or an Associated Force*, (Feb. 2, 2013), online available at http://msnbcmedia.msn.com/i/msnbc/sections/news/020413_ DOJ_White_Paper.pdf (last visited May 28, 2013); Barack Obama, Remarks by the President at the National Defense University, May 23, 2013, online available at http://www.whitehouse.gov/the-press-office/2013/05/23/remarks-president-national-defense-university (last visited May 24, 2013).

Contra Sandesh Sivakumaran, *The Law of Non-International Armed Conflict*, 234 (2012) ("[...] a conflict must have a territorial base whether a single territory, a core territory plus overspill onto different territory, or multiple territories; a global non-international armed conflict does not exist, at least as a matter of law"). However, Sivakumaran also concedes: "Ultimately, though, their [Al Qaeda's] location does not immunize them from the operation of the law and all this suggests the need to move away from geographical-based ideas of applicability of law." Sandesh Sivakumaran, *The Law of Non-International Armed Conflict*, 251 (2012).

Generalbundesanwalt [German Federal Prosecutor General] drones, just like other means of warfare, may be used only within the scope of the battlefield.[230] As far as the geographical applicability of the laws of NIACs is concerned, better arguments speak for the U.S.'s position. IHL differentiates between combatant and non-combatant, but not between battlefield and non-battlefield. Or, as *Lubell* and *Derejko* conclude, who comprehensively analyze the geographical scope of armed conflicts with respect to drone warfare:[231]

> "IHL is not in and of itself pre-determined as applying to a limited geographical scope, and its applicability is designed to follow the prevailing hostilities wherever they may spread, rather than vice versa".[232]

As a result, a NIAC could occur mainly on Afghan territory and simultaneously involve single hostilities in other states. This does not imply that the use of drones is legal in any case. There can be no global war on an abstract phenomenon such as terrorism that allows U.S. forces to strike anywhere at any time. Further dimensions of the legality of the use of drones must be considered. In their study, *Lubell* and *Derejko* clearly address these additional factors.[233] The U.S. has also considered additional dimensions of the legality of the use of force outside the U.S. and areas of active hostilities. U.S. president Barack Obama issued a Presidential Policy Guidance to address these dimensions.[234]

The first question lies in whether an armed conflict between the state and the non-state actor has even occurred. Some scholars reject the notion of one single global conflict,[235] while others remain skeptical of the ability of certain non-state

---

[230] Einstellungsvermerk des Generalbundesanwalts [Memorandum of the Federal Prosecutor General], 3 BJs 7/12-4 (June 20, 2013), online available at https://www.generalbundesanwalt.de/docs/drohneneinsatz_vom_04oktober2010_mir_ali_pakistan.pdf (last visited Feb.18, 2012).

[231] Noam Lubell & Nathan Derejko, *A Global Battlefield? Drones and the Geographical Scope of Armed Conflict*, 11 Journal of International Criminal Justice 65 (2013).

[232] Noam Lubell & Nathan Derejko, *A Global Battlefield? Drones and the Geographical Scope of Armed Conflict*, 11 Journal of International Criminal Justice 65, 88 (2013).

[233] Noam Lubell & Nathan Derejko, *A Global Battlefield? Drones and the Geographical Scope of Armed Conflict*, 11 Journal of International Criminal Justice 87-88 (2013).

[234] Presidential Policy Guidance, *U.S. Policy Standards and Procedures for the Use of Force in Counterterrorism Operations Outside the United States and Areas of Active Hostilities*, May 22, 2013, online available at http://www.whitehouse.gov/sites/default/files/uploads/2013.05.23_fact_sheet_on_ppg.pdf (last visited on May 24, 2013).

[235] Marco Sassòli, *Terrorism and War*, 4 Journal of International Criminal Justice 959, 966 (2006); Frits Kalshoven, *International Armed Conflict: Legal Qualification and IHL as Lex Specialis*, in International Humanitarian Law and Other Legal Regimes: Interplay in Situations of Violence 63, 72 (International Institute of Humanitarian Law ed. 2003); Noelle Quénivet, *The Application of International Humanitarian Law to Situa-*

actors, such as terror organizations, to be a party to a NIAC.[236] The *Generalbundesanwalt* assumes that there are two different NIACs, one taking place in Afghanistan involving mostly the Taliban and the other taking place in Pakistan involving Al Qaeda and associated groups.[237] A second dimension is the importance of determining whether the person targeted for an attack is a combatant of the other conflict party. The definition of an individual's status in a global NIAC will be addressed next. Finally, any use of force on another state's territory has a *Jus ad Bellum* dimension. The prohibition of the use of force against other states substantially limits the global use of drones.

In conclusion, the transnational character of the conflict between states and non-state armed groups, including terrorist organizations, is no longer an obstacle to applying Art. 3 GC as a subsidiary regime. Therefore, although the U.S.-Al Qaeda conflict was not internal and encompassed drone strikes in several states, it is not precluded from qualifying as a NIAC.

d) Conclusion

Art. 3 GC can be applied to transnational conflicts between states and non-state groups. The degree of organization of the non-state group, in conjunction with additional criteria, is used to assess these conflicts on a case-by-case basis. The scope of the application of Art. 3 GC leaves significant room for further development. There has been an expansion of the understanding of the NIAC regime in a direction that steers away from encompassing only internal conflicts. As a result, even if they are not bound to the territory of one state, armed conflicts between states and non-state actors can be regarded as NIACs. Therefore, the transnationality of conflicts is no longer a challenge to the application of

---

tions of a (Counter-)Terrorist Nature, in International Humanitarian Law and the 21st Century's Conflicts 25, 49 (Roberta Arnold and Pierre-Antoine Hildebrand eds. 2005).

[236] Jelena Pejic, *Terrorist Acts and Groups: A Role for International Law?* 75 British Yearbook of International Law, 71, 86 *et seq.* (2004); Marco Sassòli, *Terrorism and War*, 4 Journal of International Criminal Justice 959, 966 (2006); Claus Kreß, *Völkerstrafrecht der dritten Generation gegen transnationale Gewalt Privater?*, in Die Macht und das Recht, 323, 365. (Gerd Hankel ed., 2008); Philip Alston, *Report of the Special Rapporteur on Extrajudicial, Summary or Arbitrary Executions*, ¶ 53 *et seq.*, U.N. Doc. A/HRC/14/24/Add.6 (May 28, 2010).

[237] Einstellungsvermerk des Generalbundesanwalts [Memorandum of the Federal Prosecutor General], 3 BJs 7/12-4 (June 20, 2013), online available at https://www.generalbundesanwalt.de/docs/drohneneinsatz_vom_04oktober2010_mir_ali_pakistan.pdf (last visited Feb.18, 2012).

NIAC laws. Furthermore, the violence threshold of NIACs is met when an accumulation of events doctrine is applied, which subsequently allows for the combining of a number of isolated and sporadic acts of violence, resulting in one protracted conflict. However, it remains a crucial requirement that the non-state actor is sufficiently organized and possesses an internal disciplinary structure.

Until the end of 2001, the conflict between the U.S. and Al Qaeda qualified as a transnational NIAC. Today, given the inactivity of Al Qaeda, the death of Osama bin Laden suggests a sufficient organization may not exist. However, if the responsibility for another attack is clearly assigned to Al Qaeda, it must be assumed the group's structure has been reorganized and they can subsequently engage in a NIAC with the U.S.

2. Consequences of Applying the Laws of Non-International Armed Conflicts

As some transnational conflicts do qualify as NIACs, the consequences of applying Art. 3 GC to transnational conflicts must be analyzed considering specific challenges. In general, the legal regime of NIAC is not one of comprehensive regulations. The treaty law is rather sparse and consists only of Art. 3 GC and AP II.[238] The substance of the legal regime of NIACs must be derived though analogical and deductive reasoning,[239] in which CIL plays a major role. Many IAC law's provisions can be applied to NIACs through CIL, although it must be noted that IHL is less restrictive in NIACs than IACs.[240]

a) Legal Status of Non-State Actors

The first challenge in applying the legal regime of NIACs laws to transnational conflicts lies in determining the legal status of non-state actors. Unlike in IACs, there is no combatant-status in NIACs. It is not debated, however, that the principle of distinction also applies to NIACs. The challenge lies in implement-

---

[238] Sivakumaran suggests the conclusion of a new treaty, open to states and armed groups alike to address the gaps and difficulties of the existing law. *See* Sandesh Sivakumaran, *The Law of Non-International Armed Conflict*, 564-7 (2012).

[239] Ryan Goodman, *The Detention of Civilians in Armed Conflicts*, 103 American Journal of International Law 48, 50 (2009) ("[...] the application of IHL to noninternational conflicts[...] is often an exercise in analogical or deductive reasoning").

[240] Ryan Goodman, *The Detention of Civilians in Armed Conflicts*, 103 American Journal of International Law 48, 50 (2009) ("[...] IHL is uniformly less restrictive in internal armed conflicts than in international armed conflicts").

ing the principle of distinction given the absence of formal status of combatants during NIACs. Armed forces of a state can participate in hostilities and lawfully be attacked under IHL.[241] However, it remains difficult to determine the appropriate legal treatment of non-state actors. Two distinct approaches, of which neither appears to have assumed *lege lata* status, will be considered and discussed in the following section. The first approach characterizes members of the non-state party as civilians who directly participate in hostilities, whereas the second introduces a status based on an individual's continuous combatant function.

aa) Civilians Taking Direct Part in the Hostilities

Members of non-state groups can be regarded merely as civilians who directly participate in hostilities. They could therefore be attacked according to Art. 13.3 AP II during the period of time in which they take direct part in hostilities. This requires a further clarification of the meaning of direct participation in hostilities.

The ICRC Commentary on the APs states,

"Direct participation in hostilities implies a direct causal relationship between the activity engaged in and the harm done to the enemy at the time and the place where the activity takes place",[242]

and requires

"a sufficient causal relationship between the act of participation and its immediate consequences".[243]

---

[241] A member of a non-state group who performs the attack could however still be prosecuted under domestic law. *Cf.* Jean-Marie Henckaerts and Louise Doswald-Beck, *Customary International Humanitarian Law*, Vol. I, 13 (2005) ("The lawfulness of direct participation in hostilities in non-international armed conflicts is governed by national law").

[242] Yves Sandoz, Christophe Swinarski and Bruno Zimmermann (eds.), *Commentary on the Additional Protocols of 8 June 1997 to the Geneva Conventions of 12 August 1949*, 516 (1987).

[243] Yves Sandoz, Christophe Swinarski and Bruno Zimmermann (eds.), *Commentary on the Additional Protocols of 8 June 1997 to the Geneva Conventions of 12 August 1949*, 1453 (1987). For a broader understanding of the term participation *see* W. Hays Parks, *Air War and the Law of War*, 32 Air Force Law Review 1, 134 *et seq.* (1990) (He includes also less immediate actions like driving a military truck filled with ammunition towards the front line in the concept of participation).

The mere provision of logistic support does not suffice for direct participation.[244] Recently, in its guidance on the notion of direct participation in hostilities, the ICRC has presented a comprehensive analysis of actions which fall under direct participation.[245] At the core of the guidance lie three constitutive elements of direct participation in hostilities:

> "In order to qualify as direct participation in hostilities, a specific act must meet the following cumulative criteria: (1) The act must be likely to adversely affect the military operations or military capacity of a party to an armed conflict or, alternatively, to inflict death, injury, or destruction on persons or objects protected against direct attack (threshold of harm), and (2) There must be a direct causal link between the act and the harm likely to result either from that act, or from a coordinated military operation of which that act constitutes an integral part (direct causation), and (3) The act must be specifically designed to directly cause the required threshold of harm in support of a party to the conflict and to the detriment of another (belligerent nexus)."[246]

Although uncertainties remain, one may use the following three elements to determine direct participation: (1) threshold of harm, (2) direct causation and, (3) belligerent nexus, each of which are elaborated in the ICRC guidance.[247] However, Art. 13.3 AP II also contains a temporal element of direct participation.

According to Art. 13.3 AP II, the loss of immunity from attack is only lawful *for such time* as the civilian participates in hostilities. The determination of the temporal aspect of direct participation is unclear. The ICRC's approach is to define the temporal aspect in a rather narrow manner that encompasses only the duration of each specific act. This raises the issue of the protection of civilians, who cease to participate and subsequently regain their protection as civilians (so called revolving door effect).[248] Applying this narrow interpretation of the temporal scope of Art. 13.3 AP II to members of the non-state group creates an

---

[244] Ryan Goodman, *The Detention of Civilians in Armed Conflicts*, 103 American Journal of International Law 48, 52 (2009) ("Notwithstanding some modest, if persistent, definitional squabbles, it is well settled that providing some important logistical support to armed forces, even in a zone of active military operations, falls below the threshold for direct participation").

[245] International Committee of the Red Cross, *Interpretive Guidance on the Notion of Direct Participation in Hostilities under International Humanitarian Law* (2009).

[246] International Committee of the Red Cross, *Interpretive Guidance on the Notion of Direct Participation in Hostilities under International Humanitarian Law*, 46 (2009).

[247] International Committee of the Red Cross, *Interpretive Guidance on the Notion of Direct Participation in Hostilities under International Humanitarian Law*, 46 *et seq.* (2009).

[248] International Committee of the Red Cross, *Interpretive Guidance on the Notion of Direct Participation in Hostilities under International Humanitarian Law*, 71-2 (2009).

imbalance between non-state actors and the state's armed forces. If non-state actors are classified as civilians taking direct part in the hostilities, an attack on them would only be lawful *for such time as they take a direct part in hostilities*. On the contrary, an attack on members of the state's armed force would be lawful at any time.[249]

Ultimately, the previously mentioned circumstance involves the same obstacle that argues against the Israeli Supreme Court's approach of applying Art. 51.3 AP I to the non-state party during an IAC. In order to avoid the imbalance between the non-state actors and the state's armed forces, *Lubell* argues for broadening the definition of the temporal aspect. *Lubell* argues that the duration element should be interpreted

> "so as to include the time between repeated actions of direct participation, in that the individual is always likely to be preparing for the next engagement even when not in the midst of one".[250]

This approach is not satisfactory as it decreases civilian protection. It fails to acknowledge the difference between individuals who are not members of the non-state party but only occasionally participate in the hostilities, and individuals who participate as members of the non-state party. *Lubell* adds that it is difficult to determine whether participation was a single act or part of a chain of actions over a prolonged period of time.[251] As a result, due to Art. 13.3 AP II's temporal aspect of direct participation, characterizing non-state groups as civilians that take direct part in hostilities is not satisfactory. It either creates an imbalance between members of the non-state party and the state's armed forces, or decreases all civilians' protection without distinguishing between those who are and are not members of the non-state party.

bb) The ICRC's Approach of Continuous Combat Function

The second way to legally characterize members of non-state groups does not qualify members of the non-state party as civilians.[252] The ICRC suggests distinguishing between (1) civilians, (2) civilians who directly participate in hostilities, and (3) persons who are not protected from attacks as a result of their affili-

---

[249] Jean-Marie Henckaerts and Louise Doswald-Beck, *Customary International Humanitarian Law*, Vol. I, 21 (2005).

[250] Noam Lubell, *Extraterritorial Use of Force Against Non-State Actors*, 152 (2010).

[251] Noam Lubell, *Extraterritorial Use of Force Against Non-State Actors*, 152 (2010).

[252] International Committee of the Red Cross, *Interpretive Guidance on the Notion of Direct Participation in Hostilities under International Humanitarian Law*, 32 et seq. (2009).

ation with the non-state party. This allows for a distinction to be made between those who continuously participate in hostilities as members of the non-state armed party and those who sporadically participate without any functional allegiance. The problem lies in determining who exactly is a member of the non-state party. If these individuals are to be distinguished from civilians directly participating in the hostilities, the decisive difference must be their permanent allegiance to the non-state party.

The ICRC stresses that

"membership in such groups cannot depend on abstract affiliation, family ties, or other criteria prone to error, arbitrariness or abuse".[253]

Consequently, the ICRC proposes the concept of a functional membership:

"[...] membership must depend on whether the continuous function assumed by an individual corresponds to that collectively exercised by the group as a whole, namely the conduct of hostilities on behalf of a non-State party to the conflict."[254]

The ICRC guidance introduces the term *continuous combat function* as a key criterion to identify membership to a non-state group.[255] This is granted when an individual *"assumes a continuous function for the group involving his or her direct participation in hostilities"*.[256] The problem remains in identifying a person with a continuous combat function in the course of the battle. It is difficult for a state to know whether it is dealing with members of the non-state party or civilians who in the past may have participated in hostilities and can therefore no longer be attacked. As a result, it remains difficult for states to identify the correct targets, which inevitably entails the massive risk of misjudgment and eventual killing of civilians instead of members of the non-state group. This problem is similar to that which occurs when following the direct participation approach, where determining when a civilian directly participates in the hostilities may be problematic.[257] However, it can be argued that membership to an organization can more clearly be defined than direct participation. The ICRC presents a comprehensive list of case examples of persons who do and do not possess continu-

---

[253] International Committee of the Red Cross, *Interpretive Guidance on the Notion of Direct Participation in Hostilities under International Humanitarian Law*, 33 (2009).

[254] International Committee of the Red Cross, *Interpretive Guidance on the Notion of Direct Participation in Hostilities under International Humanitarian Law*, 33 (2009).

[255] International Committee of the Red Cross, *Interpretive Guidance on the Notion of Direct Participation in Hostilities under International Humanitarian Law*, 33 (2009).

[256] International Committee of the Red Cross, *Interpretive Guidance on the Notion of Direct Participation in Hostilities under International Humanitarian Law*, 33 (2009).

[257] Noam Lubell, *Extraterritorial Use of Force Against Non-State Actors*, 152-3 (2010).

ous combat function.[258] Without denying existing challenges, one can assume that the criterion of continuous combat function present a valuable starting point to determining the legal status of non-state party members.

cc) Conclusion

The determination of non-state actors' legal status during NIACs is an inherent difficulty of the laws of NIACs. Two approaches address this difficulty directly. Stronger arguments support the second approach, which qualifies non-state actors according to their functional membership to the non-state party, and thus distinguishes them from civilians directly taking part in hostilities. One must differentiate between, (1) immune civilians, (2) civilians who directly participate in hostilities and can be attacked according to Art. 13.3 AP II, and (3)

members of the non-state party with a continuous combat function who can be attacked at any time, in the context of permissible measures. Whether state practice ultimately adopts this approach remains to be seen.

b) Detention of Members of the Non-State Party

Developing the non-state party's status as non-civilians during NIACs leads to the next question of status post-capture. The law of NIAC, which pertains to the detention of persons *hors de combat,* is not comprehensive. The unanswered question is not whether members of non-state groups can be detained at all, but which regulation apply to their detention. The lack of adequate treaty regulation is not specific to the application of NIAC laws to transnational conflicts, but rather a general problem inherent to NIAC laws.

The regulation of detention during an NIAC must follow two principles to be deemed lawful under IHL. First, fundamental guarantees must be granted to all civilians and persons *hors de combat.* These fundamental guarantees include the requirement of humane treatment, the prohibition of torture, and the prohibition of collective punishment. This derives from Art. 3 GC and Art. 4 AP II, and has become CIL.[259] Second, members of the non-state party do not enjoy a PoW

---

[258] International Committee of the Red Cross, *Interpretive Guidance on the Notion of Direct Participation in Hostilities under International Humanitarian Law,* 34 *et seq.* (2009).

[259] For these guarantees and how they are translated into rules of CIL *see* Jean-Marie Henckaerts and Louise Doswald-Beck, *Customary International Humanitarian Law,* Vol. I, Rules 87-105 (2005).

status.[260] The PoW status in IACs is the flipside of the combatant status. International law deems the mere participation in hostilities lawful for combatants during IACs. Accordingly, combatants cannot be criminally tried for participation and enjoy PoW immunity. In the absence of combatants' status in NIACs, a PoW cannot exist either. Therefore, the lawfulness of participation in a NIAC's hostilities is governed solely by national law.[261] Art. 6.5 AP II states that

> "[a]t the end of hostilities, the authorities in power shall endeavor to grant the broadest possible amnesty to persons who have participated in the armed conflict, or those deprived of their liberty for reasons related to the armed conflict, whether they are interned or detained".

Without immunity, a PoW status cannot exist. Further issues, pertaining specifically to details of the rights of the detained, remain subject to continuing debate. Without attempting to identify and answer all remaining questions, the following sections will address the *writ of habeas corpus* and the duration of the detention during a NIAC regime.

aa) Habeas Corpus

The right to judicial review to challenge the lawfulness of one's detention, i.e. writ of habeas corpus, is regarded as a core element of the prohibition of arbitrary detention, also applicable during NIACs.[262] If and to what extent the right to judicial review can be claimed was a central dispute prior to the US Supreme Court's decision concerning prisoners detained in Guantanamo.[263] The dispute has resulted in current U.S. President Barack Obama issuing an executive order stating that

> "[t]he individuals currently detained at Guantánamo have the constitutional privilege of the writ of habeas corpus".[264]

---

[260] Jann K. Kleffner, *Operational Detention and the Treatments of Detainees*, in The Handbook of the International Law of Military Operations 465, 478 (Terry D. Gill and Dieter Fleck eds., 2010).

[261] Jean-Marie Henckaerts and Louise Doswald-Beck, *Customary International Humanitarian Law*, Vol. I, 13 (2005) ("The lawfulness of direct participation in hostilities in non-international armed conflicts is governed by national law").

[262] Jean-Marie Henckaerts and Louise Doswald-Beck, *Customary International Humanitarian Law*, Vol. I, Rule 99 (2005).

[263] *See comprehensively* Jonathan Hafetz, *Habeas Corpus After 9/11: Confronting America's New Global Detention System* (2011).

[264] Barack Obama, *Executive Order – Review and Disposition of Individuals detained at the Guantánamo Bay Naval Base and Closure of Detention Facilities,* (Jan. 01, 2009)

The form in which the judicial review is performed remains debated. *Sassòli* and *Olson* suggest applying the regime foreseen in IACs for civilians by analogy.[265] This, however, would be inconsistent with the well-supported approach that members of the non-state group are *not* civilians. As a result, there is no comparable situation for members of the non-state group and civilians, which would be required to allow for an application of the GC IV by analogy. Instead, the judicial review would have to meet minimum standards below those required in cases of PoWs or under the GC IV. This requires substantial further clarification and underlines that NIAC laws do not currently provide for a fully satisfactory answer.

bb) Duration of Detention

The duration of detention, and whether a non-civilian can be detained until the end of the hostilities, is of crucial concern.[266] It is more problematic to determine the end of a NIAC than the end of an IAC, where states may call for a ceasefire or enter into peace negotiations.[267] Additionally, a NIAC, particularly in the form of a transnational conflict, may persist for decades. According to the ICRC, in NIACs

"[p]ersons deprived of their liberty in relation to a non-international armed conflict must be release as soon as the reasons for the deprivation of their liberty cease to exist".[268]

---

online available at http://www.whitehouse.gov/the_press_office/ClosureOfGuantanamo DetentionFacilities/ (last visited Mar. 08, 2012).

[265] Marco Sassòli and Laura M. Olson, *The Relationship between International Humanitarian and Human Rights Law where it matters: Admissible Killing and Internment of Fighters in Non-International Armed Conflicts*, 90 International Review of the Red Cross 599, 627 (2008) ("While these limits have to be accepted with regard to the use of force and must be mitigated by instructions and guidelines, they may be overcome in the procedural regulation of internment by applying by analogy the regime foreseen in the humanitarian law of international armed conflicts for civilians").

[266] Art. 118 GC III ("Prisoners of war shall be released and repatriated without delay after the cessation of active hostilities").

[267] Marco Sassòli and Laura M. Olson, *The Relationship between International Humanitarian and Human Rights Law where it matters: Admissible Killing and Internment of Fighters in Non-International Armed Conflicts,* 90 International Review of the Red Cross 599, 624 (2008) ("It is also much harder to determine the actual end of hostilities than in an international armed conflict between states that may conclude a ceasefire or surrender").

[268] Jean-Marie Henckaerts and Louise Doswald-Beck, *Customary International Humanitarian Law*, Vol. I, Rule 128.C. (2005).

The point at which *the reasons for deprivation of their liberty cease to exist* remains unclear and cannot be easily determined. The states' margin of appreciation to determine that point in the absence of an independent board is far too broad. As a result, an individual may be detained simply by declaring that the conflict has not yet ended. This demonstrates that *de lege lata* the laws of NIAC provide for no suitable detention regime.

c) Protection of Civilians

This section analyzes civilian protection in circumstances of the application of NIAC law to transnational conflicts. It is pertinent to distinguish between the protection of civilians of the conflict state and of the territorial state.

Transnational conflicts are similar to ordinary NIACs as regards the conflict state's civilians. Therefore, no modifications of the protection of civilians are necessary, as they are protected by Art. 13-18 AP II and numerous rules of CIL.[269] The applicable rules of CIL in particular lead to a broad assimilation of the law of IAC and law of NIAC, as far as the protection of civilians is concerned.[270] At the core of this protection stands the general immunity from attack. According to Art. 13.3 AP II, civilians can be directly targeted only if and for such time as they directly participate in the hostilities. This provision has become CIL.[271] The detention of the conflict state's civilians is only lawful when a civilian poses a threat to the security of the state.[272] This derives from Art. 41-43 and 78 GC IV, which has been claimed to reflect a general principle applicable

---

[269] Jean-Marie Henckaerts and Louise Doswald-Beck, *Customary International Humanitarian Law*, Vol. I, Rules 1, 2, 5-24, 87-105 (2005).

[270] Hans-Peter Gasser and Knut Dörmann, *Protection of Civilian Population*, in The Handbook of International Humanitarian Law, 232 (Dieter Fleck ed. 2013) ("After the adoption of the 1977 Protocols there is hardly a significant difference between the two legal regimes, since AP II protects individuals against the misuse of power just as clearly as he law of international armed conflicts [...]. However, important parts of 'Geneva Law' [...] are relevant for international situations only").

[271] Jean-Marie Henckaerts and Louise Doswald-Beck, *Customary International Humanitarian Law*, Vol. I, Rule 6 (2005).

[272] Jean S. Pictet, *Commentary on the Geneva Convention (IV) Relative to the Protection of Civilian Persons in Times of War*, 257-8 (1958); ICTY, *Prosecutor v. Kordic' and Cerkez*, Case No. IT–95–14/2–A, Appeals Judgment, ¶ 72–73, 620 (Dec. 17, 2004); ICTY, *Prosecutor v. Delalic et al,* Case No. IT–96–21–A, Appeals Judgment, ¶ 327 (Feb. 20, 2001); Hans-Peter Gasser and Knut Dörmann, *Protection of Civilian Population*, in The Handbook of International Humanitarian Law, 315 *et seq.* (Dieter Fleck ed. 2013); Ryan Goodman, *The Detention of Civilians in Armed Conflicts*, 103 American Journal of International Law 48, 53 (2009).

to NIACs.[273] The detention of the conflict state's civilians must last as long as the persons detained pose a threat to security, rather than until the end of hostilities.[274] The question therefore lies in whether the civilian himself poses a security threat. This is evident when a civilian directly participates in hostilities. As a result, it must be lawful for a state to detain that civilian *a majore ad minus*, for it is already lawful. However, it is also possible that a civilian, although not directly participating in hostilities, poses a security threat. *Goodman* calls this *"indirect participation"*.[275] The security threat must be understood more broadly than direct participation.[276] However, if a civilian who indirectly participates in hostilities is detained, the grounds upon which he were detained would need to be concretely proven through Art. 43 and 78.2 GC IV.

With respect to the territorial state's citizens, one must consider the fact that the territorial state might not have joined either the conflict state or the non-state party.[277] This has occurred in Lebanon, is currently occurring in Somalia, and

---

[273] Ryan Goodman, *The Detention of Civilians in Armed Conflicts*, 103 American Journal of International Law 48, 53 (2009) ("The Fourth Convention, under Articles 5, 27, 41-43, and 78, plainly permits the detention, or internment, of civilians not according to status-based categories, but according to whether an individual poses a security threat. In noninternational armed conflicts, international authorities have applied the same principle").

[274] Art. 132.1 GC IV; Hans-Peter Gasser and Knut Dörmann, *Protection of Civilian Population*, in The Handbook of International Humanitarian Law, 319 *et seq.* (Dieter Fleck ed. 2013).

[275] Ryan Goodman, *The Detention of Civilians in Armed Conflicts*, 103 American Journal of International Law 48, 53 (2009).

[276] *See, e.g.*, Jean S. Pictet, *Commentary on the Geneva Convention (IV) Relative 88to the Protection of Civilian Persons in Times of War*, 257 (1958) ("It did not seem possible to define the expression 'security 88ft he State' in a more concrete fashion. It is thus left very largely to Governments to decide the measure of activity prejudicial to the internal or external security of the State which justifies internment or assigned residence"); id. At 258 ("Subversive activity carried on inside the territory of a Party to the conflict or actions which are of direct assistance to an enemy Power both threaten the security of the country; a belligerent may intern people or place them in assigned residence if it has serious and legitimate reason to think that they are members of organizations whose object is to cause disturbances... To justify recourse to such measures the State must have good reason to think that the person concerned, by his activities, knowledge or qualifications, represents a real threat to its present or future security"); Ryan Goodman, *The Detention of Civilians in Armed Conflicts*, 103 American Journal of International Law 48, 53 (2009).

[277] *See generally* Robin Geiß, *Armed Violence in Fragile States: Low-Intensity Conflicts, Spillover Conflicts, and Sporadic Law Enforcement Operations by Third States*, 873 International Review of the Red Cross 127, 139 (2009) (assessing the possible scenarios of violence within fragile states).

may be the case in Afghanistan if one were to consider that the allied forces are effectively operating independently of Afghanistan. The NIAC regime does not provide rules regarding the citizens of a state that is not party to the conflict. The regime originally regarded the conflict as purely internal, and one in which other states citizens would not be affected. As a result, the laws of NIACs did not address the status of the territorial state's citizens. Legally, the territorial state and its citizens must be treated as neutrals and therefore deserve a higher standard of protection than citizens of the conflict state. This protection can be granted to all civilians of the territorial state through the analogous application of GC IV.

3. Conclusion

Art. 3 GC is theoretically applicable to transnational conflicts between states and non-state actors. The transnational character of these conflicts is no longer an obstacle to applying the laws of NIACs. However, the requirements regarding the organization of the parties and the minimum threshold of violence must still be met. The application of the NIAC laws does not provide for a comprehensive legal regime capable of addressing all needs. This holds particularly true with respect to a correct legal qualification of the non-state party. In addition, the rules regulating detention or internment are insufficiently elaborated upon in the NIAC laws. The treaties do not address these questions and CIL cannot be detected given the lack of sufficient state practice. Hence, the application of GC IV is an urgent requirement to guarantee the protection of citizens of the territorial state.

Despite insufficient regulation, the NIAC regime entails the important advantage in that it contains an element of asymmetry: the lack of a combatant status for non-state actors. Therefore, the fact that members of the non-state party are not given the right to participate in hostilities does not run contrary to the principles of the NIAC regime and is the ultimately the key difference between the IAC and the NIAC regimes. If IHL is to be applied to transnational conflicts, the more appropriate legal regime is that of NIACs, rather than IACs.

III. New Legal Category of Armed Conflicts

This section analyzes approaches that argue in favor of a new legal category of Extra-State Armed Conflicts or Transnational Armed Conflicts to provide an adequate legal framework for transnational conflicts.[278] Although the NIAC regime can be applied to a number of transnational conflicts, an analysis of IHL would be incomplete without looking at new directions that go beyond the classic dichotomy of IHL.

1. Extra-State Armed Conflict (Schöndorf)

Schöndorf argues for a new legal regime of *Extra-State Armed Conflict* to govern transnational conflicts and outlines three major claims. First, *Schöndorf* regards the existing laws of armed conflict as insufficient, while still considering transnational conflicts as a matter of IHL.[279] This is further emphasized by classifying these conflicts as transnational *armed* conflicts; hence, the term armed conflict is used to illustrate that one continues to operate within the material field of IHL. Next, *Schöndorf* deems it insufficient to leave the classic dichotomy untouched and only adapt the existing regimes of IHL when responding to the challenges of transnational conflict.[280] The consequence of applying IHL, while simultaneously rejecting the inherent categories of IACs and NIACs, is to call for the establishment of a third category of armed conflicts. Finally, *Schöndorf* argues that a new legal category will not result in a legal void, but that,

---

[278] Roy S. Schöndorf, *Extra-State Armed Conflicts: Is there a Need for a New Legal Regime?*, 37 New York University Journal of Law and Politics 1 (2004); Geoffrey Corn and Eric Talbot Jensen, *Transnational Armed Conflict: A "Principled" Approach to the Regulation of Counter-Terror Combat Operations*, 42 Israel Law Review 46 (2009); Geoffrey Corn and Eric Talbot Jensen, *Untying the Gordian Knot: A Proposal for Determining Applicability of the Laws of War to the War on Terror*, 81 Temple Law Review 787 (2008).

[279] Roy S. Schöndorf, *Extra-State Armed Conflicts: Is there a Need for a New Legal Regime?*, 37 New York University Journal of Law and Politics 1, 19 *et seq.* (2004).

[280] Roy S. Schöndorf, *Extra-State Armed Conflicts: Is there a Need for a New Legal Regime?*, 37 New York University Journal of Law and Politics 1, 52 (2004) ("[…] the treaty regime of international humanitarian law does not properly regulate extra-state armed conflicts"); *see also* Robert D. Sloane, *Prologue to a Voluntarist War Convention*, 106 Michigan Law Review 443, 480 (2007) ("Ultimately, rather than fit a square peg of the global war on terrorism into the round hole of the existing law, IHL may well need to develop a lex specialis for conflicts with transnational terrorist networks, just as it did (albeit with limited success) for the noninternational conflicts of the latter half of the twentieth century").

"Extra-State armed conflicts are governed by specific rules that are derived from an interpretation of the general principles of International Humanitarian Law in the unique context of such conflicts [...]".[281]

In the following section, *Schöndorf's* argument that IHL is applicable but existing categories of IHL must be rejected will be addressed first. Whether his approach does indeed avoid a legal gap will be subsequently analyzed.

a) The Need for a New International Humanitarian Law Regime

Schöndorf comprehensively argues for transnational conflicts to fall under IHL regime. He states that the *"reality on the ground"* resembles an armed conflict more than an occurrence of violence during peacetime.[282] In addition, he argues that not applying IHL would have *"harsh results"*. *Schöndorf* believes the laws of peace are not fit to regulate situations of large-scale violence which occur during transnational conflicts.[283] Although transnational conflicts should fall under IHL, *Schöndorf* claims they cannot be regulated by IAC or NIAC laws, and that there is an additional armed conflict category not addressed in the Geneva Conventions.[284] *Schöndorf* puts forth the argument that the inherent categories of IHL do not encompass transnational conflicts.[285] Because IACs require two states to be parties, transnational conflicts cannot be IACs.[286] Furthermore, NIACs are traditionally regarded to be internal conflicts, hence, transnational conflicts cannot be considered NIACs.[287] This formalist argument can be rebutted as the logical connection between the existence of a new category of conflict and the *per se* inability to apply the existing laws is not evident. The old laws may not have been created with the specific purpose of addressing

---

[281] Roy S. Schöndorf, *Extra-State Armed Conflicts: Is there a Need for a New Legal Regime?*, 37 New York University Journal of Law and Politics 1, 6 (2004).

[282] Roy S. Schöndorf, *Extra-State Armed Conflicts: Is there a Need for a New Legal Regime?*, 37 New York University Journal of Law and Politics 1, 20 (2004).

[283] Roy S. Schöndorf, *Extra-State Armed Conflicts: Is there a Need for a New Legal Regime?*, 37 New York University Journal of Law and Politics 1, 21 (2004).

[284] Roy S. Schöndorf, *Extra-State Armed Conflicts: Is there a Need for a New Legal Regime?*, 37 New York University Journal of Law and Politics 1, 6-7 (2004).

[285] Roy S. Schöndorf, *Extra-State Armed Conflicts: Is there a Need for a New Legal Regime?*, 37 New York University Journal of Law and Politics 1, 52 (2004) ("Overall, the treaty regime of international humanitarian law does not properly regulate extra-state armed conflicts").

[286] Roy S. Schöndorf, *Extra-State Armed Conflicts: Is there a Need for a New Legal Regime?*, 37 New York University Journal of Law and Politics 1, 37 (2004).

[287] Roy S. Schöndorf, *Extra-State Armed Conflicts: Is there a Need for a New Legal Regime?*, 37 New York University Journal of Law and Politics 1, 40 (2004).

this specific conflict, however, they may still offer the necessary legal framework.

IHL can adjust to the changing and heterogeneous nature of armed conflicts. As previously mentioned, the transnational character of transnational conflicts does not hinder Art. 3 GC from being applied. The geographical limitation of NIACs to internal conflicts appears to be obsolete. As previously stated, the US Supreme Court has taken the position that Art. 3 GC applies to the conflict between the United States and the Taliban and Al Qaeda.[288] The Court regards Art. 3 as a substitute regime that comes into effect whenever the armed conflict does not occur between two states.[289] Arguing for a new category of IHL therefore requires substantial evidence that the existing regimes cannot be adjusted to the new conflict. *Schöndorf* does not present this evidence.

b) The Extra-State Armed Conflict Regime

Schöndorf's approach suggests the existence of a form of armed conflict outside the Geneva Conventions. As demonstrated by the Bush administration, this bears the danger of creating a legal void as opposed to providing legal regulation. *Schöndorf* claims his approach will not result in a legal void, and argues that

"extra-state armed conflicts are governed by a legal framework consisting of either basic customary norms common to all armed conflicts or general principles of international humanitarian law".[290]

He further argues that an Extra-State Armed Conflict regime would be governed by *specific rules*, although he fails to present them or further elaborate. Furthermore, he does not go into details regarding the content of his new regime.[291] *Schöndorf* presents a method of finding new norms in order to establish

---

[288] *Hamdan vs. Rumsfeld*, 548 U.S. 557, 631 *et seq.* (2006).

[289] *Hamdan vs. Rumsfeld*, 548 U.S. 557, 630 (2006) ("[…] the phrase 'not of an international character' bears its literal meaning").

[290] Roy S. Schöndorf, *Extra-State Armed Conflicts: Is there a Need for a New Legal Regime?*, 37 New York University Journal of Law and Politics 1, 48 (2004) ("[The paper] rejects the notion that extra-state armed conflicts exist in a legal vacuum, and, instead, argues that extra-state armed conflicts are governed by a legal framework consisting of either basic customary norms common to all armed conflicts or general principles of international humanitarian law").

[291] Roy S. Schöndorf, *Extra-State Armed Conflicts: Is there a Need for a New Legal Regime?*, 37 New York University Journal of Law and Politics 1, 31 (2004) ("Therefore, the laws of armed conflict should be applied only as a general framework – a starting point – within which sufficient flexibility should be preserved in its specific application

the new regime, rather than to flesh out the new set of norms in a comprehensive manner. He argues that the existing IHL can be divided into a law of combatants and a law of non-combatants.[292] By looking at single provisions rather than whole legal regimes, *Schöndorf* argues one may find a set of rules that fit transnational conflicts. Because transnational conflicts share elements of IACs and NIACs, the law of combatants from NIACs and the law of non-combatants from IACs must be combined. After having proposed this methodical approach, *Schöndorf* remains vague as far as its precise application.[293] This is especially unsatisfying in light of the three crucial elements of IHL: the legal status of the non-state actors, the acceptability of a certain amount of collateral damages, and the regulation of detention.

aa) The Legal Status of Non-State Actors

During an extra-state armed conflict, the principle of distinction must be respected.[294] The crucial problem lies in how to identify combatants of the non-state party. This problem, although addressed by *Schöndorf*,[295] is not sufficiently analyzed and no solution is suggested. *Schöndorf* mentions a limited definition of combatant status,[296] although it is vague. He ultimately accepts a form of membership based combatant status and raises the question as to whether the membership also grants a right to participate for the non-state actors. He tentatively proposes that non-state actors may be treated as legitimized participants in

---

to accommodate these concerns.") and at 57 ("[…] admittedly the foregoing principles are very general").

[292] Roy S. Schöndorf, *Extra-State Armed Conflicts: Is there a Need for a New Legal Regime?*, 37 New York University Journal of Law and Politics 1, 46 (2004) ("[…] it is arguably more useful to distinguish between the law of combatants and the law of non-combatants, rather than between the Hague Laws and the Geneva Laws").

[293] Roy S. Schöndorf, *Extra-State Armed Conflicts: Is there a Need for a New Legal Regime?*, 37 New York University Journal of Law and Politics 1, 56 (2004) ("it is not the purpose of this Article to specify particular norms that govern extra-state armed conflict").

[294] Roy S. Schöndorf, *Extra-State Armed Conflicts: Is there a Need for a New Legal Regime?*, 37 New York University Journal of Law and Politics 1, 63 (2004) ("[…] the principle of distinction [between combatants and civilians] also applies in the context of extra-state armed conflicts. Thus, combatants in extra-state armed conflicts may be targeted but civilians are immune from attack unless and for such time as they take direct part in the hostilities").

[295] Roy S. Schöndorf, *Extra-State Armed Conflicts: Is there a Need for a New Legal Regime?*, 37 New York University Journal of Law and Politics 1, 63 *et seq.* (2004).

[296] Roy S. Schöndorf, *Extra-State Armed Conflicts: Is there a Need for a New Legal Regime?*, 37 New York University Journal of Law and Politics 1, 64 (2004).

the hostilities.[297] Furthermore, *Schöndorf* states that his approach could constrain a state's action insofar as the state party may be obliged to attempt to place an arrest before actually targeting a non-state combatant.[298] This idea is not elaborated upon any further. There is also no argument for why a similar development of a limited combatant status would not be possible within the laws of NIACs. *Schöndorf's* results fit perfectly into the evolving laws of NIAC, in which the ICRC applies the concept of *continuous combat function* to specifically target persons in NIACs who regularly participate in hostilities against the state.[299] In addition, the ICRC generally claims that the principle of military necessity and humanity limits the right to target to situations in which capture is not possible.[300] Although this is highly controversial, it should still be directly addressed and resolved within the NIAC regime.

bb) Collateral Damage

An additional problem of a new legal regime of armed conflict is the extent to which collateral damage is acceptable. *Schöndorf* does not address this issue comprehensively. He applies the principle of proportionality,[301] and argues that cases where an operation resembles a law enforcement operation more than an actual battle situation, the principle of proportionality should be applied more restrictively. *Schöndorf* bases this suggestion on the stricter handling of collateral damage during law enforcement operations.[302] This, however, is not further

---

[297] Roy S. Schöndorf, *Extra-State Armed Conflicts: Is there a Need for a New Legal Regime?*, 37 New York University Journal of Law and Politics 1, 68 *et seq.* (2004) ("However, just as Additional Protocol I elevated the rights of combatants in certain intra-state armed conflicts to the rights of combatants in inter-state armed conflicts, it may be that, in certain extra-state armed conflicts – those that parallel the ones specified under article 1(4) of Additional Protocol I – a recognition of the right to engage in hostilities should be considered.") and at 72 ("This possibility is obviously not a well-analyzed, comprehensive proposal; instead, it demonstrates the advantages of the flexibility afforded by the theoretical model presented in this Article").

[298] Roy S. Schöndorf, *Extra-State Armed Conflicts: Is there a Need for a New Legal Regime?*, 37 New York University Journal of Law and Politics 1, 64 (2004).

[299] International Committee of the Red Cross, *Interpretive Guidance on the Notion of Direct Participation in Hostilities under International Humanitarian Law*, 35 (2009).

[300] International Committee of the Red Cross, *Interpretive Guidance on the Notion of Direct Participation in Hostilities under International Humanitarian Law*, 78 *et seq.* (2009).

[301] Roy S. Schöndorf, *Extra-State Armed Conflicts: Is there a Need for a New Legal Regime?*, 37 New York University Journal of Law and Politics 1, 66 (2004).

[302] Roy S. Schöndorf, *Extra-State Armed Conflicts: Is there a Need for a New Legal Regime?*, 37 New York University Journal of Law and Politics 1, 66-7 (2004).

explained and details remain vague. Yet again, why *Schöndorf's* suggestions could not also be realized within a NIAC regime remain unclear.

cc) Detention

Schöndorf addresses the issue of battlefield detention and suggests a

"specific regime designed for the regulation of the status of battlefield detainees in the context of extra-state armed conflicts".[303]

This regime should

"reflect the interpretation of two basic principles of the laws of armed conflict: humanity and military necessity".[304]

This is not a novel concept as all IHL norms derive from the balance of humanity and military necessity. However, Schöndorf proceeds to state that the detention regime should be a *"new, hybrid model"* of IAC and NIAC rules.[305] He proposes a combination of IAC and NIAC rules:

"One possibility is to afford battlefield detainees the (non-political) privileges regarding conditions of detention that are afforded to prisoners of war under the legal regime regulating inter-state armed conflicts [IACs], as this legal regime is designed to hold combatants in detention for long periods of times. At the same time, with regard to the more political aspects of detention, one could rely on the analogy between extra-state armed conflicts and intra-state armed conflicts [NIACs], which allows prosecution of detainees for their participation in hostilities."[306]

While *Schöndorf's* combination is appealing, he fails to demonstrate why it requires the development of a third regime. Instead of combining IAC and NIAC rules to create another legal regime, the existing NIAC rules could simply be

---

[303] Roy S. Schöndorf, *Extra-State Armed Conflicts: Is there a Need for a New Legal Regime?*, 37 New York University Journal of Law and Politics 1, 72 (2004) ("The specific regime designed for the regulation of the status of battlefield detainees in the context of extra-state armed conflicts should reflect the interpretation of two basic principles of the laws of armed conflict: humanity and military necessity").

[304] Roy S. Schöndorf, *Extra-State Armed Conflicts: Is there a Need for a New Legal Regime?*, 37 New York University Journal of Law and Politics 1, 72 (2004).

[305] Roy S. Schöndorf, *Extra-State Armed Conflicts: Is there a Need for a New Legal Regime?*, 37 New York University Journal of Law and Politics 1, 72 (2004) (In my view, this process of interpretation should lead to the development of a new, hybrid model that deals with the specific problems concerning the internment of battlefield detainees in the context of extra-state armed conflicts).

[306] Roy S. Schöndorf, *Extra-State Armed Conflicts: Is there a Need for a New Legal Regime?*, 37 New York University Journal of Law and Politics 1, 72 (2004).

enhanced through IAC regulation. Non-political privileges afforded to PoWs during an IAC can be applied to detainees during a NIAC. Elaborating on an existing legal regime appears to be more suitable than developing yet another legal regime which would create further uncertainties.

c) Conclusion

The analysis in the previous section demonstrates that the proposals of a new legal category of extra-state armed conflicts within the body of IHL must be rejected. *Schöndorf* is far too strict in his orientation toward the formalistic interpretation of NIACs as internal conflicts. This prevents one from considering the possibilities of the laws of NIACs to address the challenges of transnational conflicts. As a result, he fails to present a convincing argument as to why a new regime is necessary. An adjusted NIAC regime could bring the same advantages as an entirely new regime of extra-state armed conflicts.[307] By following *Schöndorf's* approach, the risks of legal voids would be immensely high as he relies only on general principles. Although he claims that specific rules can be developed, this has yet to be done. Thus, the ideas he develops should be applied within the framework of NIAC laws, which has already been done to a great extent.

By the time *Schöndorf* published his work in 2004, the development of the laws applicable during NIACs was far less progressive. This may explain why he does not sufficiently analyze them. However, his ideas are referenced in many of the new approaches that elaborate upon the laws of NIACs and are evidently very valuable. Hence, only the contextualization of his ideas within a new regime of extra-state armed conflict must be rejected.

2. Transnational Armed Conflict (Corn & Jensen)

Corn and *Jensen* also provide an approach outside the classic dichotomy of IACs and NIACs. Similar to *Schöndorf*, they claim that transnational conflicts must be characterized as armed conflicts, but do not fit into the dichotomy of

---

[307] Marco Sassòli, *Transnational Armed Groups and International Humanitarian Law*, Occasional Paper Series, Program on Humanitarian Policy and Conflict Research, 25 (Harvard University Winter 2006) online available at http://www.hpcrresearch.org/pdfs/OccasionalPaper6.pdf ("The result [of Schöndorf's approach], however, is not so different from the law of non-international armed conflicts including the customary rules recently found by the ICRC").

IHL. Hence, a new legal regime of transnational armed conflicts must be crafted.[308]

a) The Need for a New International Humanitarian Law Regime

Corn and *Jensen's* approach does not preclude the possibility that transnational conflicts that fall short of armed conflicts may exist. However, their approach is developed with respect to the conflict between the U.S. and Al Qaeda, which they argue amounts to an armed conflict. *Corn* and *Jensen* state that military operations directed against transnational terrorists must be characterized as armed conflicts, as the alternative of characterizing them as a law enforcement operation would be a *"fundamental fallacy"*.[309] They further argue that the authority to employ military means and deadly force against non-state actors is inconceivable given law enforcement regulations. It would be a mere *"legal fiction"* to understand military operations by the U.S. against a non-state actor, such as Al Qaeda, as transnational law enforcement operations.[310] This position also refers to the US Supreme Court's Hamdan decision.[311] However, *Corn* and *Jensen* claim that the Supreme Court's approach of applying Art. 3 GC

"is not sufficient to effectively regulate the conduct of hostilities between state armed forces and non-state transnational enemies".[312]

Like *Schöndorf, Corn* and *Jensen* argue for the need to develop a new legal regime within IHL to specifically address conflicts between state armed forces and non-state armed groups.

---

[308] Geoffrey Corn and Eric Talbot Jensen, *Transnational Armed Conflict: A "Principled" Approach to the Regulation of Counter-Terror Combat Operations*, 42 Israel Law Review 46 (2009); Geoffrey Corn and Eric Talbot Jensen, *Untying the Gordian Knot: A Proposal for Determining Applicability of the Laws of War to the War on Terror*, 81 Temple Law Review 787 (2008).

[309] Geoffry Corn, *Making the Case for Conflict Bifurcation in Afghanistan: Transnational Armed Conflict, Al Qaeda, and the Limits of the Associated Militia Concept*, 39 Israel Yearbook on Human Rights 27, 57 (2009).

[310] Geoffrey Corn and Eric Talbot Jensen, *Transnational Armed Conflict: A "Principled" Approach to the Regulation of Counter-Terror Combat Operations*, 42 Israel Law Review 46, 46 (2009).

[311] Geoffrey Corn and Eric Talbot Jensen, *Transnational Armed Conflict: A "Principled" Approach to the Regulation of Counter-Terror Combat Operations*, 42 Israel Law Review 46, 49 (2009).

[312] *See* Geoffrey Corn and Eric Talbot Jensen, *Transnational Armed Conflict: A "Principled" Approach to the Regulation of Counter-Terror Combat Operations*, 42 Israel Law Review 46, 49-50 (2009).

In arguing for the need for a new legal regime, *Corn* and *Jensen* claim trans-national conflicts do not fit in either regime of IHL. Attributing terrorists to a state in order to characterize the conflict as a IAC would be *"factual fiction"*.[313] *Corn* and *Jensen* argue that Al Qaeda does not act on behalf of the Taliban. As a result, the unique conflict between Al Qaeda and the U.S. must be distinguished from the U.S.'s conflict with the Taliban.[314] Thus, *Corn* and *Jensen* suggest a *lege ferenda* development of a new category of Transnational Armed Conflicts.[315] *Corn* and *Jensen's* intention is to repeal the understanding of Art. 2 and Art. 3 GC as a *"law triggering paradigm"*.[316] Instead, they argue for the possibility of identifying armed conflicts (and applying the laws of armed conflicts) given the situation on the grounds, determined from the *"perspective of the warrior"*.[317] Thus, *Corn* and *Jensen* claim the existence of an armed conflict depends not on criteria of Art. 2 or 3 GC, but whether the Rules of Engagement (RoE), which a state issues to its soldiers, are *"inherently invoking the authority of the laws of war to guide target selection and destruction decisions"*.[318] This implies that the nature of the issued RoE determines the nature of a conflict. As a result, a conflict must be qualified as an armed conflict when the conflict state has issued *status based RoE*.[319] The RoE authorize the use of deadly force against an enemy based on its status as an enemy and regardless of its conduct.

---

[313] Geoffrey Corn and Eric Talbot Jensen, *Transnational Armed Conflict: A "Principled" Approach to the Regulation of Counter-Terror Combat Operations*, 42 Israel Law Review 46, 46 (2009).

[314] Geoffrey Corn, *Making the Case for Conflict Bifurcation in Afghanistan: Transnational Armed Conflict, Al Qaeda, and the Limits of the Associated Militia Concept*, 39 Israel Yearbook on Human Rights 27, 66-7 (2009).

[315] Geoffrey Corn and Eric Talbot Jensen, *Transnational Armed Conflict: A "Principled" Approach to the Regulation of Counter-Terror Combat Operations*, 42 Israel Law Review 46, 50 (2009).

[316] Geoffrey Corn and Eric Talbot Jensen, *Untying the Gordian Knot: A Proposal for Determining Applicability of the Laws of War to the War on Terror*, 81 Temple Law Review 787, 798 Fn. 63 (2008).

[317] Geoffrey Corn and Eric Talbot Jensen, *Untying the Gordian Knot: A Proposal for Determining Applicability of the Laws of War to the War on Terror*, 81 Temple Law Review 787, 829 (2008).

[318] Geoffrey Corn and Eric Talbot Jensen, *Untying the Gordian Knot: A Proposal for Determining Applicability of the Laws of War to the War on Terror*, 81 Temple Law Review 787, 825 (2008); *see also* Geoffrey Corn, *What Law Applies to the War on Terror?*, in The War on Terror and the Laws of War: A Military Perspective 1, 26-7 (2009).

[319] *Cf.* Geoffrey Corn, W*hat Law Applies to the War on Terror?*, in The War on Terror and the Laws of War: A Military Perspective 1, 27-8 (2009).

Whether the criteria of an IAC, according to Art. 2 GC, or an NIAC, according to Art. 3 GC, are met is irrelevant for the qualification of the conflict.[320]

Corn and *Jensen's* concept of transnational armed conflicts is methodologically flawed. The characterization of a conflict as an armed conflict cannot depend on the kind of RoE a state issued. To the contrary, the kind of RoE issued by the state must depend on the nature of the conflict, and not the other way round. In addition, *Corn* and *Jensen* fail to sufficiently demonstrate why the application of the laws of NIACs is insufficient. They do not discuss the possibility of applying Art. 3 GC to non-*internal* conflict. Instead, they argue that even if one were to apply a provision such as Art. 3 GC, it would not be sufficient to govern transnational conflicts.[321] This fails to acknowledge the difference between Art. 3 GC alone and the entire legal regime of NIACs, consisting of the Additional Protocol II of the Geneva Conventions and Customary International Law. While Art. 3 GC may on its own appear insufficient to regulate transnational conflicts, the previous analysis demonstrated that the legal regime of NIACs provides for more regulation than Art. 3 GC alone.

b) The Laws of a Transnational Armed Conflict Regime

Corn and *Jensen* suggest transnational armed conflicts as a new category of IHL. However, they are vague with regard to the concrete rules that regulate the new category. They begin with the fundamental principle that

"no battlefield shall go unregulated", which "renders the application of fundamental LOAC [Laws of Armed Conflict] principles to this emerging category of armed conflict as much in the realm of lex lata as lex ferenda".[322]

---

[320] Geoffrey Corn, *What Law Applies to the War on Terror?*, in The War on Terror and the Laws of War: A Military Perspective 1, 27-8 (2009).

[321] Geoffrey Corn and Eric Talbot Jensen, *Transnational Armed Conflict: A "Principled" Approach to the Regulation of Counter-Terror Combat Operations*, 42 Israel Law Review 46, 49-50 (2009) ("[...] applying Common Article 3 to transnational armed conflicts is not sufficient to effectively regulate the conduct of hostilities between State armed forces and non-State transnational enemies. The mandate of Common Article 3 addresses only the treatment of detainees and other individuals rendered hors de combat").

[322] Geoffrey Corn and Eric Talbot Jensen, *Transnational Armed Conflict: A "Principled" Approach to the Regulation of Counter-Terror Combat Operations*, 42 Israel Law Review 46, 50 (2009) ("[...] it is the premise of the authors that the imperative that 'no battlefield go unregulated' renders the application of fundamental LOAC principles to this emerging category of armed conflict as much in the realm of lex lata as lex ferenda").

How exactly the battlefield of transnational conflicts is regulated must be assessed. *Corn* and *Jensen* speak of fundamental principles of LOAC,[323] but what exactly they mean by the fundamental LOAC principles is unclear and is less than the full body of IAC law.[324] *Corn* claims that the general LOAC principles are

"generally well understood and have formed the foundation for operational regulation of a multitude of military operations conducted by many armed forces for decades".[325]

This arguably oversimplifies the situation. Considering the difference between the laws of IACs and NIACs is absolutely essential. Corn and Jensen do not address this difference but instead state,

"what the authors believe is significant is that armed conflict must be understood as triggering the normative framework of the LOAC".[326]

This statement is unconvincing as a number of differences between the IAC and NIAC laws remain, although there may be assimilation between the two regimes.[327]

No general legal framework for armed conflicts exists. *Corn* and *Jensen* apply basic legal regulations instead of a comprehensive legal regime. This approach leads to legal uncertainties as it grants a broad margin of appreciation to states when applying general principles. Applying a general principle allows for greater flexibility than applying a concrete rule as concerns the status of non-state actors. *Corn* and *Jensen* rely on a concept of membership, which allows the state party to attack those who are considered members of the non-state group, even if

---

[323] Geoffrey Corn, *Making the Case for Conflict Bifurcation in Afghanistan: Transnational Armed Conflict, Al Qaeda, and the Limits of the Associated Militia Concept*, 39 Israel Yearbook on Human Rights 27, 68 (2009).

[324] Geoffrey Corn and Eric Talbot Jensen, *Transnational Armed Conflict: A "Principled" Approach to the Regulation of Counter-Terror Combat Operations*, 42 Israel Law Review 46, 58 (2009).

[325] Geoffrey Corn, *Making the Case for Conflict Bifurcation in Afghanistan: Transnational Armed Conflict, Al Qaeda, and the Limits of the Associated Militia Concept*, 39 Israel Yearbook on Human Rights 27, 68 (2009).

[326] *See* Geoffrey Corn and Eric Talbot Jensen, *Transnational Armed Conflict: A "Principled" Approach to the Regulation of Counter-Terror Combat Operations*, 42 Israel Law Review 46, 50 (2009).

[327] ICTY, *Prosecutor v. Tadic*, Case No. IT-94-1-I, Decision on Defence Motion for Interlocutory Appeal on Jurisdiction, ¶ 96-7 (Oct. 2, 1995); *cf.* Claus Kreß, *Friedenssicherungs- und Konfliktvölkerrecht auf der Schwelle zur Postmoderne*, 23 Europäische Grundrechte-Zeitschrift 638, 644 *et seq.* (1996).

they do not conduct a hostile act at the moment when they are targeted.[328] With respect to the regulation of detention, *Corn* and *Jensen* state the rights of those *hors de combat* emphasize the general obligation to treat persons humanely.[329] The new model does not grant PoW status, which includes full protection and rights of the GC III to non-state actors.[330] Whether armed forces of the state party should be granted PoW status is not specified.

c) A New Role for the Principle of Military Necessity

Corn and *Jensen* invoke the principle of military necessity, distinct from the existing laws of IAC, to define the allowed methods of warfare.[331] The ICRC similarly stated that the principle of military necessity and humanity must be taken into account even if an attack would be in accordance with IHL provisions.[332] In general, however, the specific provisions of IHL are understood to already include the principle of necessity.[333] Hence, there is no room for this principle except where a certain provision explicitly requires its special consideration.[334] On this same issue, the Red Cross has stated,

---

[328] Geoffrey Corn and Eric Talbot Jensen, *Transnational Armed Conflict: A "Principled" Approach to the Regulation of Counter-Terror Combat Operations*, 42 Israel Law Review 46, 61 *et seq.* (2009).

[329] Geoffrey Corn and Eric Talbot Jensen, *Transnational Armed Conflict: A "Principled" Approach to the Regulation of Counter-Terror Combat Operations*, 42 Israel Law Review 46, 69 (2009).

[330] Geoffrey Corn and Eric Talbot Jensen, *Transnational Armed Conflict: A "Principled" Approach to the Regulation of Counter-Terror Combat Operations*, 42 Israel Law Review 46, 73 (2009) ("While the humane treatment obligation does not result in the conclusion that detainees are to be treated analogously to individuals afforded special protections, such as prisoners of war [...]").

[331] Geoffrey Corn and Eric Talbot Jensen, *Transnational Armed Conflict: A "Principled" Approach to the Regulation of Counter-Terror Combat Operations*, 42 Israel Law Review 46, 57 *et seq.* (2009).

[332] International Committee of the Red Cross, *Interpretive Guidance on the Notion of Direct Participation in Hostilities under International Humanitarian Law*, 77 *et seq.* (2009); Philip Alston, *The CIA and Targeted Killings beyond Borders*, 2 Harvard National Security Journal 283, 303 (2011); Sandesh Sivakumaran, *The Law of Non-International Armed Conflict*, 251 (2012).

[333] Hans-Peter Gasser & Nils Melzer, *Humanitäres Völkerrecht*, 23-4 (2012).

[334] *Cf.* Knut Ipsen, Eberhard Menzel and Volker Epping, *Völkerrecht*, 1212 (2004).

"Considerations of military necessity and humanity neither derogate from nor override the specific provisions of IHL, but constitute guiding principles for the interpretation of the rights and duties of belligerents within the parameters set by these provisions".[335]

In a new regime, however, this principle will gain independent importance as the existing laws of IACs and NIACs do not apply.[336] In this respect, *Corn* and *Jensen's* approach differs from the recent debate on the importance of emphasizing the principles of military necessity and humanity. *Corn* and *Jensen* do not elaborate on the meaning of the application of the principle of military necessity, nor do they provide any concrete examples. *Corn* and *Jensen* state that no measures necessary to defeat Al Qaeda can be justified as militarily necessary. However, they do acknowledge that this was done by the Bush administration in the War on Terror regardless.[337] They clarify that, *"the authority derived from the contemporary principle of military necessity is not absolute"*.[338] However, the limits of authority remain unclear. *Corn* and *Jensen* summarize the (limiting) effects of the principle as such:

"This principle provides essential authority to employ the means necessary to bring a transnational non-State enemy to submission, to include detaining captured enemy operatives for so long as they continue to pose a threat of returning to the fight. However, the principle also provides an essential constraint on the authority of the State, and mandates application of the balancing principles of humane treatment and the prohibition of employing measures calculated to inflict unnecessary suffering."[339]

This explanation is unclear with respect to the relation between the principle of proportionality and the principle of military necessity. The principle of proportionality requires balancing the anticipated civilian damage and the anticipated military advantage to avoid excessive damage. The question remains as to whether the principle of proportionality is altered by the application of military necessity. According to *Corn* and *Jensen's* approach, it may be possible to use

---

[335] International Committee of the Red Cross, *Interpretive Guidance on the Notion of Direct Participation in Hostilities under International Humanitarian Law*, 78-9 (2009).

[336] Geoffrey Corn and Eric Talbot Jensen, *Transnational Armed Conflict: A "Principled" Approach to the Regulation of Counter-Terror Combat Operations*, 42 Israel Law Review 46, 58 (2009).

[337] Geoffrey Corn and Eric Talbot Jensen, *Transnational Armed Conflict: A "Principled" Approach to the Regulation of Counter-Terror Combat Operations*, 42 Israel Law Review 46, 59 (2009).

[338] Geoffrey Corn and Eric Talbot Jensen, *Transnational Armed Conflict: A "Principled" Approach to the Regulation of Counter-Terror Combat Operations*, 42 Israel Law Review 46, 58 (2009).

[339] Geoffrey Corn and Eric Talbot Jensen, *Transnational Armed Conflict: A "Principled" Approach to the Regulation of Counter-Terror Combat Operations*, 42 Israel Law Review 46, 60 (2009).

military necessity to justify an attack which leads to disproportionate civilian casualties. The Red Cross introduces the principle of military necessity and humanity to limit the authorities of the fighting parties and to introduce a capture before kill doctrine.[340] But the principle of military necessity has also often been used as a justification for the breach of the laws of war.[341] The authors do not elaborate on these concerns.

d) Conclusion

In conclusion, the application of a new legal regime of transnational armed conflicts to transnational conflicts must be rejected. A new regime that relies on *fundamental principles* without further explaining the applicable *normative framework of LOAC* cannot be regarded as more comprehensive than the existing regimes of NIACs and IACs. *Corn* and *Jensen* refer only to commonsense fundamental principles rather than stating concrete rules. Referring to the principle of military necessity without clearly determining its scope and relation to the principle of proportionality puts many civilian lives at stake. The claim that such a legal regime would be better suited to govern transnational conflicts does not hold true as far as the protection of civilians is concerned. In contrast, applying the laws of NIACs contains the advantage of reference to years of judicial practice. A new regime that has yet to be determined lacks judicial practice to rely on.

3. Conclusion

The previous analysis demonstrates that proposals of a new legal category of either extra-state or transnational armed conflicts within the body of IHL must be rejected. Both fail to present a convincing reason as to why a new regime is necessary. A new factual situation also *"does not automatically call for new laws to regulate it [...]"*.[342] The new categories do not bring substantial new advantages, but instead include propositions that are far too vague.

---

[340] International Committee of the Red Cross, *Interpretive Guidance on the Notion of Direct Participation in Hostilities under International Humanitarian Law*, 78. (2009) ("Clearly, the fact that a particular category of persons is not protected against offensive or defensive acts of violence is not equivalent to a legal entitlement to kill such persons without further considerations").

[341] Ingrid Detter, *The Law of War*, 393 *et seq.* (2000).

[342] Noam Lubell, *Extraterritorial Use of Force Against Non-State Actors*, 126 (2010).

The proposal of *Corn* and *Jensen* does not meet the requirement of predictable legal guidance. The emphasis on the principle of military necessity places a doubtful legal mechanism at the core of the new regime, thereby allowing states too wide a leeway for the application of IHL. *Schöndorf* outlines a unique way to detect new rules for a third regime within IHL. However, an adjusted NIAC regime may bring similar advantages as an entirely new category,[343] without the detriment of making existing IHL more complex by introducing a new conflict category. Therefore, if IHL is applied to transnational conflicts, one must rely on the existing categories of IACs and NIACs to determine the appropriate legal regulation for such conflicts.

IV. Conclusion

The analysis of IHL demonstrates that transnational conflicts can be addressed through an armed conflict approach. Within IHL, the only legal regime that can be applied to transnational conflicts is the NIAC regime. If understood broadly, it can be applied to a number of transnational conflicts, such as the conflict between Israel and Hezbollah.

Hezbollah qualifies as a conflict party due to its high degree of organization. Additionally, it is a party to the Lebanese parliament. The fact that the violence crosses the border of both Israel and Lebanon no longer presents an obstacle to a qualification as a NIAC. Furthermore, the threshold of violence was crossed during the summer of 2006. However, this does not imply that the conflict will always remain a NIAC. It is more plausible to argue that, after the end of the hostilities in 2006, the NIAC has ended as the nature of the conflict decreased to one below the threshold of an armed conflict. Evidently, the conflict is of a changing nature.

---

[343] Marco Sassòli, *Transnational Armed Groups and International Humanitarian Law*, Occasional Paper Series, Program on Humanitarian Policy and Conflict Research, 25 (Harvard University Winter 2006) online available at http://www.hpcrresearch.org/pdfs /OccasionalPaper6.pdf ("The result [of Schöndorf's approach], however, is not so different from the law of non-international armed conflicts including the customary rules recently found by the ICRC"); Noam Lubell, *Extraterritorial Use of Force Against Non-State Actors*, 133 (2010); Sandesh Sivakumaran, *The Law of Non-International Armed Conflict*, 228-9 (2012) ("[...] it is submitted that the better view is that, from a legal standpoint, such [transnational armed] conflicts are but a subset of the category of non-international armed conflicts, even if, from a descriptive perspective, they can be characterized as transnational armed conflicts").

The conflict between the U.S. and Al Qaeda has led to a different result than that of Israel and the Hezbollah. During the period between 1998 and 2001, the conflict reached the NIAC threshold. However, in the aftermath of the first phase of the war in Afghanistan, the conflict dwindled below the armed conflict threshold, mainly due to Al Qaeda's loss of organizational structure and stability. Thus, this transnational conflict does not qualify as a NIAC at this point.

These examples and the previous analysis demonstrate that not even the broadest possible understanding of NIACs allows *de lege lata* application of the regime to all transnational conflicts and during all phases of the conflict. This holds especially true due to the sporadic nature of violence and the loose organization of the non-state actors in some of the conflicts. Some transnational conflicts are left unregulated by IHL, or change and ultimately fall below the NIAC threshold.[344] Consequently, these very instances of violence are governed exclusively by the affected state's domestic law and IHRL. This, however, raises the question as to whether the legitimate security interests of the conflict states can be fully met, or if the laws of NIACs must be further expanded. Accordingly, the potential of an approach that addresses transnational conflicts through a transnational law enforcement regime based on IHRL will be discussed in the following chapter.

---

[344] *Cf.* Noam Lubell, *Extraterritorial Use of Force against Non-State Actors*, 159 *et seq.* (2010) (Lubell describes those situations as „small-scale operations against individuals").

D. Transnational Law Enforcement

In this chapter, whether an IHRL based transnational law enforcement regime can adequately regulate transnational conflicts will be examined. In Section I brief remarks on a state's justification to excercise extraterritorial law enforcement are presented.[1] Section II analyzes the rules of conduct under a transnational law enforcement regime and focuses on the regulation and limitation of the conflict state's powers, with respect to the rights of those affected by the law enforcement operations.

I. The Justification for Extraterritorial Action

In order to implement extraterritorial law enforcement, states require extraterritorial jurisdiction in addition to the authority to enforce it.[2] For example, the U.S. needs such jurisdiction and the authority to enforce it in the event they intend to fight members of Al Qaeda on territories outside the U.S., such as Afghanistan of Pakistan. According to the classic *Territorial Principle*, a state exercises jurisdiction only within its territory.[3] However, in transnational conflicts, extraterritorial jurisdiction may be based on the *Protective Principle*[4] or the *Universality Principle*.[5] To enforce this jurisdiction and take action against foreign citizens on the territory of another state, the conflict state must be authorized by international law.[6] This may occur by obtaining the territorial state's consent, a Security Council Resolution, or when a conflict state acts in self-defense under Art. 51 of the UN Charter.

The preferred method to authorize the conflict state's actions is through obtaining the territorial state's consent. Under a law enforcement regime, the territorial state may be more likely to consent to the conflict state's operations as the conflict state's authorities are more restricted than under an armed conflict para-

---

[1] For a comprehensive analysis of the jus ad bellum questions see Noam Lubell, *Extraterritorial Use of Force against Non-State Actors*, 25-84 (2010).

[2] On the differences between Jurisdiction to Prescribe, Jurisdiction to Adjudicate and Jurisdiction to Enforce *see generally* Sean D. Murphy, *International Law*, 253 (2006).

[3] Sean D. Murphy, *International Law*, 237 and 241 *et seq.* (2006).

[4] Markus Volz, *Extraterritoriale Terrorismusbekämpfung*, 92 *et seq.* (2007); Sean D. Murphy, *International Law*, 245 (2006).

[5] Markus Volz, *Extraterritoriale Terrorismusbekämpfung*, 102 *et seq.* (2007); Sean D. Murphy, *International Law*, 246-9 (2006).

[6] Markus Volz, *Extraterritoriale Terrorismusbekämpfung*, 117 (2007).

digm. However, even without the territorial state's consent, the conflict state can be authorized by the Security Council. For example, in the fight against piracy in Somalia and the Horn of Africa, the Security Council Resolution 1851, in conjunction with Resolution 1846, authorized a mission that qualifies as a transnational law enforcement mission.[7] Resolution 1851 addressed the need to *"effectively investigate and prosecute piracy and armed robbery at sea offences"*.[8] The key element of this resolution was a time-limited permission to use all necessary measures that were consistent with applicable international humanitarian and human rights law and appropriate for the purpose of suppressing acts of piracy and armed robbery.[9]

Finally, in the case of an armed attack, a state may act in self-defense under Art. 51 of the UN Charter, which does not require a Security Council authorization.[10] Whether non-state actors can be held responsible for an armed attack and subsequent involvement by the state remains highly debated.[11] The type of entity involved in the armed attack is not specified in Art. 51 UN Charter, thereby making the requirements to invoke Art. 51 UN Charter unclear. In its Advisory Opinion on the Legal Consequences of the Construction of a Wall in the Occupied Palestinian Territory, the ICJ states,

"Article 51 of the Charter thus recognizes the existence of an inherent right of self-defense in the case of armed attack by one State against another State. However, Israel does not claim that the attacks against it are imputable to a foreign State. [...] Conse-

---

[7] S.C. Res. 1851, U.N. Doc. S/RES/1851 (Dec. 16, 2008); S.C. Res. 1846, U.N. Doc. S/RES/1846 (Dec. 2, 2008); Robin Geiß, *Armed Violence in Fragile States: Low-intensity Conflicts, Spillover Conflicts, and Sporadic Law Enforcement Operations by Third Parties*, 91 International Review of the Red Cross 127, 139 *et seq.* (2009); Douglas Guilfoyle, *Counter-Piracy Law Enforcement and Human Rights*, 59 International and Comparative Law Quarterly 141, 148 (2010).

[8] S.C. Res. 1851, ¶ 5, U.N. Doc. S/RES/1851 (Dec. 16, 2008).

[9] S.C. Res. 1851, ¶ 6, U.N. Doc. S/RES/1851 (Dec. 16, 2008).

[10] Art. 51 UN Charta ("Nothing in the present Charter shall impair the inherent right of individual or collective self-defence if an armed attack occurs against a Member of the United Nations, until the Security Council has taken measures necessary to maintain international peace and security. Measures taken by Members in the exercise of this right of self-defence shall be immediately reported to the Security Council and shall not in any way affect the authority and responsibility of the Security Council under the present Charter to take at any time such action as it deems necessary in order to maintain or restore international peace and security").

[11] *See* Noam Lubell, *Extraterritorial Use of Force Against Non-State Actors*, 30 *et seq.* (2010).

quently, the Court concludes that Article 51 of the Charter has no relevance in this case."[12]

The ICJ's stance on Art. 51 UN Charter is that self-defense can be invoked only in response to an attack by a state or by an entity acting on behalf of a state. This view is shared by the UN Special Rapporteur on Extrajudicial, Summary or Arbitrary Executions.[13]

In its judgment on Armed Activities on the Territory of the Congo, however, the ICJ states that,

> "the Court has no need to respond to the contentions of the parties as to whether and under what conditions contemporary international law provides for a right of self-defense against large-scale attacks by irregular forces".[14]

Here, the ICJ leaves room for debate as it does not deny the possibility of a non-state group executing an armed attack. The U.S. stance is that a non-state group can perform an armed attack and that Art. 51 UN Charter applies even to terror-ist violence. According to the U.S., 9/11 was an armed attack by Al Qaeda that triggered the U.S.'s right to self-defense.[15] A number of commentators support this view.[16] The UN pactice supports the possibility of an armed attack perfor-med solely by a non-state group, such as Al Qaeda. In its Resolutions 1368 (2001) and 1373 (2001), the UN Security Council invoked the right to self-defense in response to the terror attacks of September 11th.[17] Similarly, NATO qualified the attacks as an armed attack and subsequently invoked collective

---

[12] ICJ, *Legal Consequences of the Construction of a Wall in the Occupied Palestinian Territory*, Advisory Opinion, 2004 ICJ 136, ¶ 139 (July 9).

[13] Philip Alston, *Report of the Special Rapporteur on Extrajudicial, Summary or Arbitrary Executions*, ¶ 40, U.N. Doc. A/HRC/14/24/Add.6 (May 28, 2010).

[14] ICJ, *Armed Activities on the Territory of the Congo* (Dem. Rep. Congo v. Uganda), ICJ GL No 116, ¶ 146-7 (Dec. 19, 2005).

[15] *See* the position of the Bush-Administration expressed by John B Bellinger III, Legal Advisor to the Secretary of State in John Bellinger, *Legal Issues in the War on Terrorism*, 8 German Law Journal, 735, 736 *et seq.* (2007); *See* the position of the Obama-Administration expressed by Attorney General Eric Holder at Northwestern University School of Law, Mar. 5, 2012 available at http://www.justice.gov/iso/opa/ag /speeches/2012/ag-speech-1203051.html (last visited Mar. 8, 2012).

[16] Roy S. Schöndorf, *Extra-State Armed Conflicts: Is there a Need for a New Legal Regime?*, 37 New York University Journal of Law and Politics 1, 22-3 (2004); Yoram Dinstein, *War, Aggression and Self-Defence*, 227 *et seq.* (2011); Carsten Stahn, *Terrorist Acts as "Armed Attack": The Right to Self-Defense, Article 51(1/2) of the UN Charter, and International Terrorism*, 27/2 Fletcher Forum of World Affairs 35, 44 and 47 (2003); Noam Lubell, *Extraterritorial Use of Force Against Non-State Actors*, 35 (2010).

[17] S.C. Res. 1368, U.N. Doc. S/RES/1368 (Sep. 16, 2001); S.C. Res. 1373, U.N. Doc. S/RES/1373 (Sep. 28, 2001).

self-defense in accordance with Art. 5 of the North Atlantic Treaty.[18] If it were to be accepted that non-state actors can perform armed attacks that trigger states' right to self-defense, the point at which the non-state group's actions reach the threshold of an armed attack must be specified within the context of Art. 51 UN Charter, in each case.[19] Additionally, the type of response lawfully taken by the conflict state must be specified within the self-defense parameters of necessity and proportionality.[20]

In conclusion, various justifications for a state's extra-territorial actions can be found in international law. Whether an operation is lawful must be determined given the specific case.

II. The Scope of States' Authority

This section aims to discuss the authorities granted to states by law enforcement regimes during transnational conflicts. The possibly applicable legal frameworks are the respective states' domestic law enforcement laws and International Human Rights law.[21] As the scope of this thesis is to bring light to a possible international legal framework for transnational law enforcement operations, the focus of the analysis will be on the application of IHRL. In particular, the analysis focuses on the ECHR as it provides the most substantive case law and on the ICCPR due to its global applicability.

---

[18] *See* NATO Press Release 124 (Sep. 12, 2001) online available at http://www.nato.int/docu/pr/2001/p01-124e.htm (last visited Mar. 8, 2012).

[19] Philip Alston, *Report of the Special Rapporteur on Extrajudicial, Summary or Arbitrary Executions*, ¶ 41, U.N. Doc. A/HRC/14/24/Add.6 (May 28, 2010).

[20] These issues are not part of this book. *Cf.* Noam Lubell, *Extraterritorial Use of Force Against Non-State Actors*, 43 *et seq.* (2010); Philip Alston, *Report of the Special Rapporteur on Extrajudicial, Summary or Arbitrary Executions*, ¶ 41, U.N. Doc. A/HRC/14/24/Add.6 (May 28, 2010); Christian J. Tams and James G. Devaney, *Applying Necessity and Proportionality to Anti-Terrorist Self-Defence*, 45 Israle Law Review 91-106 (2012).

[21] Michael N. Schmitt, *Targeted Killings in International Law: Law Enforcement, Self-defense, and Armed Conflict*, in International Humanitarian Law and Human Rights Law 525, 528 (Roberta Arnold and Noelle Quénivet eds. 2008) ("In the first instance, therefore, a state's own laws govern whether its law enforcement, military, or intelligence authorities may lethally 'target' an individual. International human rights norms further restrict a state's resort to potentially deadly law enforcement methods"); Nils Melzer, *Targeted Killing in International Law*, 86 (2008) ("The exact scope and content of 'police powers' depend largely on domestic law and, therefore, may vary considerably").

Whether IHRL binds states extraterritorially will be briefly addressed, as the debate on the extraterritorial application of IHRL is crucial to the application of IHRL to transnational conflicts. However, whether IHRL binds states even outside their territory remains controversial.[22] All human rights treaties require that states protect everyone *"within their jurisdiction"*.[23] Art. 2.1 ICCPR refers to the state's territory as such:

> "Each State Party to the present Covenant undertakes to respect and to ensure to all individuals within its territory and subject to its jurisdiction the rights recognized in the present Covenant [...]."

Therefore, the question arises as to whether the word *and* between *within its territory* and *subject to its jurisdiction* is to be read as conjunctive or disjunctive. Whether both territory and jurisdiction are simultaneously needed, or if territory or jurisdiction alone is sufficient, is highly debated. The U.S. and Israel constantly assert that both territory and jurisdiction are required.[24] Others argue that jurisdiction alone is sufficient, but that states only have jurisdiction within their own territory.[25] The central debate appears to be in regards to when a state has jurisdiction.[26] The general consensus of the ICJ,[27] the European Court on

---

[22] For a comprehensive analysis *see* Marko Milanovic, *Extraterritorial Application of Human Rights Treaties: Law, Principles and Policy* (2011).

[23] *See* Art. 1 ECHR, Art. 1.1 ACHR and Art. 2.1 ICCPR.

[24] *Contra* United States Responses to Selected Recommendations of the Human Rights Committee Oct. 10, 2007; available at http://www.state.gov/documents /organization/100845.pdf (last visited Jan. 24, 2011).
For the Israeli position *see* UN Human Rights Committee, *International Covenant on Civil and Political Rights Second Periodic Report*, U.N Doc. CCPR/C/ISR/2001/2, ¶ 8 (Nov. 20, 2001); *cf.* on the Israeli position Orna Ben-Naftali and Yuval Shany, *Living in Denial: The Application of Human Rights in the Occupied Territories*, 37 Israel Law Review 17, 25 *et seq.* (2003-2004).

[25] Yoram Dinstein, *The Conduct of Hostilities under the Law of International Armed Conflict*, 25 (2004) (Dinstein comes to his conclusion based on the Bankovic case of the ECtHR).

[26] Jurisdiction in general is understood as the ability and competence of a State to adopt legislation, to enforce it and to adjudicate it. *See* Bernard H. Oxman, *Jurisdiction of States*, Max Planck Encyclopedia of Public International Law (Nov 2007), http://www.mpepil.com/subscriber_article?script=yesandid=/epil/entries/law-978019923 1690-e1436andrecno=8andsearchType=Advancedandtitle=Jurisdiction; Matthias Herdegen, *Völkerrecht*, §§ 23-28 (2013);
For a model, that suggests distinguishing between positive and negative obligations of states in ordert o determine jurisdiction *see* Marko Milanovic, *Extraterritorial Application of Human Rights Treaties: Law, Principles and Policy*, 119, 208 *et seq.* (2011).

[27] ICJ, *Legal Consequences of the Construction of a Wall in the Occupied Palestinian Territory*, Advisory Opinion, 2004 ICJ 136, ¶ 11-113 (July 9); ICJ, Armed Activities on

Human rights (ECtHR),[28] the Inter American Commission of Human Rights,[29] the UN Human Rights Committee, other UN treaty organs[30] and national courts,[31] is that, at least under certain circumstances, a state exercises jurisdiction outside its national territory. The territory is only one very clear indicator of a state's jurisdiction. However, a state's jurisdiction and legal responsibility are not limited to internal situations.[32] Rather, a state performs (executive) jurisdiction whenever it is engaged in law enforcement. Therefore, within a coherent transnational law enforcement regime, IHRL must be applied extraterritorially because the state is performing (extraterritorial) jurisdiction.[33] In addition, it is imperative that the transnational law enforcement approach is understood as one within an IHRL framework, rather than as an alternative to an IHRL framework. If IHRL is not applied, the modalities of the state's action would be entirely dependent on the state's own domestic law, thereby yielding an unsatisfactory result. The following analysis outlines options states have to effectively engage

---

the Territory of the Congo (Dem. Rep. Congo v. Uganda), ICJ GL No 116, ¶ 216 (Dec. 19, 2005).

[28] ECtHR, *Loizidou v. Turkey*, Application No. 15318/89 (Merits) (Dec. 18, 1996), ¶ 62; ECtHR, Bankovic et al. v. Belgium et al., Application No. 52207/99 (Dec. 12, 2001), ¶ 67 et seq.; ECtHR, Ilaşcu et al. v. Moldova and Russia, Application No. 48787/99 (Judgment, Merits and Just Satisfaction) ¶ 310 *et seq.*

[29] Inter-American Commission on Human Rights, Coard et al. v. United States, Case No. 10.951, Report No. 109/99, Sep. 29, 1999, OAS Doc. OEA/Ser.L/V/II.106 Doc. 3 rev. ¶ 37 (Sep. 29, 1999).

[30] UN Human Rights Committee, General Comment 31, *Nature of the General Legal Obligation Imposed on States Parties to the Covenant*, U.N. Doc. CCPR/C/21/Rev.1/Add.13, ¶ 10 (May 26, 2004); UN Human Rights Committee, *Delia Saldias de* Lopez v. Uruguay, UN Doc CCPR/C/13/D/52/1979, ¶ 12.1 et seq., and individual opinion by Christian Tomuschat, Appendix (July 29, 1981); *cf.* documents concerning CESCR, CERD, CAT, CEDAW, CRC cited by Bernhard Schäfer, *Zum Verhältnis Menschenrechte und humanitäres Völkerrecht*, 22 Fn. 57 & 58 (2006).

[31] UK House of Lords, Al-Skeini v Secretary of State for Defence (Application for Judicial Review) (June 13, 2007) [2007] UKHL 26, ¶ 105 *et seq.*; UK House of Lords, Al-Jedda v Secretary of State for Defence (Appeal Judgment) (Dec. 12, 2007) [2007] UKHL 58, ¶ 48.

[32] Ilaşcu et al. v. Moldova and Russia, Application No. 48787/99 (Judgment, Merits and Just Satisfaction) ¶ 314 ("Moreover, the Court observes that, although in Bankovic and Others [...] it emphasised the preponderance of the territorial principle in the application of the Convention, it has also acknowledged that the concept of 'jurisdiction' within the meaning of Article 1 of the Convention is not necessarily restricted to the national territory of the High Contracting Parties").

[33] For a comprehensive account of the debate about when a state is bound by IHRL extraterritorially *see* Bernhard Schäfer, *Zum Verhältnis Menschenrechte und humanitäres Völkerrecht*, 25 et seq. (2006).

in transnational conflicts within a human rights framework. Transnational conflicts can be differentiated from ordinary threats, which are generally addressed through law enforcement regulations.

First, transnational conflicts inherently possess a cross-border dimension. Additionally, the posed threat is likely to be more severe. In the event of an exceptionally severe threat, human rights provisions must be interpreted and applied such that the extraordinary nature of the situation is reflected. This does not automatically imply that a new legal body of *"Human Rights at War"* must be developed;[34] however, it is imperative to note that the exigencies of the situation consequently affect the understanding of the corresponding human right, as well as the necessity and proportionality considerations.

The next subsections examine three core issues central to the authority of law enforcement agents under a transnational law enforcement approach: (1) the use of lethal force against persons suspected of being members of the non-state party, (2) the acceptability of civilian casualties, and (3) the authority to detain persons suspected of causing a threat.

1. Use of Lethal Force against Non-State Actors

The present section focuses on the killing of alleged terrorists or other non-state actors under an IHRL-based transnational law enforcement regime. Under IHRL, any killing of a suspected terrorist by state agents may infringe on the right to life, a right that has acquired *jus cogens* status,[35] and is counted among

---

[34] For a discussion of that possibility *see* Naz Modirzadeh, *The Dark Sides of Convergence: A Pro-Civilian Critique of the Extraterritorial Application of Human Rights Law in Armed Conflict*, 86 U.S. Naval War College International Law Studies (Blue Book) Series 349, 393 *et seq.* (2010); William Abresch, *A Human Rights Law of Internal Armed Conflict: the European Court of Human Rights in Chechnya*, 16 European Journal of International Law 741, 767 (2005) ("[…] the ECtHR has taken a new approach, and one that shows great promise. It is providing rules for the conduct of hostilities where, as it applies to internal armed conflicts, humanitarian law that is accepted as legally binding is inadequate and seldom obeyed. Moreover, with rules that treat armed conflicts as law enforcement operations against terrorists, the ECtHR has begun to develop an approach that may prove both more protective of victims and more politically viable than that of humanitarian law").

[35] Restatement of the Law Third: Foreign Relations of Law of the United States (1987), ¶ 702; Noelle Quénivet, *The Right to Life in International Humanitarian Law and Human Rights Law*, in International Humanitarian Law and Human Rights Law, 331 (Roberta Arnold and Noelle Quénivet, eds. 2008).

the supreme values of international law and domestic law in most states.[36] All major human rights treaties address the protection of the right to life, of which three specifically refer to the prohibition of *arbitrary* deprivation of life.[37] This inevitably brings into question the circumstances under which the deprivation of life is not arbitrary.

In the *Elettronica Sicula* case, the ICJ stated that the term *arbitrary* specifically implies *"opposed to the rule of law"*.[38] However, the term arbitrary is vague and requires further interpretation.[39]

The Human Rights Committee, the Inter-American Commission on Human Rights, the Inter-American Court of Human Rights, and the African Commission on Human and Peoples' Rights have set standards for determining the arbitrariness of an act, which include sufficient legal basis, necessity, proportionality and precaution.[40] The European Convention on Human Rights presents a slightly different approach to the protection of the right to life. According to Art. 2.1 ECHR, one shall not be deprived of life intentionally:

> "Everyone's right to life shall be protected by law. No one shall be deprived of his life intentionally save in the execution of a sentence of a court following his conviction of a crime for which this penalty is provided by law."

Instead of using a term that permits flexibility, such as *arbitrary*, the previously mentioned clause prohibits all intentional killings and inevitably calls for various exceptions in Art. 2.2 ECHR:

> "Deprivation of life shall not be regarded as inflicted in contravention of this article when it results from the use of force which is no more than absolutely necessary: a) in defense of any person from unlawful violence; b) in order to effect a lawful arrest or to

---

[36] Georg Nolte, *Preventive Use of Force and Preventive Killings: Moves into a Different Legal Order*, 5 Theoretical Inquiries in Law 111, 118 (2004).

[37] Art. 6.1 ICCPR ("Every human being has the inherent right to life. This right shall be protected by law. No one shall be arbitrarily deprived of his life"); Art. 4.1 American Convention of Human Rights ("Every person has the right to have his life respected. This right shall be protected by law and, in general, from the moment of conception. No one shall be arbitrarily deprived of his life"); Art. 4 African Charter on Human and Peoples' Rights ("Human beings are inviolable. Every human being shall be entitled to respect for his life and the integrity of his person. No one may be arbitrarily deprived of this right").

[38] ICJ, *Elettronica Sicula Case* (United States v. Italy.), ICJ GL No 76, ¶ 128 (July 20, 1989).

[39] Nils Petersen, *Life, Right to, International Protection*, Max Planck Encyclopedia of Public International Law ¶ 16 (2010) available at http://www.mpepil.com/subscriber_article?script=yesandid=/epil/entries/law-9780199231690-e841andrecno=2 andsearchType=Quickandquery=right+to+life (last visited Jan. 30, 2011).

[40] Nils Melzer, *Targeted Killing in International Law*, 100 *et seq.* (2008).

prevent the escape of a person lawfully detained; c) in action lawfully taken for the purpose of quelling a riot or insurrection."

The key element of Art. 2.2 ECHR is the outlining of the three exceptions to the right to life and the requirement of absolute necessity. The state is not only bound by the Principle of Proportionality, which is essentially a version of the Prohibition of Arbitrariness, but is also limited to act within one or more of the three explicit exceptions. The concepts of absolute necessity and arbitrariness both require further examination. Although the concepts differ, *Melzer* correctly concludes that,

> "[...] there is no or no significant discrepancy between deprivations of life that are unlawful under Article 2 ECHR, and deprivations of life that are arbitrary within the meaning of Article 6 ICCPR, Article 4 ACHR and 4 ACHPR."[41]

During a law enforcement operation, the right to life cannot be derogated from or suspended. The right to life, as per the ICCPR, the ACHR and the ACHPR, is not subject to derogations at all.[42] However, as conceptualized by *Melzer*, during times of armed conflict, *"the standards by which the 'arbitrariness' of a deprivation of life is assessed are adapted to the circumstances".*[43] The ECHR, on the other hand, allows for the derogation from the right to life in one exceptional case, namely *"in respect of deaths resulting from lawful acts of war".*[44] In general, states must act in accordance with the right to life almost exclusively, regardless of the exigencies of the given situation. The challenge, however, lies in the obligation that states must *"at once respect and ensure the right to life".*[45] As noted by the ECtHR, this presents states with the *"fundamental dilemma"* that, in the event of a terrorist threat, they must protect the life of its citizens, including law enforcement agents, while simultaneously abstaining from the use of lethal force against those suspected of posing this threat.[46] IHRL takes this

---

[41] Nils Melzer, *Targeted Killing in International Law*, 118 (2008).

[42] Nils Melzer, *Targeted Killing in International Law*, 120 *et seq.* (2008); Philip Alston, *Report of the Special Rapporteur on Extrajudicial, Summary or Arbitrary Executions*, ¶ 47, U.N. Doc. A/HRC/2/2 (Oct. 2, 2006) ("No derogation is permitted from the right to life, and none is needed").

[43] Nils Melzer, *Targeted Killing in International Law*, 121 (2008).

[44] Art. 15.2 ECHR.

[45] Philip Alston, *Report of the Special Rapporteur on Extrajudicial, Summary or Arbitrary Executions*, ¶ 47, U.N. Doc. A/HRC/2/2 (Oct. 2, 2006).

[46] ECtHR, *McCann et al v. U.K.*, Application No 18984/91 (Judgment, Merits and Just Satisfaction) (Sep. 27, 1995) ¶ 192 ("In carrying out its examination under Article 2 (art. 2) of the Convention, the Court must bear in mind that the information that the United Kingdom authorities received that there would be a terrorist attack in Gibraltar presented them with a fundamental dilemma. On the one hand, they were required to have

dilemma into account when limiting the protection of the right to life to arbitrary deprivations of life as in Art. 6.1 ICCPR and Art. 4.1 ACHR or by listing exceptions, as in Art. 2.2 ECHR. Therefore, it is plausible that a law enforcement agent uses lethal force without violating the right to life, so long as he does not act arbitrarily but within these exceptions.

The treaty bodies of the respective IHRL treaties have subsequently developed four requirements the state must abide by to lawfully use lethal force, (1) the requirement of sufficient legal basis, (2) the requirement of necessity, (3) the requirement of proportionality, and (4) the requirement of precaution.[47] The following subsections assume that states provide sufficient legal basis for their transnational law enforcement actions, thereby satisfying the first requirement. The subsections then examine the requirements of, a) absolute necessity, b), proportionality, and c) requirement of precautions. The results will be analyzed with the use of further empirical evidence in section d).

a) Absolute Necessity

In Art 2.2 the ECHR explicitly requires state action to be *"absolutely necessary"*. This reflects the principle of necessity, which argues that the use of lethal force is not permitted as long as other less harmful means may be used as an alternative to pursue the respective aim.[48] When assessing the necessity of a state's action, the aims pursued by the state must be the starting point.

Aims that can lawfully be pursued by a law enforcement agent through the use of force are limited. The UN has adopted the *Basic Principles on the Use of Force and Firearms by Law Enforcement Officials* of which Principle 9 outlines the grounds for the possible use of force as the following:

"Law enforcement officials shall not use firearms against persons except in self-defence or defence of others against the imminent threat of death or serious injury, to prevent the perpetration of a particularly serious crime involving grave threat to life, to arrest a person presenting such a danger and resisting their authority, or to prevent his or her escape, and only when less extreme means are insufficient to achieve these objectives. In any event, intentional lethal use of firearms may only be made when strictly unavoidable in order to protect life."

---

regard to their duty to protect the lives of the people in Gibraltar including their own military personnel and, on the other, to have minimum resort to the use of lethal force against those suspected of posing this threat in the light of the obligations flowing from both domestic and international law").

[47] Nils Melzer, *Targeted Killing in International Law*, 100-2 and 116-8 (2008).

[48] *See* Jan Römer, *Killing in a Gray Area between Humanitarian Law and Human Rights Law*, 103-4 (2010).

This UN approach strictly limits the lethal use of firearms to situations in which a life must be protected. In Art. 2.2., the ECHR lists three purposes for which the state is permitted to resort to lethal force: a) in defense of any person from unlawful violence, b) in order to effect a lawful arrest or prevent escape of a person lawfully detained, and c) in action lawfully taken for the purpose of quelling a riot or insurrection. The third legitimate purpose stated in the ECHR, quelling a riot or insurrection, is not of relevance to the context of transnational conflicts. It refers only to instances where the masses, who are citizens, commit violent crimes in large quantities,[49] and not situations where the state fights against terrorists or other foreign non-state groups. The ICCPR and the ACHR do not list purposes a state may legitimately pursue when resorting to lethal force as strictly. However, the general prohibition of arbitrary deprivation of lives suggests that the resort to lethal force is lawful only for certain legitimate purposes. This includes any action for self-defense, or the defense of others against imminent threat of death or serious injuries,[50] and actions to lawfully arrest or prevent escape from arrest.[51] According to *Melzer's* analysis of the

---

[49] Jochen Abr. Frowein, *Artikel 2 (Recht auf Leben)*, in Europäische Menschenrechts-konvention – EMRK-Kommentar, ¶ 15 (Jochen Abr. Frowein and Wolfgang Peukert eds., 3rd ed. 2009).

[50] Inter-American Commission on Human Rights, *Report on Terrorism and Human Rights*, IACHR OAS-Doc. OEA/Ser.L/V/II.116 Doc. 5 rev. 1 corr., ¶ 92 (Oct. 22, 2002) („[...] the amount of force used must be justified by the circumstances, for the purpose of, for example, self-defense or neutralizing or disarming the individuals involved in a violent confrontation");
UN Code of Conduct, Art. 3 Commentary C (Dec. 17, 1979) („In general, firearms should not be used except when a suspected offender offers armed resistance or otherwise jeopardizes the lives of others [...]");
Office of the UN High Commissioner for Human Rights, *Basic Principles on the Use of Firearms by Law Enforcement Officials*, § 9 („Law enforcement officials shall not use firearms against persons except in self-defence or defence of others against the imminent threat of death or serious injury, to prevent the perpetration of a particularly serious crime involving grave threat to life, to arrest a person presenting such a danger and resisting their authority, or to prevent his or her escape, and only when less extreme means are insufficient to achieve these objectives");
Philip Alston, *Report of the Special Rapporteur on Extrajudicial, Summary or Arbitrary Executions*, ¶ 48, U.N. Doc. E/CN.4/2006/53 (March 8, 2006) ("For lethal force to be considered to be lawful it must be used in a situation in which it is necessary for self-defence or the defence of another's life") online available at http://daccess-ods.un.org/TMP/4071096.77791595.html (last visited March 8, 2012); *cf.* Jan Römer, *Killing in a Gray Area between Humanitarian Law and Human Rights Law*, 97 et seq. (2010).

[51] UN Code of Conduct Art. 3 Commentary A (Dec. 17, 1979) ("[...] law enforcement officials may be authorized to use force as is reasonably necessary under the circum-

interpretation by the respective treaty bodies, a legitimate purpose for a state to resort to lethal force can be

> "to protect any person, including the law enforcement officials themselves, from imminent death or serious injury, to effect an arrest or prevent the escape of a person suspected of a serious crime, or to otherwise maintain law and order or to protect the security of all".[52]

It is imperative to emphasize that the killing of a terrorist suspect can never be the sole purpose of a state's use of force.[53] Instead, it must serve another purpose such as to protect other individual's lives.[54] Here, the law enforcement model differs substantially from an IHL approach, in which the killing of a combatant by another combatant is regarded as legitimate during the armed conflict. Thus, the law enforcement approach is much less permissive for states than an IHL approach, as it requires every state action to be justified by a legitimate purpose.

The two legitimate purposes relevant to the transnational law enforcement approach are, (aa) the protection of any person from unlawful violence, and (bb) the arrest of a person suspected of a serious crime, such as of being a terrorist, or to prevent his escape. In the following section, the requirement of absolute necessity will be discussed with respect to these two purposes.

aa) Necessity to Protect any Person from Unlawful Violence

The use of force by a state may be justified to protect any person from unlawful violence. As a result, the state is permitted to act in the event of danger of unlawful violence. The practical challenge lies in correctly determining the

---

stances for the prevention of crime or in effecting or assisting in the lawful arrest of offenders or suspected offenders [...]").

[52] Nils Melzer, *Targeted Killing in International Law*, 101 (2008).

[53] Philip Alston, *The CIA and Targeted Killings Beyond Borders*, 2 Harvard National Security Journal 283, 304 (2011); The only exception is contained in Art. 2.1 ECHR with respect to the death penalty, but its practical relevance is minimal for the death penalty was abolished by the Protocol No. 13 to the Convention for the Protection of Human Rights and Fundamental Freedoms, concerning the abolition of the death penalty in all circumstances. This protocol has been signed by more than 40 members of the ECHR. *See* Isabel Schübel-Pfister, *Art. 1 ZP XIII – Abschaffung der Todesstrafe*, in EMRK – Konvention zum Schutz der Menschenrechte und Grundfreiheiten 428, 429 (Ulrich Karpenstein and Franz C. Mayer eds., 2012).

[54] Philip Alston, *Report of the Special Rapporteur on Extrajudicial, Summary or Arbitrary Executions*, ¶ 33, U.N. Doc. A/HRC/14/24/Add.6 (May 28, 2010).

degree of danger, which allows the state to resort to lethal force.[55] In order to determine the degree of danger, concreteness and immediacy of danger must be simultaneously considered. Only in the presence of both would a state's use of force be deemed lawful.

(1) Concrete Danger

The criterion of concrete danger serves as a first threshold for state action. Only concrete danger allows and obliges a state to take action. Concrete danger is that which is based on concrete circumstances of a specific case and, with sufficient probability, may be realized within the foreseeable future.[56] Abstract danger, on the other hand, is not characterized by the concrete circumstances of a specific case, but rather by the inherent dangerous nature of the behavior. The terms concrete and abstract danger regularly cause confusion. This is due mainly to the fact that they are misunderstood as criteria which determine probability. It is therefore important to clarify that the criterion of concrete danger does not serve to determine the probability of a terrorist attack's occurrence. Both concrete and abstract danger require sufficient probability that the event will occur. The difference lies in that a concrete danger emanates from a specific situation, whereas an abstract danger derives from the typical nature of a certain type of situation.[57]

---

[55] Georg Nolte, *Preventive Use of Force and Preventive Killings: Moves into a Different Legal Order*, 5 Theoretical Inquiries in Law 111, 114 (2004) ("The main legal problem with preventive self-defense against states and with preventive killings of individual persons is the degree of danger that is necessary so that such action may legally be taken").

[56] Anna Goppel speaks of an undeterminable abstract harming act and a determinable harming act. She agrees that self-defence [of the state] can only be applied in the context of a determinable harming act., *see* Anna Goppel, *Killing Terrorists – A Moral and Legal Analysis*, 269 (2013).

[57] *See* Bundesverwaltungsgericht (Federal Administrative Court) *Judgment of June 26 1970*, 23 Neue Juristische Wochenschrift, 1890, 1892 (1970) ("Solche hinreichende oder auch 'bloße' Wahrscheinlichkeit gehört zur abstrakten genauso wie zur konkreten Gefahr; beide Gefahrenbegriffe stellen, was den zu erwartenden Eintritt eines Schadens anlangt, die gleichen Anforderungen der Wahrscheinlichkeit. Der Unterschied liegt nur in der Betrachtungsweise: bei der konkreten Gefahr 'konkret', d.h. auf den Einzelfall, bei der abstrakten Gefahr 'abstrakt-generell', also auf den typischen Fall bezogen. Eine konkrete Gefahr liegt danach vor, wenn in dem zu beurteilenden konkreten Einzelfall irgendwann, freilich in überschaubarer Zukunft, mit dem Schadenseintritt hinreichend wahrscheinlich gerechnet werden muß; eine abstrakte Gefahr ist gegeben, wenn eine generell-abstrakte Betrachtung für bestimmte Arten von Verhaltensweisen oder Zuständen zu dem Ergebnis führt, daß mit hinreichender Wahrscheinlichkeit ein Schaden im Einzelfall einzutreten

In order to determine concreteness, the relevant point of reference must be a concrete situation as opposed to an abstract-general examination. An airplane flown by a terrorist with a bomb approaching a skyscraper is considered a concrete danger. Even if the terrorist had not yet boarded the plane, but instead had prepared the bomb, picked a target and was on his way to the airport, the danger would still be considered concrete as it is based on the specific circumstances of the case. While additional steps are necessary to realize the danger, it is evident that these circumstances would not qualify the danger as abstract.

Law enforcement rules and IHL appear as similar in the context of the element of concreteness. According to the ICRC, preparatory measures for a specific act are a form of direct participation in the hostilities. As a result, the individual responsible for carrying out preparatory measures may also be targeted under IHL.[58] However, law enforcement law differs from IHL in that an individual's mere membership to a terrorist organization and the planning of a terrorist attack does not suffice to qualify as concrete danger. Prior to beginning concrete preparatory measures to execute an act of violence, the individual is only generally dangerous and cannot justifiably be attacked under a law enforcement regime.[59]

(2) Immediacy

The element of immediacy will be introduced in this section as an additional criterion upon which the degree of danger necessary to allow a state to resort to lethal force can be determined. The criterion of immediacy determines whether or not the state's action is absolutely necessary as a last resort.[60]

---

pflegt (vgl. z.B. Drews-Wacke, aaO S. 390) und daher Anlaß besteht, diese Gefahr mit generell-abstrakten Mitteln, also einem Rechtssatz, insbesondere einer PolizeiVO zu bekämpfen, was wiederum zur Folge hat, daß auf den Nachweis der Gefahr eines Schadenseintritts im Einzelfall verzichtet werden kann").

[58] *See* International Committee of the Red Cross, *Interpretive Guidance on the Notion of Direct Participation in Hostilities under International Humanitarian Law,* 65 (2009) ("Measures preparatory to the execution of a specific act of direct participation in hostilities, as well as the deployment to and the return from the location of its execution, constitute an integral part of that act").

[59] A person might, however, be wanted for arrest because of this membership, hence the use of force might be lawful with respect to the attempt of arrest.

[60] Anna Goppel, *Killing Terrorists – A Moral and Legal Analysis,* 273 (2013) ("Only imminence determines whether or not lethal force ist he least harmful means of defence available").

In *Guerrero v. Colombia,* the Human Rights Committee demanded that, if possible, one should be given the opportunity to surrender.[61] Only when both, the arrest and the opportunity to surrender, are not possible may a state resort to lethal force. For example, *Nolte* would describe a terrorist placing his finger on the detonator of a bomb as *"visible immediacy"*.[62] There is not sufficient time to make an arrest and dismantle the bomb prior to its detonation. The only action a law enforcement agent can take to prevent the detonation is to shoot the terrorist before he is able to detonate the bomb. As a result, the use of lethal force is necessary. However, even if a suspected terrorist were not to have his finger on the detonator, the threat may still be considered immediate. If the terrorist were to put on an explosive belt set to detonate in five hours and then proceed toward a densely populated city, the danger is immediate not only in the moment prior to the detonation of the explosives. The immediacy of the threat depends on the law enforcement agent's ability to eliminate the threat. If the law enforcement agents are only able to track the suspected person for a limited time, the threat becomes immediate in the final moment when the agents are able to eliminate the threat. As a result, a danger is immediate when immediate action is required to reliably avert the danger.[63] Determining immediacy requires an *ex ante* point of view.

Nolte argues that law enforcement agents' powers of prevention must not be a factor in determining the immediacy of a threat.[64] According to *Nolte,* the im-

---

[61] UN Human Rights Committee, *Suarez de Guerrero v. Colombia,* Communication No. 45/1979, Merits, U.N. Doc. CCPR/C/15/D/45/1979, ¶ 13.2 (Mar. 31, 1982).

[62] Georg Nolte, *Preventive Use of Force and Preventive Killings: Moves into a Different Legal Order,* 5 Theoretical Inquiries in Law 111, 119 *et seq.* (2004).

[63] *Contra* Georg Nolte, *Preventive Use of Force and Preventive Killings: Moves into a Different Legal Order,* 5 Theoretical Inquiries in Law 111, 117 *et seq.* (2004).

[64] Georg Nolte, *Preventive Use of Force and Preventive Killings: Moves into a Different Legal Order,* 5 Theoretical Inquiries in Law 111, 117 (2004) ("The decisive step is the move away from a concept of immediacy that looks at the relationship between the attacker and the attacked in a specific situation to a concept of immediacy that looks at the threat from the perspective of the state authorities and their powers of prevention. It may well be true that a state has one last opportunity to prevent the hiding of a weapon of mass destruction for the purpose of using it later, and it may well be true that the police authorities have one last opportunity to stop a terrorist before he or she goes into hiding and gives the order to blow up a bomb. In both cases, however, there is, as yet, no immediate threat to the potential victims. A number of other factors can intervene that might stop the pariah state or the prospective terrorist individual from carrying out their evil intentions. Therefore, for all practical purposes, a concept of immediacy that depends on the powers of the allegedly threatened state to prevent is a move away from a requirement of concrete danger to one of abstract danger or even of mere risk prevention").

mediacy of a threat depends solely on the temporal relationship between the attacker and the attacked. *Nolte* argues that

"[a] number of other factors can intervene that might stop [...] the prospective terrorist individual from carrying out their evil intentions".[65]

This is unconvincing as factors may intervene at any given time, even in instances of *visible immediacy*. Even if the terrorist were to have his finger on the detonator, the bomb may be faulty and not detonate. As a result, uncertainty can never be fully avoided. *Nolte* does not accept the perspective of the law enforcement agent who persistently acts based on assumptions. However, a law enforcement agent must always act based on a certain assessment of danger. Certainty is never a given. All the agent must be convinced of is that his action is the last resort. Similarly, *Goppel* refuses to accept this result and argues,

"imminence may only be understood as describing the moment just prior to the accomplishment of the harming act [i.e. the terrorist attack]".[66]

Her reasoning is based on the assumption that the requirement of imminence fulfills not one but two functions.[67] The first is providing the required certainty that an attack cannot be prevented by means less harmful than killing. This reflects the previously mentioned last-resort function. However, *Goppel* claims that the second function of imminence is to provide the required certainty that the individual to be attacked is an object to the right of self-defense. The second function introduces a strict temporal threshold of imminence. *Goppel* holds that someone can be an object of self-defense only when he is performing an attack. Furthermore, the state agent must be certain, although this can occur only in the moment just prior to the attack. Therefore, only at that time can an individual be an object to the right of self-defense. *Goppel* understands imminence as the moment just prior to accomplishment of the harming act.

Goppel's claim is a misunderstanding of the last-resort function and an inappropriate application of the concept of self-defense. Last-resort describes not only the type of action (i.e. killing or less harmful means), but also the time of action (i.e. now or later). There is no reason to claim that last-resort is only given in the moment prior to the accomplishment of the harming act. This is essentially a repetition of *Nolte's* requirement of *visible immediacy* which is a sufficient but not necessary requirement for a state agent to lawfully act. Introducing the concept of self-defense does not raise the temporal threshold. The last-resort

---

[65] Georg Nolte, *Preventive Use of Force and Preventive Killings: Moves into a Different Legal Order*, 5 Theoretical Inquiries in Law 111, 117 (2004).

[66] Anna Goppel, *Killing Terrorists – A Moral and Legal Analysis*, 275 (2013).

[67] Anna Goppel, *Killing Terrorists – A Moral and Legal Analysis*, 274 (2013).

function alone defines immediacy. If an action is the last resort to avoid a concrete danger, the person from which that danger emanates is an object to the right of self-defense. Similarly, in his authoritative commentary of Section 34 of the German Criminal Codes, *Fischer* defines imminent danger as a danger that can be averted only by immediate action, irrespective of whether the actual dangerous action has been started.[68] The defenders point of view, not the attackers, is of utmost importance.

One must remember that the purpose of the criteria of immediacy determines whether a state action is necessary. For this, a concrete and sufficiently dangerous situation is a prerequisite. The criterion of concrete danger prevents a state to act in mere risk prevention. Immediacy determines whether the law enforcement agent action is *his* last resort. It may be that this last resort occurs just prior to the execution of the harming act. However, this last resort may also occur hours before the moment prior to executing the harming act. Immediacy depends on the last possible window of opportunity for a law enforcement agent to act and reflect the state's duty to protect its citizens.

Furthermore, if the terrorist resorts to tactics that hinder the state agent from acting at a later point in time, the terrorist must accept that he may face law enforcement measures even prior to executing the attack. Therefore, the relationship between the attacker and the attacked is not crucial to immediacy. Instead, the relationship between the attacker and the law enforcement agent is crucial.[69]

A danger is immediate when the final opportunity for the law enforcement agent to stop an attack has come. *Schmitt* correctly argues, that

"a targeted killing will comport with human rights norms only if the authorities harbor a reasonable belief, in the circumstances holding at the time, that they are acting in the last possible window of opportunity to prevent a terrorist attack that is almost certainly going to be perpetrated by their target(s)".[70]

The existence of both a concrete and immediate danger satisfies the requirement of necessity.

---

[68] Thomas Fischer, *Strafgesetzbuch mit Nebengesetzen*, § 34 Fn. 7 (2012).

[69] *See* Jens David Ohlin, *It's 'Immediately Necessary' for Eric Holder to Clarify 'Imminence'*, Lieber Code Blog (Mar. 7, 2012) online available at http://www.liebercode.org/2012/03/its-immediately-necessary-for-eric.html (last visited May 31, 2013).

[70] Michael N. Schmitt, *Targeted Killings in International Law: Law Enforcement, Self-defense, and Armed Conflict*, in International Humanitarian Law and Human Rights Law 525, 530 (Roberta Arnold and Noelle Quénivet eds. 2008).

bb) Necessity to Arrest or Prevent Escape

The second aim a state may lawfully pursue is to arrest or prevent the escape of a person suspected of a serious crime. According to the ECtHR's jurisdiction,

> "[T]here can be no such necessity [to put human life at risk] where it is known that the person to be arrested poses no threat to life or limb and is not suspected of having committed a violent offence, even if a failure to use lethal force may result in the opportunity to arrest the fugitive being lost." [71]

Reasons to suspect that the individual has committed a serious crime is of importance. While there is no status of combatants under a law enforcement regime, membership in a terrorist organization may suffice as a serious crime.

According to German criminal law, the leadership (*Rädelsführer* or *Hintermann*) of a terrorist organization is a crime (*Verbrechen*) in itself as per §§ 129a Abs. 4, 12 StGB, and could thus be the relevant serious crime. In addition, the judicial branch must be involved prior to state action. According to German law, an arrest usually requires an arrest warrant (*Haftbefehl*), issued by a judge (§ 114 StPO).[72] An exception of this general procedure is stated in § 127 StPO,[73]

---

[71] ECtHR, *Nachova et al. v. Bulgaria*, Application Nos. 43577/98 and 43579/98 (Judgment, Merits and Just Satisfaction) (July 6, 2005) ¶ 95; Lousie Doswald-Beck, *The Right to Life in Armed Conflict: Does International Humanitarian Law Provide all Answers?*, 88 International Review of the Red Cross 881, 886 (2006) ("In several cases treaty bodies have considered that the use of lethal force against persons who are not dangerous to be excessive, even in situations where arrest is not possible").

[72] § 114 StPO "(1) Remand detention shall be imposed by the judge in a written warrant of arrest.

(2) The warrant of arrest shall indicate

1. the accused;

2. the offence of which he is strongly suspected, the time and place of its commission, the statutory elements of the criminal offence and the penal provisions to be applied;

3. the ground for arrest; as well as

4. the facts disclosing the strong suspicion of the offence and the ground for arrest, unless disclosure would endanger national security.

(3) If it appears that Section 112 subsection (1), second sentence, is applicable, or if the accused invokes that provision, the grounds for not applying it shall be stated."

Online available at http://www.gesetze-im-internet.de/englisch_stpo/index.html (last visited Mar. 9, 2012).

[73] §127 StPO "(1) If a person is caught in the act or is being pursued, any person shall be authorized to arrest him provisionally, even without judicial order, if there is reason to suspect flight or if his identity cannot be immediately established. The establishment of the identity of a person by the public prosecution office or by officials in the police force shall be governed by Section 163b subsection (1).

which would eventually allow for the use of force against a suspected terrorist who has just acquired a weapon of mass destruction with which he is about to disappear into a diffuse global network of terrorism. Intentionally using lethal force would, however, not be lawful as it cannot lead to an arrest.[74] In sum, lethal force can only be used intentionally to prevent harm, and would be lawful if the suspected terrorist already poses a concrete and immediate danger.

b) Proportionality

The legality of the use of lethal force against a suspected terrorist further depends on the value judgment contained in the proportionality assessment. The principle of proportionality is *"firmly established"* [75] in IHRL and requires weighing the aim pursued against the means employed to achieve it.[76] The Human Rights Committee highlights the importance of the principle of proportionality in addition to the requirement of necessity in *Baumgarten v. Germany*, stating that,

> "even when used as a last resort lethal force may only be used, under article 6 of the Covenant, to meet a proportionate threat".[77]

---

(2) Furthermore, in exigent circumstances, the public prosecution office and officials in the police force shall be authorized to make a provisional arrest if the prerequisites for issuance of a warrant of arrest or of a committal order have been fulfilled.

(3) In the case of a criminal offence which can only be prosecuted upon application, provisional arrest shall also be admissible where no application has yet been filed. This shall apply *mutatis mutandis* if a criminal offence may be prosecuted only with authorization or upon request for prosecution.

(4) Sections 114a to 114c shall apply *mutatis mutandis* to provisional arrest by the public prosecution office and by officials in the police force."

Online available at http://www.gesetze-im-internet.de/englisch_stpo/index.html (last visited Mar. 9, 2012).

[74] Christoph Grabenwarter and Katharina Pabel, *Europäische Menschenrechtskonvention*, 153 (5th ed. 2012) ("Eine absichtliche Tötung kann gemäß Art. 2 Abs. 2 lit. B nicht gerechtfertigt werden, weil sie das Ziel der Festnahme und Fluchtverhinderung nicht erreichen kann und daher unverhältnismäßig ist").

[75] Jost Delbrück, *Proportionality*, in Encyclopedia of Public International Law, Vol. 3, 1140, 1143 (1984).

[76] ECtHR, *Gülec v Turkey*, Application No. 21593/93 (Merits and Just Satisfaction) (July 27, 1998) ¶ 71.

[77] UN Human Rights Committee, *Baumgarten v. Germany*, Communication No 960/2000, Merits, UN Doc CCPR/C/78/D/960/2000, ¶ 9.4 (July 31, 2003).

When assessing the proportionality of a state's law enforcement action, it is difficult to draw solid conclusions outside of instances involving excessive state action. *Delbrück* therefore correctly states, that

"[The principle of proportionality] primarily fulfills a guiding function for the law-applying authorities rather than in itself being a substantive, concrete legal norm."[78]

The difference between an individual planning to assassinate a single person and someone preparing for the use of a weapon of mass destruction is significant. As a result, both call for measures of differing proportions. However, complex cases, such as during an attempt to arrest a person suspected of having committed a serious crime, beg the question as to at which point the use of lethal force is deemed disproportionate. The answer varies based on a variety of factors, including the degree of suspicion and the type of crime the person is suspected of having committed.

The state is given discretion by the principle of proportionality. Hence, the proportionality requirement must not be overvalued. If the use of force has proven to be necessary, the principle of proportionality will not present a substantive threshold for the state to act, unless its action is excessive. Evidently, the vagueness of the principle of proportionality places emphasis on the aforementioned requirement of necessity. It is important to emphasize that, until this point, the possible effects of a state's action on innocent civilians has not been taken into consideration. This will be addressed separately in the following section. In the previous sections of this book, proportionality was regarded only in a narrow sense and in reference to weighing the harm done to the alleged terrorist and the prevention of harm on possible victims of a terrorist attack. As will be discussed, the anticipation of what is euphemistically called *collateral damages* will make an otherwise lawful use of force unlawful.

c) Requirement of Precautions

The state is required to take precautions to avoid situations in which it has no choice but to resort to lethal force. This reflects the understanding of immediacy as one that looks at the state's ability to avert concrete danger. In turn, the state is required to take precautionary measures to strengthen the ability to act. In *McCann v. U.K.*, the ECtHR analyzed the deliberate shooting of three suspected IRA terrorists and distinguished between the force used directly by U.K. agents

---

[78] Jost Delbrück, *Proportionality*, in Encyclopedia of Public International Law, Vol. 3, 1140, 1140-1 (1984).

and supervising authorities' organization and planning of the operation.[79] The court drew a distinction between the planning of a police operation and the actual use of force by the law enforcement agents.[80] In order to remain lawful, the state would not only have to consider the actual exercising of lethal force, but also be required to make adequate preparations to avoid the use of lethal force, if at all possible. The ECtHR described this as follows:

> "In particular, the force used must be strictly proportionate to the achievement of the aims set out in sub-paragraphs 2 (a), (b) and (c) of Article 2 (art. 2-2-a-b-c). In keeping with the importance of this provision (art. 2) in a democratic society, the Court must, in making its assessment, subject deprivations of life to the most careful scrutiny, particularly where deliberate lethal force is used, taking into consideration not only the actions of the agents of the State who actually administer the force but also all the surrounding circumstances including such matters as the planning and control of the actions under examination."[81]

Poor planning and insufficient control of the action, such as poor communication between the acting law enforcement agents and a controlling officer with greater knowledge of the situation, can render state action unlawful.

In *McCann,* the ECtHR saw no breach of Art. 2 ECHR on behalf of the soldiers, despite having fired with the intention to kill. Additionally, the assumption that one of the IRA terrorists was carrying a detonator to blow up a car bomb was false:

> "It [the Court] considers that the use of force by agents of the State in pursuit of one of the aims delineated in paragraph 2 of Article 2 (art. 2-2) of the Convention may be justified under this provision (art. 2-2) where it is based on an honest belief which is perceived, for good reasons, to be valid at the time but which subsequently turns out to be mistaken."[82]

This privilege, which allows a state agent to act based on an ex-ante assessment, derives from the legal duty of the state to protect its citizens. As stated by the ECtHR:

---

[79] ECtHR, *McCann et al v. U.K.*, Application No 18984/91 (Judgment, Merits and Just Satisfaction) (Sep. 27, 1995) ¶ 194.

[80] Lousie Doswald-Beck, *The Right to Life in Armed Conflict: Does International Humanitarian Law Provide all Answers?*, 88 International Review of the Red Cross 881, 885 (2006) ("[S]everal cases before the ECHR have underlined a distinction between the planning of a police operation and the actual use of force by police officers").

[81] ECtHR, *McCann et al v. U.K.*, Application No 18984/91 (Judgment, Merits and Just Satisfaction) (Sep. 27, 1995) ¶ 149-150.

[82] ECtHR, *McCann et al v. U.K.*, Application No 18984/91 (Judgment, Merits and Just Satisfaction) (Sep. 27, 1995) ¶ 200.

"To hold otherwise would be to impose an unrealistic burden on the State and its law-enforcement personnel in the execution of their duty, perhaps to the detriment of their lives and those of others. It follows that, having regard to the dilemma confronting the authorities in the circumstances of the case, the actions of the soldiers do not, in themselves, give rise to a violation of this provision (art. 2-2)." [83]

However, in *McCann*, the ECtHR deemed the operation illegal due to poor planning. Had the terrorist been arrested earlier, the state may have avoided the use of lethal force altogether. Only here did the court eventually find a violation of Art. 2 ECHR.[84] The *McCann* case demonstrates that a state must take sufficient precautions to avoid the use of lethal force if the eventual, unavoidable use of lethal force is to be deemed lawful.

d) Assessment of the Results in Practice

The following sections outline the lawfulness of the use of lethal force with respect to specific events which occurred post-9/11.[85]

aa) Shoot-To-Kill Tactics – The Case of Jean Charles de Menezes

Shortly after 9/11, the UK developed a shoot-to-kill tactic to fight suspected suicide bombers.[86] This policy, also known as *Operation Kratos*, attracted attention and criticism over the killing of the innocent Brazilian, Jean Charles de Menezes, by British police officers.[87] In the report on the investigation following the incident (so called *Stockwell 1*), the Independent Police Complaints Commission emphasized that, *"[t]o be lawful, a deliberate killing has to be an action of last resort"*.[88] While the endorsement of the shoot-to-kill policy has been

---

[83] ECtHR, *McCann et al v. U.K.*, Application No 18984/91 (Judgment, Merits and Just Satisfaction) (Sep 27, 1995) ¶ 200.

[84] Even this decision was a very close with 10 to 9 vote.

[85] For a comprehensive list of U.S. practice of use of lethal force *see* Philip Alston, *The CIA and Targeted Killings beyond Borders*, 2 Harvard National Security Journal 283, 323 *et seq.* (2011).

[86] John Steele, *Shoot-to-kill Tactic still Viable say Police Chiefs*, Telegraph, March 8, 2006, available at: http://www.telegraph.co.uk/news/uknews/1512406/Shoot-to-kill-tactic-still-viable-say-police-chiefs.html.

[87] *See* Independent Police Complaints Commission, *Stockwell One – Investigation into the Shooting of Jean Charles de Menezes at Stockwell Underground Station on 22 July 2005*, 40 *et seq.* (2007) available at http://www.ipcc.gov.uk/stockwell_one.pdf.

[88] Independent Police Complaints Commission, *Stockwell One – Investigation into the Shooting of Jean Charles de Menezes at Stockwell Underground Station on 22 July 2005*, ¶ 19.13 (2007) available at http://www.ipcc.gov.uk/stockwell_one.pdf.

repeatedly criticized,[89] the Stockwell 1 report eventually stated that the tactic of Operation Kratos is not per se unlawful under Art. 2 ECHR.[90] The arguments in this book support this result.

In the event of an identified suicide bomber, the targeted killing must be considered a legitimate aim. The threat that the bomber poses is deemed concrete in that it is specific and likely to occur. One can assume the bomber will blow himself up during an attempt to arrest him. No other means, including firing at body parts, would prevent him from doing so. No argument suggests that the killing would be disproportionate, given the lethal threat to innocent bystanders posed by the bomb. Ultimately, even *Alston*, a critic of the shoot-to-kill tactics, accept that,

> "States have a legal duty to exercise 'due diligence' in protecting the lives of individuals from attacks by criminals, including terrorists [...]. This may require the use of lethal force against a suspect, but only when doing so is proportionate and strictly unavoidable to prevent the loss of life."[91]

Therefore, one can conclude that shoot-to-kill tactics to stop identified suicide bombers are lawful.[92] However, identifying the suicide bomber remains a crucial problem.

According to *Melzer,* state agents must possess a *"subjectively honest"* and *"objectively reasonable"* belief that an individual may be a suicide bomber within a concrete situation.[93] During the suicide-bomb attacks on the London

---

[89] Philip Alston, *Report of the Special Rapporteur on Extrajudicial, Summary or Arbitrary Executions*, ¶ 44-54, U.N. Doc. A/HRC/2/2 (Oct. 2, 2006); Philip Alston, *Report of the Special Rapporteur on Extrajudicial, Summary or Arbitrary Executions*, ¶ 33, U.N. Doc. A/HRC/14/24/Add.6 (May 28, 2010).

[90] Independent Police Complaints Commission, *Stockwell One – Investigation into the Shooting of Jean Charles de Menezes at Stockwell Underground Station on 22 July 2005*, ¶ 19.16 (2007) available at http://www.ipcc.gov.uk/stockwell_one.pdf. ("It follows from the above that a properly structured and properly managed operation which borrows 'KRATOS' strategy and tactics is not unlawful per se. Those who manage such an operation and those who act on instruction or, in extremis, act instinctively, are not acting unlawfully if they abide by the general principles set out above [i.e. test of 'strict proportionality']").

[91] Philip Alston, *Report of the Special Rapporteur on Extrajudicial, Summary or Arbitrary Executions*, ¶ 47, U.N. Doc. A/HRC/2/2 (Oct. 2, 2006).

[92] Nils Melzer, *Targeted Killing in International Law*, 230-1 and 233 (2008); *see also* Antonio Cassese, *Expert Opinion on Whether Israel's Targeted Killings of Palestinian Terrorists is Consonant with International Humanitarian Law*, submitted on July 18, 2003 to the Israel Supreme Court, available at http://www.stoptorture.org.il/files/cassese.pdf (last visited Feb. 2, 2011).

[93] Nils Melzer, *Targeted Killing in International Law*, 231 (2008).

underground system in 2005, Jean Charles de Menezes wore a voluminous coat, large enough to conceal an explosive belt, and ran away from the police and entered the underground system. No additional evidence that de Menezes was preparing a suicide attack was found. His behavior and attire are not at all sufficient to form an *objectively reasonable* belief that he was a suicide bomber preparing to commit a terrorist attack. If de Menezes was an identified member of Al Qaeda, or the IRA, as in the *McCann Case*,[94] and was seen carrying a bomb, there may have been sufficient grounds to form objective reasonability. However, in this case, law enforcement agents acted on mere assumptions, which is unlawful.

In conclusion, while shoot-to-kill tactics are not unlawful per se, the lawfulness of a state's actions is dependent on how the tactic is applied. Most importantly, it is imperative that the targeted person is properly identified. Law enforcement agents must not act on simple assumptions.

bb) The Use of Drones

Drones are remotely piloted aircrafts that carry missiles and are used to kill individuals through a targeted airstrike.[95] Recently the U.S. is employing more and more drones in its fight against Al Qaeda. Reportedly, the U.S. runs two drone programs, one operated by the military and one covertly operated by the CIA.[96] While the program operated by the military is part of the conventional war efforts in Afghanistan and Iraq, the CIA program is designed to operate globally and target suspected terrorists.

In the context of the right to life, the CIA drone program is not lawful under a law enforcement paradigm. The assessment of the concreteness of threat emanating from the attacked individual is questionable. Instead of referring to a concrete threat, the drone tactic is based more on the general assessment of an individual as dangerous. This is insufficient and alien to a law enforcement regime

---

[94] ECtHR, *McCann et al v. U.K.*, Application No 18984/91 (Judgment, Merits and Just Satisfaction) (Sep. 27, 1995).

[95] *See* Chris Jenks, Law From Above – Unmanned Aerial Systems, Use of Force, and the Law of Armed Conflict, 85 North Dakota Law Review 649, 652-656 (2009); Nils Melzer, Targeted Killing in International Law, 40-3 (2008); Bob Woodward, CIA Told to Do 'Whatever Necessary' to Kill Bin Laden, Washington Post, Oct. 21, 2001, available at http://www.washingtonpost.com/wp-dyn/content/article/2007/11/18/AR2007111800 655.html (last visited Feb. 2, 2011).

[96] Jane Mayer, *The Predator War: What Are The Risks Of The CIA's Covert Drone Program?*, The New Yorker, Oct. 28, 2009, available at http://www.newyorker.com/ reporting/2009/10/26/091026fa_fact_mayer (last visited Feb. 2, 2011).

where a death list of individuals is not permitted. Furthermore, no attempt to capture the individual is even considered. The use of drones implies a *per se* assumption that capture is impossible, which is unlawful as the necessity of the killing is not proven in each case. In addition, the necessity to use lethal force is not assessed with respect to a specific moment, which contradicts IHRL's temporal element of necessity. Therefore, the CIA drone program does not conform with the human right to life and is therefore open to justification only within the framework of an armed conflict model.[97]

cc) The Shooting of Osama Bin Laden

The law enforcement approach can be applied to the killing of Osama Bin Laden, on May 1st 2011.[98] Assuming that the U.S. raid aimed to kill Bin Laden from the outset, the action would have been illegal under a law-enforcement paradigm. However, if the goal were to apprehend Bin Laden according to an indictment, such as the one issued in 1998 for the bombings of the U.S. embassies in Kenya and Tanzania,[99] then the operation could be deemed justifiable under certain circumstances.[100] This begs the question as to whether U.S. forces were allowed to shoot Bin Laden. If he surrendered, his killing would not have

---

[97] With respect to the military drone program, the legality is not a question of IHRL but of IHL, as long as it is used as part of an armed conflict in Afghanistan and Iraq. Whether the use of drones is legal under the laws of armed conflict is a different question and although also debated, more likely to be answered affirmatively. *See* Chris Jenks, *Law From Above – Unmanned Aerial Systems*, Use of Force, and the Law of Armed Conflict, 85 North Dakota Law Review 649, 66 *et seq.* (2009).
However, Alston has pointed out that the lack of transparency itself has consequences regarding the legality of the use of drones, Philip Alston, The CIA and Targeted Killings Beyond Borders, 2 Harvard National Security Journal 283, 352 *et seq.* (2011).
[98] Helene Cooper, *Obama Announces Killing of Osama bin Laden*, N.Y. Times, May 1st, 2011 online availabel at http://thelede.blogs.nytimes.com/2011/05/01/bin-laden-dead-u-s-official-says/ (last visited Mar. 9, 2012).
[99] Chad Bray, *U.S. Formally Drops Charges Against bin Laden*, Wall Street Journal, June 17, 2011 online available at http://online.wsj.com/article/SB1000142 40527023044533045763915635244822274.html (last visited Mar. 9, 2012).
[100] *See* Christof Heynes and Martin Scheinin, *Osama bin Laden: Statement by the UN Special Rapporteurs on Summary Executions and on Human Rights and Counter-Terrorism* (May 6, 2011). ("In respect of the recent use of deadly force against Osama bin Laden, the United States of America should disclose the supporting facts to allow an assessment in terms of international human rights law standards. For instance it will be particularly important to know if the planning of the mission allowed an effort to capture Bin Laden") online available at http://www.ohchr.org/en/NewsEvents/Pages/Display News.aspx?NewsID=10987andLangID=E (last visited May 31, 2012).

been justified. However, if he resisted his arrest by possibly firing at the U.S. agents, the use of force would have been permitted on grounds of self-defense. Similarly, the use of force would have also been permitted had Bin Laden attempted to flee as a result of the threat he posed and the violent offenses he committed. The use of force to prevent him from evading arrest would have therefore been deemed lawful. However, in this case, proportionality would have required the U.S. agents to prevent his escape not by deliberately killing him, but by attempting non-lethal shots. Even without having full knowledge of the exigencies of the situation, it seems unlikely that it was impossible to arrest Bin Laden without killing him. Therefore, the legality of the U.S. operation against Bin Laden is seriously questionable under a law enforcement paradigm.

2. Permissibility of Collateral Damages

In IHL, collateral damage is defined as the unintended death of civilians, who do not directly partake in hostilities, as a consequence of an attack against a military target. In an armed conflict, collateral damage is, although morally questionable,[101] legally permissible within the limits of proportionality.[102] Whether the infliction of collateral damage can ever be justified under a law-enforcement paradigm governed by IHRL will be addressed in this section.

a) Position of the German Constitutional Court

In its decision on the *Luftsicherheitsgesetz* (Aviation Security Act), the German Constitutional Court ruled against the justifiability of collateral damage during law enforcement operations.[103] The Court ruled that even to avert an immediate and massive threat to the life of other persons, the state cannot shoot down a hijacked plane:

"The armed forces' authorisation pursuant to § 14.3 of the Aviation Security Act (Luftsicherheitsgesetz – LuftSiG) to shoot down by the direct use of armed force an aircraft that is intended to be used against human lives is incompatible with the right to life un-

---

[101] *See* David Lefkowitz, *Collateral Damage in War – Esssays in Political Philosophy*, 145-164 (Larry May ed. 2008).

[102] Art. 51.5 b) AP I; Art. 23.1 g) Hague Regulation; *cf.* Hans-Peter Gasser and Knut Dörmann, *Protection of Civilian Population*, in The Handbook of International Humanitarian Law, 243 *et seq.* (Dieter Fleck ed. 2008).

[103] Bundesverfassungsgericht (Federal Constitutional Court), 1 BvR 357/05 (Feb. 15, 2006) english version, online available at http://www.bverfg.de/entscheidungen /rs20060215_1bvr035705en.html (last visited Mar. 9 2012).

der Article 2.2 sentence 1 of the Basic Law in conjunction with the guarantee of human dignity under Article 1.1 of the Basic Law to the extent that it affects persons on board the aircraft who are not participants in the crime."[104]

The Court's central argument stated that shooting down the plane would deprive the hostages of their human dignity by using them as a means to an end.[105] It states that

"[...] it is absolutely inconceivable under the applicability of Article 1.1 of the Basic Law to intentionally kill persons such as the crew and the passengers of a hijacked plane, who are in a situation that is hopeless for them, on the basis of a statutory authorisation which even accepts such imponderabilities if necessary".[106]

The court's reasoning remains unchanged despite the fact that shooting the plane down may be the only way to prevent harm to those who would subsequently be the victims of the attack. The court held that human dignity is an absolute right and cannot be weighed against other rights. As a result, any proportionality assessment is precluded from the outset. This court's rigid understanding of the right to human dignity has been criticized for setting unnecessary stringent limits for state action.[107]

One argument in support of the German Constitutional Court's strict position and granting permission to shoot down hijacked airplanes, is that there are always uncertainties within concrete situations. Making an accurate assessment of whether the plane is truly taken over by terrorists is close to impossible. The communication between the cabin and cockpit, and the communication between the cockpit and the authorities on the ground, may not be sufficiently reliable. In addition, visual contact with the hijacked plane is difficult. Finally, conditions onboard may change at any moment, thereby denying any possibility for authorities on the ground to adapt their decisions and halt the orders to shoot down the

---

[104] Bundesverfassungsgericht (Federal Constitutional Court), 1 BvR 357/05, Headnote 3 (Feb. 15, 2006) english version, online available at http://www.bverfg.de/entscheidungen/rs20060215_1bvr035705en.html (last visited Mar. 9 2012).

[105] Bundesverfassungsgericht (Federal Constitutional Court), 1 BvR 357/05, ¶ 122 (Feb. 15, 2006) english version, online available at http://www.bverfg.de/entscheidungen/rs20060215_1bvr035705en.html (last visited March 9 2012); Christian Starck, Anmerkung, 61 Juristenzeitung 417 (2006) ("Das BverfG aktiviert erneut die Objektformel zur Auslegung der Menschenwürdegarantie [...]").

[106] Bundesverfassungsgericht (Federal Constitutional Court), 1 BvR 357/05, ¶ 128 (Feb. 15, 2006) english version, online available at http://www.bverfg.de/entscheidungen/rs20060215_1bvr035705en.html (last visited Mar. 9 2012).

[107] Nina Naske and Georg Nolte, *Aerial Security Law*, 101 American Journal of International Law 466, 470 *et seq.* (2007) (Although both authors disagree with the Courts arguments, they agree with the Courts decision).

plane. As a result, it can never be stated with utmost certainty that a state's last possible option is shooting the plane down.

The inability to perform an accurate assessment of the situation was yet another argument put forth by the German Constitutional Court's to reject the Aerial Security Act.[108] Lastly, the Court's decision does not preclude the shooting down of hijacked airplanes under all circumstances. The German Constitutional Court was fully aware of the difference between an armed conflict situation and a law enforcement framework. The court's ruling is applicable only to a *"mission by the armed forces of a non-warlike nature"*,[109] not addressing the possibility of legally shooting-down a plane in an armed conflict scenario. It is remarkable that no other state has included an authorization similar to that in § 14.3 LuftSiG in their respective aviation security laws, nor have similar provisions been issued by the EU.[110] In conclusion, the German Constitutional Court established a strict position against the permissibility of collateral damage during law enforcement operations. However, it accepts different results for armed conflict situations.

b) Positions of the European Court of Human Rights and the Inter-American Court of Human Rights

If one were to focus on Europe, the jurisprudence of the ECtHR can be understood as introducing a different conception of the right to life, which allows for law enforcement actions that entail civilian casualties.[111] Instead of considering each operation that accepts the killing of innocents as unlawful, the ECtHR requires the state to plan and conduct an operation

---

[108] Bundesverfassungsgericht (Federal Constitutional Court), 1 BvR 357/05, ¶ 123 (Feb. 15, 2006) english version, online available at http://www.bverfg.de/entscheidungen/rs20060215_1bvr035705en.html (last visited Mar. 9 2012).

[109] Bundesverfassungsgericht (Federal Constitutional Court), 1 BvR 357/05, ¶ 128 (Feb. 15, 2006) english version, online available at http://www.bverfg.de/entscheidungen/rs20060215_1bvr035705en.html (last visited Mar. 9 2012).

[110] *See* Mathias Bug et al., *Strategien gegen die Unsicherheit. Europäische Sicherheitsmaßnahmen nach 9/11*, 86 Friedenswarte 53, 66 *et seq.* (2011).

[111] *See* David Kretzmer, *Rethinking the Application of IHL in Non-International Armed Conflicts*, 42 Israel Law Review 8, 29 (2009); Georg Nolte, *The Bundesverfassungsgericht on the German Aerial Security Law: A Sonderweg from Perspective of International Law?*, in The Right to Life 83, 91 *et seq.* (Christian Tomuschat, Evelyne Lagrange and Stefan Oeter, eds. 2010).

"in such a way as to avoid or minimize, to the greatest extent possible, damage to civilians".[112]

This obligation is similar to the obligation to take precautionary measures under IHL.[113] According to the ECtHR jurisprudence, a state is not precluded from taking action when it expects civilian casualties. Instead, as long as it takes sufficient precautions to keep damage to civilians to a minimum, the death of civilians during a law-enforcement operation does not violate those civilians' rights to life. These precautions involve planning prior to the operation, the respect for necessity and proportionality while conducting the operation, and an effective *ex-post* investigation. Therefore, the ECtHR would not follow the German Constitutional Court's categorical understanding of human dignity during transnational conflicts.[114] According to the ECtHR, collateral damages would be permissible if necessary and proportionate.

Outside Europe, the IACtHR has not yet explicitly dealt with the question of collateral damage under IHRL. However, when addressing the right to life and its possible limitations, it has only referred to the principles of necessity and proportionality. This is more similar to the ECtHR's position than that of the German Constitutional Court.

In the case of *Montero-Aranguren and others v. Venezuela* (Detention Center of Caita), the guards of a Venezuelan prison and intervening National Guard an Metropolitan Police *"shot indiscriminately at the prisoners using firearms and tear gas"*[115] to prevent a suspected attempt to escape. The IACtHR did not distinguish between the legality of shooting those who wanted to escape and those

---

[112] ECtHR, *Isayeva, Yusupova and Bazayeva v Russian Federation*, App Nos. 57947/00, 57948/00 and 57949/00 (Admissibility, Merits and Just Satisfaction) (Feb. 24, 2005) ¶ 177; *See also* ECtHR, Ergi v. Turkey, Application No. 23818/94 (Judgment, Merits and Just Satisfaction) (July 28, 1998) ¶ 79.

[113] Noelle Quénivet, *The Right to Life in International Humanitarian Law and Human Rights Law*, in International Humanitarian Law and Human Rights Law, 347 (Roberta Arnold and Noelle Quénivet, eds. 2008) ("The approach adopted by the European Court of Human Rights can generally be associated to the concept of precautionary measures established in IHL"); William Abresch, *A Human Rights Law of Internal Armed Conflict*, 16 European Journal of International Law 741, 762 ("The ECtHR has developed a vigorous jurisprudence on the planning and execution of military operations in internal conflicts. Here the rules it has promulgated largely track those that humanitarian law provides for international conflicts").

[114] Georg Nolte, *The Bundesverfassungsgericht on the German Aerial Security Law: A Sonderweg from Perspective of International Law?*, in The Right to Life 83, 89 *et seq.* (Christian Tomuschat, Evelyne Lagrange and Stefan Oeter, eds. 2010).

[115] Montero-Aranguren and others v. Venezuela (Detention Center of Caita), IACtHR Series C No 150 (5 July 2006) ¶ 60(19).

who did not. In addition, the Court made no statement that suggests shooting at escaping prisoners is unlawful if it willfully accepts the death of prisoners who did not want to escape. Instead, the Court refers only to the necessity and proportionality of the action, in that

> "the actions of the security forces that participated in the above mentioned events were neither proportionate to the then existing threat or danger, nor the strictly necessary to keep the peace and order in the Detention Center of Catia".[116]

However, the IACtHR's decision must not necessarily be read as an argument in favor of the permissibility of collateral damages under IHRL. The Court did not address this question as it first applied the principles of necessity and proportionality and then deemed the state authority's indiscriminate actions unlawful. Through the application of the principles of necessity and proportionality, the Court has so far avoided directly addressing the question of collateral damages in IHRL.

c) Conclusion

It must be first noted that there is no comprehensive discussion of the question of collateral damage under IHRL. The most prominent argument against collateral damages was made by the German Constitutional Court in the case of the Arial Security Act. Strong arguments support the position of the German Constitutional Court. The Court's approach to the right to life and the categorical interpretation of human dignity deserves approval on an international level as well as it is necessary to protect innocents from any intentional killing by the state during peacetime. Allowing states to deliberately accept the death of innocents as long as they are proportionate would eliminate the difference between peace and war. During an armed conflict, collateral damage is justifiable. On the contrary, collateral damage has no place during peacetime as it puts civilian lives at permanent risk. While citizens can be required to take this risk during times of war, the same demand must be rejected in times of peace.

Safety from a terrorist attack can never be guaranteed, however, law-abiding citizens must be guaranteed safety from an attack by their state. Only then is a life in dignity possible. Furthermore, the indeterminacy of what would be *proportionate* gives states too much of a leeway and opens the door for abuse. The dangers resulting from an introduction of collateral damages to IHRL are greater than those resulting from the prohibition of collateral damages during peacetime.

---

[116] *Montero-Aranguren and others v. Venezuela* (Detention Center of Caita), IACtHR Series C No 150 (5 July 2006) ¶ 74.

Therefore, as long as transnational conflicts do not amount to NIAC, the applicable IHRL must not be interpreted as permitting an action that anticipates the killing of innocent civilians.

3. Detention of Non-State Actors

The legal standards governing the detention of non-state actors under a law enforcement regime will be addressed in this section. These standards derive from the human right to liberty, addressed in all human rights treaties despite their varying description.[117] The focus of this section will be on the ECHR and the ICCPR.[118]

a) Preventive Detention for Security Purposes

An individual may be detained after being convicted of a crime or pending trial. In transnational conflicts, a non-state actor may be charged with offenses ranging from mere membership to a terrorist organization, to attempted murder or manslaughter. Recently, a case in Germany involved individuals suspected of being Al Qaeda members. The individuals were detained on April 29, 2011 and are still awaiting their trial.[119] Now, the question is whether a state can lawfully detain enemy fighters to protect public security without planning an impending trial. This question becomes particularly relevant when the state has not collected sufficient evidence to convict the suspected terrorists or when the evidence cannot be disclosed due to intelligence reasons.[120] The key issue is then whether preventive detention for security purposes is possible under IHRL.

---

[117] Art. 9 ICCPR, Art. 5 ECHR, Art. 7 ACHR and Art. 6 ACHPR.

[118] For an assessment of the ACHR *see* Michelangela Scalabrino, *Fighting Against International Terrorism: The Latin American Response*, in Enforcing International Law Norms Against Terrorism 163 (Andrea Bianchi ed., 2004).

[119] Bundesgerichtshof, Beschluss, AK 19-21/11, Nov. 23. 2011.

[120] Colin Warbrick, *The European Response to Terrorism in an Age of Human Rights*, 15 European Journal of International Law 989, 1007 (2004) ("The [UK] Government had identified a problem of brining suspected terrorist to trial in the UK where the evidence against them would not be admissible because the Government did not want to reveal its source in the intelligence-gathering processes or because it was hearsay.") In Germany, the Case of Mounir El Motassadeq demonstrated the difficulties of a trial against an alleged terrorist. The first conviction of Mr. El Motassadeq was rescinded by Germany's federal court of justice (BGH) because Mr. Ramzi Binalshib, a crucial witness, could not be heard in the trial. Additionally, transcripts of his interrogations were declassified by U.S. authorities. *See* Bundesgerichtshof [German Federal Court of Justice], Judgment of

Under the ICCPR, the protection of public security can be a valid reason for detention.[121] Art. 9.1 ICCPR does not limit valid reasons for detention, provided it is not arbitrary or discriminatory, and as long as the further procedural requirements of Art. 9 ICCPR are met (see below). The UN Human Rights Committee states that preventive detention for reasons of public security falls under Art. 9 ICCPR.[122] A deprivation of liberty for purposes of national security does not violate Art. 9.1 ICCPR.[123] As a result, an Al Qaeda fighter can be preventively detained under a law enforcement regime so long as the detention is neither arbitrary nor discriminatory.

The ECHR presents a more restrictive legal framework than the ICCPR. Art. 5.1 ECHR presents a list of reasons for which detention is permissible. Prolonged preventive detention for security purposes is not among those reasons. Art. 5.1 c ECHR authorizes detention

"when it is reasonably considered necessary to prevent [a person] committing an offence".

However, the ECtHR states that a prolonged preventive detention would be repugnant to the fundamental principles of the Convention.[124] In the court's

---

Mar. 4, 2004, 3 Str 218/03 Neue Juristische Wochenschrift, 1259 (2004) *cf.* Timo Kost, *Mounir El Motassadeq – A missed Chance for Weltinnenpolitik*, 8 German Law Journal, 443 (2007); Christoph J.M. Safferling, *Terror and Law – Is the German Legal System able to deal with Terrorism? – The Bundesgerichtshof (Federal Court of Justice) decision in the case against El Motassadeq*, 5 German Law Journal, 515 (2004).

[121] Douglas Cassel, *Pretrial and Preventive Detention of Suspected Terrorists: Options and Constraints under International Law*, 98 Journal of Criminal Law and Criminology 811, 850 (2008); Monica Hakimi, *International Standards for Detaining Terrorism Suspects: Moving Beyond the Armed Conflict-Criminal Divide*, 33 Yale Journal of International Law 369, 407 (2008) ("an alternative legal framework already exists under human rights law in the form of administrative detention").

[122] UN Human Rights Committee, *General Comment No 8, Right to Liberty and Security of Persons*, ¶ 4 (June 30, 1982) online available at http://www.unhchr.ch/tbs/doc.nsf/%28Symbol%29/f4253f9572cd4700c12563ed00483bec?Opendocument (last visited Jan. 27, 2011).

[123] UN Human Rights Committee, *Mansour Ahani vs. Canada*, Communication No. 1051/2002, CCPR/C/80/D/1051/2002, ¶ 10.2 (June 15, 2004), online available at http://www.unhcr.org/refworld/docid/4162a5a50.html (last visited Mar. 9, 2012) ("The Committee observes, consistent with its earlier jurisprudence, that detention on the basis of a security certification by two Ministers on national security grounds does not result ipso facto in arbitrary detention, contrary to article 9, paragraph 1").

[124] ECtHR, *Lawless v Ireland* (No 3), Application No. 332/57 (July 1, 1961) ¶ 14 ("whereas it must be pointed out in this connexion that, if the construction placed by the Court on the aforementioned provisions were not correct, anyone suspected of harbouring an intent to commit an offence could be arrested and detained for an unlimited period on

reading, Art. 5.1 c ECHR only affords the contracting parties a *"means of preventing a concrete and specific offence"*,[125] thereby allowing for a brief preventive detention. It follows from this rather restrictive reading of Art. 5.1 ECHR that a preventive detention for security purposes, under the ECHR, is permissible only by derogating from Art. 5 ECHR.[126] The following section analyzes ECtHR jurisprudence to determine whether transnational conflicts are sufficient grounds for derogation as per the ECtHR.

b) Derogability from Art. 5 of the European Convention on Human Rights

Derogation from provisions of the ECHR is regulated in Art. 15.1 ECHR:

"In time of war or other public emergency threatening the life of the nation any High Contracting Party may take measures derogating from its obligations under this Convention to the extent strictly required by the exigencies of the situation, provided that such measures are not inconsistent with its other obligations under international law."

War must be classified as a subcategory of public emergencies that threatens the life of a nation.[127] Like war, IACs and NIACs are situations in which a state can derogate from the ECHR. Transnational conflicts that amount to NIACs would therefore allow the state to derogate from the ECHR. The crucial question is whether transnational conflicts that do not amount to NIACs can also constitute a public emergency that poses a threat to the life of a nation. From the out-

---

the strength merely of an executive decision without its being possible to regard his arrest or detention as a breach of the Convention; whereas such an assumption, with all its implications of arbitrary power, would lead to conclusions repugnant to the fundamental principles of the Convention").

[125] ECtHR, *Guzzardi v Italy*, Application No. 7367/76 (A/39) (Merits, Just Satisfaction) (Nov 6, 1980) ¶ 102 ("[Art. 5.1 c] does no more than afford the Contracting States a means of preventing a concrete and specific offence").

[126] In fact the IACHR foresees similar regulation than the ECHR in Art. 7 IACHR. Therefore, only where a state derogates from Art. 7 IACHR can it detain a person preventively for security reasons. *Cf.* Florian Prill, *Präventivhaft zur Terrorismusbekämpfung*, 296-7 (2009); Inter-American Commission on Human Rights, *Report on Terrorism and Human Rights*, IACHR OAS-Doc. OEA/Ser.L/V/II.116 Doc. 5 rev. 1 corr., ¶ 138 (Oct. 22, 2002) ("In circumstances not involving a state of emergency as strictly defined under applicable human rights instruments, states are fully bound by the restrictions and limitations under international human rights law governing deprivations of personal liberty").

[127] Christian Johann, *Art. 15 – Abweichen im Notstandsfall*, in EMRK – Konvention zum Schutz der Menschenrechte und Grundfreiheiten 433, 436 ¶ 6 (Ulrich Karpenstein and Franz C. Mayer eds., 2012); Christoph Grabenwarter and Katharina Pabel, *Europäische Menschenrechtskonvention*, 11 (5th ed. 2012).

set, the term public emergency is not limited to armed conflicts, as they are al-ready encompassed by the term war.[128] The ECtHR understands a public emergency to be

"an exceptional situation of crisis or emergency which affects the whole population and constitutes a threat to the organized life of the community of which the state is composed".[129]

The ECtHR therefore concluded that, the unlawful activities in Northern Ire-land by the IRA and various associated groups constituted a public emergency.[130] These situations do not necessarily need to affect the entire coun-try. They can be limited to a specific region such as Northern Ireland or Southeast Turkey, as the ECtHR clarified in subsequent judgments.[131] As a re-sult, the fight against terrorism that occurs in a limited region of a state may qualify as a public emergency, even if it is not a NIAC.

In a recent case concerning legislation in the U.K., the ECtHR confirmed that terrorism may amount to a public emergency, and therefore allowed for deroga-tion from Art. 5 ECHR.[132] In the U.K., the Anti-Terrorism, Crime and Security Act 2001 (ATCSA) foresaw an authorization for the Home Secretary to detain non-U.K. nationals if the Home Secretary *"reasonably believes"* that a person is a threat to national security and if he *"suspects"* that the person is a terrorist.[133] This detention, as part of the immigration law, was not time-limited, and the detained individual need not be charged with a crime. In order to comply with the ECHR, derogation is required according to Art. 15 ECHR and Art. 4 ICCPR.

---

[128] On the debate whether NIAC are "wars" or rather "public emergencies" according to Art. 15 ECHR *see* Christian Johann, *Art. 15 – Abweichen im Notstandsfall*, in EMRK – Konvention zum Schutz der Menschenrechte und Grundfreiheiten 433, 435 ¶ 5 (Ulrich Karpenstein and Franz C. Mayer eds., 2012).

[129] ECtHR, *Lawless v Ireland* (No 3), Application No. 332/57 (July 1, 1961) ¶ 28.

[130] ECtHR, *Lawless v Ireland* (No 3), Application No. 332/57 (July 1, 1961) ¶ 29.

[131] ECtHR, *Brannigan and McBride v. U.K.*, Application Nos. 14553/89 and 14554/89 (Decision on the Merits) (May 25, 1993) ¶ 47 ("[…] in the light of all the material before it as to the extent and impact of terrorist violence in Northern Ireland and elsewhere in the United Kingdom […], the Court considers there can be no doubt that such a public emergency existed at the relevant time"); ECtHR, *Aksoy v. Turkey*, Application No. 21987/93 (Judgment, Merits and Just Satisfaction) (Dec. 18, 1996) ¶ 70 (The Court considers, in the light of all the material before it, that the particular extent and impact of PKK terrorist activity in South-East Turkey has undoubtedly created, in the region con-cerned, a "public emergency threatening the life of the nation").

[132] ECtHR, *A and others v. UK.*, Application No. 3455/05 (Feb. 19, 2009).

[133] Section 21 of the ATCSA; For a critical comment on that Act *see* Colin Warbrick, *The European Response to Terrorism in an Age of Human Rights*, 15 European Journal of International Law 989, 1007 *et seq.* (2004).

Hence, whenever an individual was detained, the Home Secretary was required to declare a state of emergency. This law served as a special law enforcement measure for states of emergency. Although the House of Lords, in *A and others v Secretary of State for the Home Department*, ruled that this authorization violated the ECHR,[134] the ruling was based not on the possible indefinite detention, but on its discriminatory application to non-U.K. nationals.[135] The determination of the existence of a public emergency was not challenged. Here, the ECtHR followed the House of Lords. The ECtHR granted the U.K. a wide margin of appreciation.[136] The ECtHR accepted that the threat of international terrorism following the 9/11 attacks was an emergency that threatened the life of the nation as per the definition in Art. 15 ECHR. Additionally, according to the ECtHR, an emergency does not need to be temporary.[137] The Court concluded that *"the danger from al'Qaeda"* constitutes a public emergency within the concrete situation, and that the U.K.'s assessment of the situation was therefore correct.[138]

---

[134] UK House of Lords, *A et al v Secretary of State for Home Department* (Dec. 16, 2004) [2004] UKHL 56.

[135] David Weissbrodt, *Immigration*, in Max Planck Encyclopedia of Public International Law, Vol 5, 84, (Rudiger Wolfrum, ed., Oxford University Press, 2012). The U.K. government has responded to this decision by passing the Prevention of Terrorism Act 2005 (Available at http://www.statutelaw.gov.uk/content.aspx?active TextDocId=1414108) which allows the Home Secretary to impose "control orders" on people who are suspected to be terrorists or involved in terrorism. These control orders are essentially a restriction on liberty but do not go so far as to completely deprive the suspected person of his liberty. *See, Control Orders Explained*, BBC News (March 12, 2005) http://news.bbc.co.uk/2/hi/uk_news/politics/4343081.stm (last visited Jan. 27, 2011).

[136] ECtHR, *A and others v. UK.*, Application No. 3455/05 (Feb. 19, 2009) ¶ 173 ("The Court recalls that it falls to each Contracting State, [...] to determine whether that life is threatened by a 'public emergency' [...]. By reason of their direct and continuous contact with the pressing needs of the moment, the national authorities are in principle better placed than the international judge to decide both on the presence of such an emergency and on the nature and scope of the derogations necessary to avert it. Accordingly, in this matter a wide margin of appreciation should be left to the national authorities"); On the ECtHR decision *see* Marco Milanovic, *European Court decides A and others v. United Kingdom*, EJIL: Talk! Blog (Feb. 19, 2009) online available at http://www.ejiltalk.org/european-court-decides-a-and-others-v-united-kingdom/ (last visited May 31, 2013).

[137] ECtHR, *A and others v. UK.*, Application No. 3455/05 (Feb. 19, 2009) ¶ 178.

[138] ECtHR, *A and others v. UK.*, Application No. 3455/05 (Feb. 19, 2009) ¶ 180-1. The U.K. still lost the case before the ECtHR as the measures it had taken in response to the public emergency were not strictly required by the exigencies of the situation, but were disproportionate, *see* ECtHR, *A and others v. UK.*, Application No. 3455/05 (Feb. 19, 2009) ¶ 190.

In conclusion, according to the ECtHR's jurisprudence, a threat posed by a transnational conflict, if sufficiently severe, allows the state to derogate from Art. 5 ECHR. Therefore, according to the ECHR, detaining violent non-state actors in a transnational conflict as a preventative measure is possible if the state has derogated from Art. 5 ECHR. However, even during a public emergency, the response measures taken must be strictly required by the exigencies of the situation. Thus, an individual assessment of the required measures must be performed in all cases.

c) Procedural Dimension of Detention

This section examines the procedural dimension of the detention that aims at eventually putting fighters on trial within the context of a transnational conflict. The right to liberty inherently contains a procedural dimension, in that even if certain circumstances permit a state to detain a person, specific procedural requirements must also be met. This procedural dimension is explained in Art. 5.2-5.5 ECHR or Art. 9.2-9.5 ICCPR, and consists of four core elements, 1) the detained individual must be informed of the reasons for his detention, 2) the detained person must promptly be brought before a judge, 3) access to judicial (not only administrative) review must be granted so as to allow the detainee to challenge the legality of their detention, and 4) if the detention is deemed unlawful, the detainee has a right to enforceable compensation.

As per the principle of legality, all procedures of detention must be previously established by law,[139] in that they must include safeguards, such as the registration of the detainee. This allows the detainee to communicate and grants judicial control of the detention.[140] The permissible duration of a detention prior to a trial is crucial to transnational conflicts. Under an IHL regime, an enemy may be detained until hostilities have ended. By contrast, the permissible duration of detention under IHRL must be developed through the interpretation of the relevant provisions in the human rights treaties, such as Art. 5.3 and 5.4 ECHR, or Art. 9.4 ICCPR.[141] The *promptness* and *without delay* requirements set forth by these articles must be properly determined.

---

[139] Art. 9.1 ICCPR; Art. 5.1 ECHR; Art. 7.2 ACHR; Art. 6 ACHPR.

[140] *Cf.* Douglas Cassel, *Pretrial and Preventive Detention of Suspected Terrorists: Options and Constraints under International Law*, 98 Journal of Criminal Law and Criminology 811, 844 *et seq.* (2008).

[141] Art. 9.3 ICCPR is not applicable because it is milited to detention on criminal charges.

States' domestic law regulates the maximum length of time a suspect can be detained. In Germany, a suspect is put before a judge within 48 hours of his arrest,[142] although in extreme cases this period may be exceeded. The ECtHR has issued a number of judgments and decisions regarding the amount of time a suspect may be detained prior to being brought before a judge.

In Brogan v. U.K., the court generally accepted longer periods of detention stating that,

> "subject to the existence of adequate safeguards, the context of terrorism in Northern Ireland has the effect of prolonging the period during which the authorities may, without violating Article 5 para. 3 (art. 5-3), keep a person suspected of serious terrorist offences in custody before bringing him before a judge or other judicial officer".[143]

However, the ECtHR also ruled that a particular case, with a four day and six hour detention that was not brought before a judge, violated Art. 5.3, and added that

> "[t]he undoubted fact that the arrest and detention of the applicants were inspired by the legitimate aim of protecting the community as a whole from terrorism is not on its own sufficient to ensure compliance with the specific requirements of Article 5 para. 3 (art. 5-3)".[144]

Art. 5.3 was violated as, despite the threat of terrorism, the suspect could have been brought before a judge sooner. The length of detention, in this particular case, was not justified by the concrete situation. Under alternative circumstances, e contrario, a longer detention may have been justified. This was confirmed by the ECtHR in Brogan, when the Court regarded the general *context of terrorism* as grounds to permit a prolonged detention. Although the Court did not rule on the basis of a state of emergency in Brogan, in all cases, including public emergencies, circumstances must be considered individually as per Art. 15 ECHR.

In another case, *Aksoy v. Turkey*, the ECtHR ruled that a detention for at least 14 days (the facts of the exact duration were debated) violated Art. 5.3 ECHR:

> "The Court has taken account of the unquestionably serious problem of terrorism in South-East Turkey and the difficulties faced by the State in taking effective measures against it. However, it is not persuaded that the exigencies of the situation necessitated the holding of the applicant on suspicion of involvement in terrorist offences for four-

---

[142] *See Grundgesetz der Bundesrepublik Deutschland* (Federal Constitution), Art. 104 (2).

[143] ECtHR, *Brogan et al. v. U.K.*, Application Nos. 11209/84, 11234/84, 11266/84 and 11386/85 (Judgment, Merits) (Nov. 29,1988) ¶ 61.

[144] ECtHR, *Brogan et al. v. U.K.*, Application Nos. 11209/84, 11234/84, 11266/84 and 11386/85 (Judgment, Merits) (Nov. 29,1988) ¶ 62.

teen days or more in incommunicado detention without access to a judge or other judicial officer."[145]

Regardless of whether the state is confronted with a context below or at the threshold of a public emergency, the actual exigencies of the situation are crucial. In any given situation, the possibility and feasibility of bringing a suspect before a judge must be assessed.[146] The question lies in whether an individual suspected of being a participant in a transnational conflict can be detained for as long as necessary to bring him before a judge, even if the arrest were to take place in another country or on the high seas.

In *Rigopoulos v. Spain,* the court dismisses the application due to *"wholly exceptional circumstances",* where a detention of 16 days was not a violation of Art. 5.3 ECHR.[147] The individual had been arrested on board a vessel on the high seas more than 5500 km away from Spanish Territory, thus making this an exceptional circumstance. The court considered *"that it was therefore materially impossible to bring the applicant physically before the investigating judge any sooner".*[148]

Similarly, in *Medvedyev v. France,* the court stated a 13 day detention was not a breach of Art. 5.3 ECHR as the suspects were arrested at sea and could not physically be brought before a judge any earlier.[149] The ECtHR's application of Art. 5.3 ECHR demonstrates that, although the state is obliged to bring a suspected terrorist before a judge promptly, IHRL still grants states the flexibility necessary to meet the requirements for detention in transnational conflicts.

Other human rights bodies provide a less comprehensive response than the ECtHR. The Human Rights Committee states that indefinite detention for security purposes is not permissible under Art. 9 ICCPR.[150] Furthermore, it argues for

---

[145] ECtHR, *Aksoy v. Turkey,* Application No. 21987/93 (Judgment, Merits and Just Satisfaction) (Dec. 18, 1996) ¶ 84.

[146] The main difference might be that during a situation of public emergency the states margin of appreciation with respect to that possibility and feasibility is greater.

[147] ECtHR, *Rigopoulos v. Spain,* Application No. 37388/97 (Decision) (Jan. 12, 1999).

[148] ECtHR, *Rigopoulos v. Spain,* Application No. 37388/97 (Decision) (Jan. 12, 1999).

[149] ECtHR, *Medvedyev et al. vs. France,* App no. 3394/03 (Judgment, Merits and Just Satisfaction) (Mar. 29, 2010) ¶ 131-134.

[150] UN Human Rights Committee, *Concluding Observations: Zambia,* U.N. Doc. CCPR/C/79/Add.62 (Apr. 3, 1996) ¶ 14 ("The Committee is concerned that three journalists were found to be in 'gross contempt of the National Assembly' without any of the procedural guarantees of fair trial provided for by articles 9 and 14 of the Covenant and that two of these journalists were held in indefinite detention before release, contrary to the provisions of article 9 of the Covenant [...]"); UN Human Rights Committee, *Concluding Observations: Israel,* U.N. Doc. CCPR/C/79/Add.93 (Aug. 18, 1998) ¶ 21. ("The Committee remains concerned that despite the reduction in the number of persons held in

a more comprehensive approach to the issue of detention duration and paints out, that preventive detention is missing from the clause.

The Human Rights Committee does not see a fundamental difference between the application of Art. 9 ICCPR for detention on criminal charges and preventive detention for security reasons.[151] However, Art. 9.3 ICCPR, the parallel provision to Art. 5.3 ECHR, cannot be applied to preventive detention as it only applies to *"anyone arrested or detained on a criminal charge [...]"*.[152] The crucial provision of the ICCPR is Art. 9.4, which clearly outlines the detainee's *habeas corpus* right, which grants every individual the right to challenge his or her detention *without delay* in a court. [153] As this must occur on the instigation of the detainee, rather than *ex officio*,[154] the individual must be given the right to a lawyer within a 48 hour time period.[155] The right to be brought before a judge, however, may occur within two weeks, as per Art. 9.4 ICCPR.[156] In the absence of further clarification, the permissible length of time that may pass prior to the

---

administrative detention on security grounds, persons may still be held for long and apparently indefinite periods of time in custody without trial. It is also concerned that Palestinians detained by Israeli military order in the occupied territories do not have the same rights to judicial review as persons detained in Israel under ordinary law. [...] The Committee takes due note that Israel has derogated from article 9 of the Covenant. The Committee stresses, however, that a State party may not depart from the requirement of effective judicial review of detention").

[151] UN Human Rights Committee, General Comment No 8, *Right to Liberty and Security of Persons*, ¶ 4 (June 30, 1982) online available at http://www.unhchr.ch/tbs/doc.nsf/%28Symbol%29/f4253f9572cd4700c12563ed00483be c?OpendocumentU (last visited Jan. 27, 2011).

[152] Art. 9.3 ICCPR.

[153] Sarah Jones, Jenny Schulz, Melissa Castan, *The International Covenant on Civil and Political Rights*, 330 *et seq.* (2004).

[154] Sarah Jones, Jenny Schulz, Melissa Castan, *The International Covenant on Civil and Political Rights*, 331 (2004).

[155] UN Human Rights Committee, *Concluding Observations: Israel*, U.N. Doc. CCPR /CO/78/ISR (Aug. 21, 2003) ¶ 13 ("The Committee is concerned that the use of prolonged detention without any access to a lawyer or other persons of the outside world violates articles the Covenant (arts. 7, 9, 10 and 14, ¶ 3 (b). The State party should ensure that no one is held for more than 48 hours without access to a lawyer").

[156] UN Human Rights Committee, *Torres v. Finland*, U.N. Doc. CCPR/C/38/D/291 /1988 (Apr. 5, 1990) ¶ 7.4 ("The committee notes that the Helsinki City Court reviewd the author's detention under the Extradition Act at two-week intervals. The Committee find that such reviews satisfy the requirements of article 9, paragraph 4, of the Covenant").

review of lawfulness of detention by a judge remains unclear under the ICCPR.[157]

During transnational conflicts, states are permitted to adapt the procedural safeguards outlined by IHRL to protect the right to liberty, given the exigencies of transnational conflicts. This may be done when absolutely necessary, provided the state does not act arbitrarily or undermine the procedural safeguards intentionally. To verify this, every state action is subject to judicial review by both national and supranational courts, including the ECtHR.

III. Conclusion

A Transnational Law Enforcement Regime presents an adequate legal framework to regulate transnational conflicts which fall below the threshold of armed conflicts. This approach foresees the deployment of state forces, police and military alike, to perform law enforcement operations against non-state groups under an IHRL framework.

Under a transnational law enforcement regime, states have authority to kill members of non-state groups, although not to the same extent as in armed conflicts. The necessity requirement always limits states' use of force to the extent necessary to avert the concrete and imminent threat that the non-state actors pose. With respect to collateral damages, an IHRL-based transnational law enforcement regime would be more restrictive than an IHL approach. The killing of innocent bystanders is not permissible under an IHRL framework. Although death and the wounding of civilians may still occur, a state cannot legally perform an attack where it anticipates the loss of civilian lives. Lastly, the IHRL framework allows for preventive detention only under certain circumstances, provided that strict procedural safeguards are respected. While under the ICCPR, a preventive detention for security reasons is possible, even without derogating from Art. 9 ICCPR. Under Art. 5 ECHR, preventive detention for security purposes is possible only after derogating from Art. 5 ECHR, whereby transnational conflicts are a valid reason for derogation. Detention cannot be and is not indefinite. The concrete duration, however, must be determined by the exigencies of the concrete situation. Even a prolonged detention of several days and weeks may be lawful if the state presents valid grounds and does not act arbitrarily. In conclusion, the application of a transnational law enforcement regime limits

---

[157] Sarah Jones, Jenny Schulz, Melissa Castan, *The International Covenant on Civil and Political Rights*, 347 (2004).

state powers more than an IHL regime, but still leaves the state with effective means.

E. Prospects on the Regulation of Transnational Conflicts

The existing IHRL provides a framework to govern transnational conflicts which fall below the threshold of NIACs. The question lies in whether an IHRL based law enforcement regime is sufficient to meet legitimate state security demands or whether the scope of application of the law of NIAC should be expanded.

I. Rejecting the Expansion of the Armed Conflict Approach

A state's way of fighting in transnational conflicts resembles its way of fighting in armed conflicts. In the U.S. – Al Qaeda conflict in particular, the U.S. resorts to military means and deploys armed forces, which operate in accordance with military rules of engagement.[1] The military nature of most of the state's responses in transnational conflicts leads some authors to conclude that the conflicts themselves can only be of an armed conflict kind.[2] Accordingly, it is demanded that the laws of armed conflict, IHL, should be applied, as no other law would fulfill the state's requirements to prevail in conflict.

The NIAC regime remains the only possible IHL regime that can be applied to transnational conflicts.[3] However, the limitations in applying NIAC laws include that some non-state armed groups do not qualify as parties to a NIAC. Additionally, some transnational conflicts do not meet the violence threshold necessary to characterize them as NIACs. Therefore, the laws of NIAC, as they stand, do not sufficiently cover all transnational conflicts. As a result, one may argue for an expansive understanding of NIACs. This would include the application of the

---

[1] Geoffrey Corn and Eric Talbot Jensen, *Transnational Armed Conflict: A "Principled" Approach to the Regulation of Counter-Terror Combat Operations*, 42 Israel Law Review 46, 65 (2009) ("[...] because the threshold of armed conflicts against transnational non-state enemies is crossed when armed forces operate pursuant to status based rules of engagement, these operations defy a law enforcement characterization").

[2] Geoffrey Corn and Eric Talbot Jensen, *Transnational Armed Conflict: A "Principled" Approach to the Regulation of Counter-Terror Combat Operations*, 42 Israel Law Review 46, 78 (2009) ("[...] the legal fiction that the use of military combat power to respond to such threats is in reality just extraterritorial law enforcement, fails to acknowledge the essential nature of such operations").

[3] Noam Lubell, *Extraterritorial Use of Force against Non-State Actors*, 133 (2010) ("In most cases, conflicts between a state and a non-state actor would be classified as non-international armed conflicts").

laws to all actors capable of massive violence, regardless of organization, and all conflicts, despite the sporadic nature of the violence, if the violence were performed by the same non-state group. The argument in favor of an even broader application of the laws of NIACs would be that it fills a legal gap.

Prior to IHRL, the laws of NIACs were the sole international legal source that provided protection for civilians during internal conflicts. The application of NIAC laws was advantageous to civilians as they imposed legal restraints on the state through international law in cases that were previously the state's own legal domain. However, as *Kretzmer* correctly states, with the existence of IHRL, the application of a NIAC regime no longer suggests an increase in legal protection.[4] Presently, states are bound by IHRL at all times. As a result, the application of the laws of NIACs no longer fills an *"international legal vacuum"*.[5] Instead, it may supersede the higher protections now granted through IHRL. The application of the laws of NIACs is cause for concern when motivated solely by the state's intention to obtain the right to kill and detain alleged terrorists, without the constraints of IAC or IHRL laws.[6]

If the laws of NIACs are applied to all transnational conflicts, one must be aware that the consequential *"liberty costs"* are immense and perhaps prohibitive.[7] The rules for the use of lethal force and detention are more permissive under an armed conflict paradigm than under a law enforcement paradigm.[8] Although it is widely accepted that IHRL is still generally applicable in armed

---

[4] David Kretzmer, *Rethinking the Application of IHL in Non-International Armed Conflicts*, 42 Israel Law Review 8, 18 (2009) ("To the extent that IHL is less protective of certain rights, such as the right to life, than the applicable human rights regime, its application as lex specialis narrows protection of these rights"); *See also* Marko Milanovic & Vidan Hadzi-Vidanovic, *A Taxonomy of Armed Conflict*, in Research Handbook of International Conflict and Security Law 256, 305 *et seq.* (Nigel White & Christian Henderson, eds. 2013).

[5] David Kretzmer, *Rethinking the Application of IHL in Non-International Armed Conflicts*, 42 Israel Law Review 8, 39 (2009).

[6] David Kretzmer, *Rethinking the Application of IHL in Non-International Armed Conflicts*, 42 Israel Law Review 8, 23 *et seq.* (2009).

[7] Monica Hakimi, *International Standards for Detaining Terrorism Suspects: Moving Beyond the Armed Conflict-Criminal Divide*, 33 Yale Journal of International Law 369, 395 (2008) ("[...] its [the armed-conflict model's] liberty costs are prohibitive: innocents easily could be detained, for extended periods if not for life, based only on a reasonable suspicion of threat and without judicial guarantees").

[8] Philip Alston, *Report of the Special Rapporteur on Extrajudicial, Summary or Arbitrary Executions*, ¶ 47, U.N. Doc. A/HRC/14/24/Add.6 (May 28, 2010) ("[...] the IHL applicable in armed conflict arguably has more permissive rules for killing than does human rights law or a State's domestic law, and generally provides immunity to State armed forces").

conflict,[9] the laws of NIACs, will be the *lex specialis*.[10] The ICJ elaborates on the *lex specialis* nature of IHL towards IHRL, in the context of the right to life:

---

[9] ICJ, *Legality of the Threat or Use of Nuclear Weapons*, Advisory Opinion, 1996 ICJ 226, ¶ 25 (July 8) ("The Court observes that the protection of the International Covenant of Civil and Political Rights does not cease in times of war, except by operation of Article 4 of the Covenant whereby certain provisions may be derogated from in a time of national emergency"); ICJ, *Legal Consequences of the Construction of a Wall in the Occupied Palestinian Territory*, Advisory Opinion, 2004 ICJ 136, ¶ 106-113 (July 9); ICJ, *Armed Activities on the Territory of the Congo* (Dem. Rep. Congo v. Uganda), ICJ GL No 116, ¶ 216 (Dec. 19, 2005);

European Commission on Human Rights, *Cyprus v. Turkey*, App. Nos. 6780/74 and 6950/75 (Preliminary Objections) (May 26, 1975) DR 2 (1975) 125, 136 (No. 8); ECtHR, *Isayeva, Yusupova and Bazayeva v Russian Federation*, App Nos. 57947/00, 57948/00 and 57949/00 (Admissibility, Merits and Just Satisfaction) (Feb. 24, 2005) ¶ 177;

Inter American Court of Human Rights, *Bamaca Velásquez v. Guatemala*, Judgement, Nov. 25, 2000, ¶ 207 ("The Court considers that it has been proved that, at the time of the facts of this case, an internal conflict was taking place in Guatemala (supra 121 b). As has previously been stated (supra 143 and 174), instead of exonerating the State from its obligations to respect and guarantee human rights, this fact obliged it to act in accordance with such obligations");

UN Human Rights Committee, General Comment 31, *Nature of the General Legal Obligation on States Parties to the Covenant*, U.N. Doc. CCPR/C/21/Rev.1/Add.13, ¶ 11 (May 26, 2004).; The Committee has further dealt with the question in its observations on States' Periodic Reports: United States, UN Doc. CCPR/C/USA/CO/3 (2006), ¶ 10; Democratic Republic of Congo, UN Doc. CCPR/C/COD/CO/3 (2006), ¶ 13; Israel, UN Doc. CCPR/CO/78/ISR (2003); Sri Lanka, UN Doc. CCPR/CO/79/LKA (2003); Colombia, UN Doc. CCPR/CO/80/COL (2004); S.C. Res. 237, U.N. Doc. S/RES/237 (June 14, 1967) ("Considering that the essential and inalienable human rights should be respected even during the vicissitudes of war [...]"); G.A. Res. 2675 (XXV), ¶ 1, U.N. Doc. A/RES/2675 (Dec. 9, 1970). Knut Ipsen, Eberhard Menzel and Volker Epping, *Völkerrecht*, 795 ¶ 55 (2004); Christopher Greenwood, *Scope of Application of Humanitarian Law*, in The Handbook of International Humanitarian Law, 74 (Dieter Fleck ed. 2008); Bernhard Schäfer, *Zum Verhältnis Menschenrechte und humanitäres Völkerrecht*, 17 (2006); David Zechmeister, *Die Erosion des humanitären Völkerrechts in den bewaffneten Konflikten der Gegenwart*, 123-4 (2007); David Kretzmer, *Rethinking the Application of IHL in Non-International Armed Conflicts*, 42 Israel Law Review 8, 14 *et seq.* (2009); Jann K. Kleffner, *Scope of Application of International Humanitarian Law, in* The Handbook of International Humanitarian Law, 72 (Dieter Fleck ed. 2013).

[10] ICJ, *Legality of the Threat or Use of Nuclear Weapons*, Advisory Opinion, 1996 ICJ 226, ¶ 25 (July 8); ICJ, *Legal Consequences of the Construction of a Wall in the Occupied Palestinian Territory*, Advisory Opinion, 2004 ICJ 136, ¶ 106 (July 9); Philip Alston, *The CIA and Targeted Killings Beyond Borders*, 2 Harvard National Security Journal 283, 301 (2011).

"The test of what is an arbitrary deprivation of life, however, then falls to be deter-mined by the applicable lex specialis, namely, the law applicable in armed conflict which is designed to regulate the conduct of hostilities."[11]

This concept, outlined by the ICJ, can be further demonstrated with the principle of proportionality, which applies to both IHL and IHRL. This principle differs when applied to IHL versus law enforcement.[12]

In IHL, the principle of proportionality requires weighing the intended military aim with the unintended side effects, which includes the loss of civilian life. In law enforcement, a balance must be obtained between a law enforcement aim (i.e. averting imminent threat) and avoiding unintended side effects. Both circumstances require a balance of two factors, of which one is the scale of the unintended side effects. The difference between the two regimes, however, lies in the second factor: the pursued aim against which the side effects must be weighed. In IHL, this may be any military aim, while in law enforcement the only permissible aim is averting an imminent threat.

In order to deem a military aim as legitimate, IHL *a priori* distinguishes between persons and objects based on whether they can be (combatants and military objects) or cannot be (civilians and civilian objects) attacked. Therefore, under IHL, it is permissible to target anyone who has been identified as an enemy combatant, without specific justification or further assessment of necessi-ty.[13] In law enforcement, the state is limited to defensive actions when averting a threat. In order to determine who qualifies as a target under a law enforcement regime, an assessment of whether the attacked person or object poses as a threat must be conducted. Therefore, the attack must be proportionate, even with respect to the targets, under a law enforcement paradigm.[14]

---

[11] ICJ, *Legality of the Threat or Use of Nuclear Weapons*, Advisory Opinion, 1996 ICJ 226, ¶ 75 (July 8).

[12] David Kretzmer, *Rethinking the Application of IHL in Non-International Armed Conflicts*, 42 Israel Law Review 8, 26 (2009); Noam Lubell, *Extraterritorial Use of Force against Non-State Actors*, 238-9 (2010).

[13] *Contra* International Committee of the Red Cross, *Interpretive Guidance on the No-tion of Direct Participation in Hostilities under International Humanitarian Law*, 77 et seq. (2009); Philip Alston, *The CIA and Targeted Killings beyond Borders*, 2 Harvard National Security Journal 283, 303 (2011); Sandesh Sivakumaran, *The Law of Non-International Armed Conflict*, 251 (2012).

[14] Noam Lubell, *Extraterritorial Use of Force against Non-State Actors*, 238-9 (2010) ("Other differences include the notion of proportionality, which under IHL is used prima-rily with reference to the 'side-effects' and collateral damage, ie the effect upon people and objects other than the target, whereas in law enforcement, in addition to the effect on others, proportionality also refers to the effect of the force on the targeted individual").

An additional effect of the application of IHL as *lex specialis* is the acceptance of civilian casualties as collateral damage. The authority of states to sacrifice civilians to achieve a military objective is unique to IHL. As previously discussed, the *ex-ante* acceptance of civilian casualties, during a peacetime law enforcement operation, is not permissible. Finally, only under an IHRL paradigm do civilians have access to judicial fora such as the ECtHR[15] or the IACtHR,[16] which enables them to have a supranational judicial review over state actions.[17] *Alston* therefore concludes that while

"international mechanisms for exacting compliance with IHL norms are both under-developed and under-utilized, [...] those relating to IHRL are beginning to have some bite".[18]

In conclusion, although state action must be proportionate under both IHL and IHRL, the state has significantly more authority to interfere with individuals' lives and freedom under the IHL paradigm.[19] While the ICRC has recently introduced a least harmful means requirement for operations within IHL as well,[20] this is not applicable international *lege lata*.[21] The IHL approach is harsher.

---

[15] *See* Art. 34 ECHR: "The Court may receive applications from any person, non-governmental organisation or group of individuals claiming to be the victim of a violation by one of the High Contracting Parties of the rights set forth in the Convention or the protocols thereto. The High Contracting Parties undertake not to hinder in any way the effective exercise of this right."

[16] *See* Art. 44 IACtHR: "Any person or group of persons, or any nongovernmental entity legally recognized in one or more member states of the Organization, may lodge petitions with the Commission containing denunciations or complaints of violation of this Convention by a State Party."

[17] Adam Roberts, *Transformative Military Occupation: Applying the Laws of War and Human Rights*, 100 American Journal of International Law 580, 620 (2006) ("[...] individuals can press cases in certain regional courts (specifically, the European Court of Human Rights and the Inter-American Court of Human Rights) in ways that the laws of war do not offer"); Yoram Dinstein, *The Conduct of Hostilities under the Law of International Armed Conflict*, 25 (2004); René Provost, *International Human Rights and Humanitarian Law*, 45 (2004).

[18] Philip Alston, *The CIA and Targeted Killings Beyond Borders*, 2 Harvard National Security Journal 283, 305 (2011).

[19] For a further analysis of the differences in the principles necessity and proportionality in IHL and IHRL *see* Noelle Quénivet, *The Right to Life in International Humanitarian Law and Human Rights Law*, in International Humanitarian Law and Human Rights Law 331, 340 *et seq.* (Roberta Arnold and Noelle Quenivet, eds. 2008).

[20] International Committee of the Red Cross, *Interpretive Guidance on the Notion of Direct Participation in Hostilities under International Humanitarian Law* (2009) ("In addition to the restraints imposed by international humanitarian law on specifc means and methods of warfare, [...] the kind and degree of force which is permissible against per-

In the context of transnational conflicts where the non-state group is loosely organized and the violence occurs sporadically, the application of IHL is excessive. It is likely to cause more damage than it prevents, particularly in instances of the radicalization of once-innocent civilians, who become victims of state violence or suffer from unjustified use of force by the state.[22] An IHRL-based transnational law enforcement regime is capable of striking the balance between the protection of innocents and a state's security demands in situations of transnational conflicts below the existing threshold of armed conflict.

II. The Right to Self-Defense as a Regulating Regime

An approach that characterizes transnational conflicts based on a state's right to self-defense will be addressed in this section.

Some scholars have argued for a robust self-defense regime that exists between IHRL and IHL.[23] They claim that conflicts that take place outside state borders and do not cross the threshold of armed conflict are neither regulated by

---

sons not entitled to protection against direct attack must not exceed what is actually necessary to accomplish a legitimate military purpose in the prevailing circumstances").

[21] Jann K. Kleffner, *Section IX of the ICRC Interpretive Guidance on Direct Participation in Hostilities: The end of Jus in Bello Proportionality as We know it?* 45 Israel Law Review 35 -52 (2012).

[22] *See* Dale Stephens, *Military Involvement in Law Enforcement*, 92 International Review of the Red Cross 453, 465 (2010) ("In short, an approach modeled on law enforcement, in terms of calibrated application and anticipated effect, is likely to be strategically more productive than relying upon traditional rights (and methodologies) under the law of armed conflict").

[23] Michael N. Schmitt, *Targeted Killings in International Law: Law Enforcement, Self-defense, and Armed Conflict*, in International Humanitarian Law and Human Rights Law 525, 528 (Roberta Arnold and Noelle Quénivet eds. 2008); Kenneth Anderson, *Targeted Killing in US Counterterrorism Strategy and Law*, (2009), online available at http://www.brookings.edu/~/media/Files/rc/papers/2009/0511_counterterrorism_anderson/0511_counterterrorism_anderson.pdf (last visited Jan. 27, 2011); Kenneth Anderson, *Predators over Pakistan*, The Weekly Standard, March 8, 2010; Jorden J. Paust, *Self-Defense Targetings of Non-State Actors and Permissibility of U.S. Use of Drones in Pakistan*, 19 Journal of Transnational Law and Policy 237, 279-80 (2010) online available at http://papers.ssrn.com/sol3/papers.cfm?abstract_id=1520717 (last visited Jan. 27, 2011); W. Hays Parks, Memorandum of Law: Executive Order 12333 and Assassination, 1989 Army Lawyer 4, 7-8 (1989).
Very critical Philip Alston, Report of the Special Rapporteur on Extrajudicial, Summary or Arbitrary Executions, ¶ 42, U.N. Doc. A/HRC/14/24/Add.6 (May 28, 2010).

law enforcement rules nor by IHL. Instead, the state can rely solely on its right to self-defense.

Koh, the former U.S. Legal Adviser to the Department of State, has endorsed the approach of relying on the right to self-defense,[24] based on the criteria of necessity, proportionality and perhaps immediacy, to determine if an attack against an alleged terrorist is lawful.[25] This approach relies on the criteria of necessity and proportionality, which are considered equivalent in *jus ad bellum* and in *jus in bello*.[26] One can, however, assume that proponents intend to apply a more lenient version of these criteria by expanding the state's authority to take coercive measures. The approach is also applied in the U.S. Policy Standard and Procedures for the Use of Force in Counterterrorism Operations Outside the United States and Areas of Active Hostilities, which speaks of individuals who are *"targetable in the exercise of national self-defense"*.[27] This approach is inherently flawed as it conflates *jus ad bellum* and *jus in bello*.[28] It reflects a misunderstanding of the concept of self-defense, intended primarily to serve as an exception to the general prohibition of the use of force explained in Art. 2.4

---

[24] Harold Koh, Legal Advisor of the Department of State, Keynote Address at the Annual Meeting of the ASIL: *The Obama Administration and International Law* (Mar. 25, 2010).

[25] Michael N. Schmitt, *Targeted Killings in International Law: Law Enforcement, Self-defense, and Armed Conflict*, in International Humanitarian Law and Human Rights Law 525, 534 (Roberta Arnold and Noelle Quénivet eds. 2008).

[26] *See e.g.*, Michael N. Schmitt, *Targeted Killings in International Law: Law Enforcement, Self-defense, and Armed Conflict*, in International Humanitarian Law and Human Rights Law 525, 529 (Roberta Arnold and Noelle Quénivet eds. 2008); *contra* Raphaël van Steenberghe, *Proportionality under Jus ad Beluum and Jus in Bello: Claryfying their Relationship*, 45 Israel Law Review 107, 112 (2012) ("Although they share basic common features, proportionality under jus ad bellum and proportionality under jus in bello remain two independent notions, this independent nature ultimately deriving from their different rationales").

[27] Presidential Policy Guidance, *U.S. Policy Standards and Procedures for the Use of Force in Counterterrorism Operations Outside the United States and Areas of Active Hostilities*, May 22, 2013, online available at http://www.whitehouse.gov/sites/default/files/uploads/2013.05.23_fact_sheet_on_ppg.pdf (last visited on May 24, 2013).

[28] Philip Alston, *Report of the Special Rapporteur on Extrajudicial, Summary or Arbitrary Executions*, ¶ 42-44, U.N. Doc. A/HRC/14/24/Add.6 (May 28, 2010); *cf.* Marko Milanovic, *Drones and Targeted Killings: Can Self-Defense Preclude their Wrongfulness?* (2010) http://www.ejiltalk.org/drones-and-targeted-killings-can-self-defense-preclude-their-wrongfulness/; Marko Milanovic, *More on Drones, Self-Defense, and the Alston Report on Targeted Killings* (2010) and http://www.ejiltalk.org/more-on-drones-self-defense-and-the-alston-report-on-targeted-killings/.

UN Charter Therefore, it is relevant only *if* a state can use force, but does not provide legal guidelines for *how* the particular use of force may be conducted.

The criteria of proportionality, necessity and immediacy serve to determine whether the violation of another state's sovereignty can be justified as an act of self-defense. The justification of the violation of another state's territory by the right to self-defense may be possible. However, the legality of *how* to use force is not a question of *jus ad bellum,* but depends on IHL, in the event of armed conflict, and on IHRL, in all other situations.

In transnational conflicts, the rights in question are not another state's sovereignty, but rather, the affected person's individual rights under IHRL or IHL. Inevitably, a legal gap would arise if the situation does not amount to an armed conflict and the application of IHRL is denied due to the extraterritorial character of the situation. However, this gap cannot be closed by referring to the *jus ad bellum* concept of self-defense. Instead, the presence of the gap itself clearly demonstrates that IHRL must be applied extraterritorially. In conclusion, the application of a legal regime based on a state's right to self-defense must be refuted. The existing legal regimes of IHL and IHRL provide for sufficient regulation of transnational conflicts where the challenge lies in determining the scope of their application.

III. Introducing an Integrated Approach

Although an expansion of the laws of NIACs should be rejected, a transnational law enforcement approach has its limits. A non-state group may reorganize and the conflict may increase in intensity at any given point in time. Subsequently, the conflict may cross the threshold of an armed conflict, which shifts the applicable legal framework to the IHL regime.

The regulation of transnational conflicts is not the sole issue of either IHL or transnational law enforcement, but of both. States should seek an integrated approach that allows them to apply, with necessary flexibility, transnational law enforcement rules whenever the conflict falls below the level of an armed conflict and NIAC rules whenever the conflict reaches the armed conflict threshold. States should apply different legal frameworks to the same conflict, depending on its current stage.

An integrated approach of IHL and IHRL should not appear as a theoretical concept as it reflects the legal reality. Conflicts are not static, but rather change in nature, calling for the application of IHL as well as law enforcement. The challenge lies in finding and establishing legal mechanisms that allow for the integration of IHL and law enforcement to function more effectively. The following section focuses on a case where an integrated IHL and IHRL approach has been taken: the case of Colombia.[29]

1. The Colombian Approach

Colombia encounters various forms of internal violence from a variety of non-state actors. The violence ranges from guerilla groups, such as the FARC or EPL (*Ejército Popular de Liberación*), to state-sponsored paramilitaries, to criminal bands and drug cartels. While the conflict between the Colombian authorities and the guerilla groups, particularly the FARC, must qualify as a NIAC,[30] the fight against the criminal band and drug cartels cannot qualify similarly.

From a legal perspective, the varying conflicts in Colombia have distinctive corresponding applicable legal frameworks. The laws of NIAC govern conflicts with guerilla groups that cross the NIAC threshold. Other conflicts are regulated exclusively by national rules of law enforcement and IHRL.[31]

Colombia has reacted to its multifaceted internal situation by issuing a manual for its armed forces that distinguishes between two different operational frameworks: operations during hostile scenarios and operations to maintain security.[32] Although military forces are deployed in both cases, the rules they are required to abide by differ.[33] In operations during hostile scenarios, the concrete case exceeds a specified threshold of violence. Armed forces are subsequently

---

[29] *See* Constantin von der Groeben, *The Conflict in Colombia and the Relationship between Humanitarian Law and Human Rights Law in Practice*, 16 Journal of Conflict and Security Law 141 (2011).

[30] Jan Römer, *Killing in a Gray Area between Humanitarian Law and Human Rights Law*, 26 (2010); Constantin von der Groeben, *The Conflict in Colombia and the Relationship between Humanitarian Law and Human Rights Law in Practice*, 16 Journal of Conflict and Security Law 141, 145-7 (2011).

[31] It has to be noted that despite the fact that it applies IHL Colombia rejects the view that it is involved in a NIAC, because it fears that admitting to be involved in a NIAC implies a lack of control over its own territory and puts its full sovereignty into question. *See* Constantin von der Groeben, *The Conflict in Colombia and the Relationship between Humanitarian Law and Human Rights Law in Practice*, 16 Journal of Conflict and Security Law 141, 148-9 (2011); *cf.* Andreas Paulus and Mindia Vashakmadze, *Asymmetrical War and the Notion of Armed Conflict – A Tentative Conceptualization*, 91 International Review of the Red Cross 95, 103 (2009).

[32] Comando General Fuerzas Militares, *Manual de Derecho Operacional*, 94 *et seq.* (2009).

[33] For an analysis how the Colombian National Police deals with the legal uncertainties *see* Jan Römer, *Killing in a Gray Area between Humanitarian Law and Human Rights Law* (2010).

deployed under the so-called *red-card-rules,* which allow them to execute full force authorized under IHL.[34] Simultaneously, operations that maintain security are regulated by a set of law enforcement rules referred to as *blue-card-rules.*[35] Colombia foresees a role for its military, even in mere law enforcement operations. In other words, one state agent, the military, must address various situations and apply different corresponding operational rules.

Colombia has established a legal framework that allows for the parallel application of IHL and IHRL, as well as a gradual application of IHL, when the internal situation transitions from an operation to maintain security (law enforcement) into a hostile scenario (armed conflict). Three elements in the Colombian legal framework are highlighted to demonstrate the mode of operation of the combined approach of IHL and law enforcement. This includes, (1) how to determine which set of rules must be applied, (2) how to oversee that the military abides by the rules, and (3) how to perform post operational investigations.

Colombia has introduced a *Grupo Asesor* (advisory board) in light of the first element. This advisory board is comprised of members of the police force, the military forces and intelligence agencies.[36] The *Grupo Asesor* determines whether the military should act under red-card or blue-card rules based on the level of hostilities, and the structure and degree of organization of the non-state group. The assessment is not made with respect to a specific situation on the ground, but rather in reference to a certain group. The *Grupo Asesor* also provides an annual or semi-annual evaluation of the conflict between Colombia and a non-state armed group to determine the applicable law.[37] For Colombia, this subsequently implies that the *Grupo Asesor* determines that a well-organized guerilla group, with a clear structure of command like the FARC, that is engaged in protracted violence against the state's forces, should be fought under a red-card rules framework. Simultaneously, the *Grupo Asesor* determines that other criminal bands (so called *bandas criminals* or *BACRIM*) lacking these features may be fought under a blue-card rules framework. The *Grupo Asesor de facto*

---

[34] Constantin von der Groeben, *The Conflict in Colombia and the Relationship between Humanitarian Law and Human Rights Law in Practice,* 16 Journal of Conflict and Security Law 141, 151 *et seq.* (2011).

[35] Constantin von der Groeben, *The Conflict in Colombia and the Relationship between Humanitarian Law and Human Rights Law in Practice,* 16 Journal of Conflict and Security Law 141,154 (2011).

[36] Comando General Fuerzas Militares, *Manual de Derecho Operacional,* 96 *et seq.* (2009).

[37] At the time of writing the efficiency of the Grupo Asesor is questionable for no records of their meetings can be found.

determines whether a conflict between the Colombian authorities and a certain non-state actor qualifies as a NIAC or not.

Once the *Grupo Asesor* makes the decision concerning the applicable legal framework, legal advisors, called AJOs (*Asesor Jurídico Operacional*), supervise military compliance with this legal framework.[38] They serve to accompany the armed forces and are consulted prior to any military operation. AJOs serve as any other legal advisor to armed forces, however, they uniquely also determine whether red-card or blue-card rules are applicable given the concrete case. AJOs rely on the *Grupo Asesor's* general qualification of the conflict. However, they are authorized to qualify a concrete situation on the ground as a blue-card situation, even if the *Grupo Asesor* has generally qualified the conflict with the respective non-state actor as a red-card conflict. This way the abstract determination of the *Grupo Asesor* is adapted to the concrete situation on the ground. This ability of the AJO guarantees that only the minimum force required is actually used.

Finally, every operation by the military is subject to an investigation performed by the Office of the Prosecutor General, i.e. the ordinary justice system and not the military criminal jurisdiction. Technical investigation units (CTIs) have been created to investigate operations in combat zones from all sides.[39] Hence, they investigate possible human rights violations committed by the armed forces, as well as criminal acts performed by the non-state actors. The CTI's main tasks include the collection of evidence, which can later be used against the non-state actors when charged under criminal law. The ultimate purpose is to bring the non-state actors to justice by putting them before the court and charging them with violations of criminal law, rather than placing an arrest as Prisoners of War.

The interplay between the *Grupo Asesor*, the AJOs and the Office of the Prosecutor General, is the basis for the integrated approach of IHL and IHRL as foreseen in the new Colombian military operational law. Presently, it is difficult to assess the effectiveness of the Colombian model and determine whether the institutions work efficiently given its very recent introduction. However, it demonstrates what institutions and mechanisms are required to foster in terms of the integration of IHL and law enforcement in the face of transnational conflicts.

---

[38] Comando General Fuerzas Militares, *Manual de Derecho Operacional*, 141 (2009).

[39] Ministry of National Defence, *Comprehensive Human Rights and IHL Policy*, ¶ 167 (2007) ("In June 2006 the Ministry of Defence and the Prosecutor General's Office signed a document supporting Military Criminal Justice, in which it was specified that CTI officials should carry out inspections in locations where combat deaths had occurred during the conduct of military operations").

On a final note, the Colombian approach is limited in that it applies its rules only to conflict situations that take place inside Colombia. Colombia rejects the extra-territorial application of IHRL, thus Colombian armed forces acting outside Colombia are only bound by IHL.

In its armed incursion into Ecuador to fight FARC members,[40] Colombia based its operation solely on IHL. The hybrid approach that encompasses the blue-card rules is applied only to internal Colombian situations. The Colombian approach does not provide answers to the problems that arise from the transnational character of transnational conflicts. As a result, the Colombian approach does not provide an answer with respect to *jus ad bellum* questions when fighting non-state actors abroad. Questions pertaining to the legitimacy of extra-territorial law enforcement are particularly not dealt with. Nevertheless, on the whole, the Colombian approach serves to provide practical guidance on how to apply an integrated approach of IHL and IHRL to regulate transnational conflicts. It demonstrates that a further integration of IHL and IHRL is possible and feasible.

2. The Application of an Integrated Approach

The present section proposes suggestions on how an integrated approach can be applied in practice and how the applicability of IHL or IHRL is determined.

At the outset, it is imperative to emphasize the ICTR's dictum that

"whether or not a situation can be described as an 'armed conflict', meeting the criteria of Common Article 3, is to be decided upon a case-by-case basis".[41]

For this purpose, no independent authority exists and, in most cases, the involved state controls the flow of facts necessary to make the required determination of the situation, particularly concerning the organization of the non-state group. Therefore, although Sassòli correctly noted, *"[...] legal classifications depend upon the facts themselves and not upon the views on the facts of those subject to the law".*[42] It is often inevitable that *"the question whether an armed*

---

[40] *See* Simon Romero, *Files Suggest Venezuela Bid to Aid Colombia Rebels*, N.Y. Times, March 30, 2008 (the incident led to the killing of top FARC commander Raul Reyes).

[41] ICTR, *The Prosecutor vs. Rutaganda*, Case No. ICTR-96-3-T, Judgment and Sentence, ¶ 93 (Dec. 6, 1999).

[42] Marco Sassòli, *Transnational Armed Groups and International Humanitarian Law*, Occasional Paper Series, Program on Humanitarian Policy and Conflict Research, 7 (Harvard University Winter 2006) online available at http://www.hpcrresearch.org/pdfs/OccasionalPaper6.pdf.

conflict exists or not will be left to the State".[43] Even if with the International Criminal Tribunals and the ICC, the states' discretion was and will occasionally be reviewed by a Court, this is only an ex-post review. The following section addresses the analytical steps required to legally qualify a transnational conflict to allow for the verification of a state's qualification of a conflict.

a) Identifying the Conflict Parties

Identifying conflict parties is absolutely essential prior to legally qualifying a conflict. By doing so, all political rhetoric, such as *War on Terrorism* or *War on Drugs,* can be excluded from further legal examination. Clearly, a conflict cannot occur between an international entity and a phenomenon, such as terrorism. As a result, it is imperative to identify the concrete parties involved. Furthermore, conflicts, such as the Israel-Palestine conflict, may consist of several other sub-conflicts between multiple actors. On the Palestinian side, several non-state groups are involved, including Fatah, the Al-Aqsa-Brigades, Hamas, Islamic Jihad and PFLP.[44] It would be inaccurate to state that all Palestinian non-state groups form one conflict party in one conflict against Israel, as each of these non-state groups operates independently and follows its own political agenda. This is particularly important as some non-state groups, such as Hamas can be viewed as *de facto* regimes in Gaza. This would ultimately transform the conflict into an IAC. Similarly, it is necessary to avoid including sympathizers of Al Qaeda in conflict between the U.S. and Al Qaeda. Only a person or a group of persons within the organizational structure of Al Qaeda can be regarded as part of Al Qaeda's conflict. Although they may share a similar ideology, organizations other than Al Qaeda that separately fight against the U.S. must be assessed differently within the legal context.

b) Identifying Clear Cases

Whether a conflict between two parties qualifies as an IAC must be addressed as a next step and is conducted by analyzing the party structure of the conflict. If two states or a state and a *de-facto* regime are facing each other, then an IAC exists. The same holds true if the activities of a non-state group are attributed to a state. Lastly, a situation amounts to an IAC if the state party recognizes the non-state group as belligerent.

---

[43] Lindsay Moir, *The Law of Internal Armed Conflict*, 45 (2002).

[44] For an overview over the conflict parties *see* Friederike Bredt, *Anwendbarkeit der humanitären Völkerrechts im Israel-Palästina-Konflikt*, 192 *et seq.* (2009).

If the possibility that the conflict qualifies as an IAC has been excluded, whether the situation can then be identified as either NIAC or non-NIAC must be examined. This is more difficult than identifying an IAC, as the threshold of violence becomes an additional factor to be considered. However, no in-depth analysis should be performed. Instead, only situations that clearly qualify as NIACs should be singled out. Such clear situations exist when a non-state group has gained territorial control over parts of the country and established adminis-trative function. Additionally, the intensity and duration of the hostilities must have risen to the extent that both sides protractedly use military means. Lastly, the numbers of casualties must have increased beyond that which is justifiable during a law-enforcement situation. The conflict between Israel and Hezbollah in the summer of 2006 serves as an example of a conflict that can be clearly identified as a NIAC. On the contrary, when a single person acts, such as during the massacre in a youth camp in Norway in 2011,[45] or when the violence is of the level of a riot, as in the U.K. in 2011,[46] the situation can be characterized as below the threshold of a NIAC.

c) Assessing the Controversial Cases

Once it is clear that a conflict cannot be easily characterized as an IAC or NI-AC, the third, and most challenging, step follows. Here, the integrated approach of IHL and IHRL becomes relevant as it aids in establishing mechanisms, as opposed to determining the nature of a conflict, to enable states to legally char-acterize conflicts at any given time. One must first determine where exactly the problem in characterizing the conflict lies. The party structure or violence threshold itself may not permit a clear characterization to occur. With respect to Al Qaeda, it is the party structure that makes it difficult to qualify the conflict. The question lies in how Al Qaeda is truly structured and whether it can qualify as a party to a NIAC. In order to make a credible assessment, it may be wise to establish an authority that resembles the *Group Asesor* in Colombia. The respon-sibility of this advisory board could be that of a national security council, or it could operate at the multinational level e.g. within the European Union, or even a global level within the UN System. The latter would be the most appropriate approach.

---

[45] *Norway massacre: Anders Behring Breivik 'acted alone'*, BBC News, July 21, 2011, http://www.bbc.co.uk/news/world-europe-14266815 (last visited Mar. 9, 2012).

[46] *UK riots: Trouble erupts in English cities*, BBC News, Aug. 10, 2011, online available at http://www.bbc.co.uk/news/uk-england-london-14460554 (last visited Mar. 9, 2012).

The responsibility for determining the correct legal framework for a transnational conflict should be placed in the hands of a supranational body such as the UN. One could rely on the already existing terrorism committees, such as the Counter-Terrorism Committee or the 1566 Working Group, or establish yet another committee through a UN Security Council Resolution.[47] This committee would assess whether a non-state group sufficiently encompasses an internal organizational structure for it to qualify as a party to a NIAC. An annual report would then be published on every relevant non-state group. The assessment of the committee would require access to classified information that cannot be published. However, a mechanism for persons to challenge the assessment in court must be established and regular judicial review should be performed. Here, lessons can be learned from the listing and delisting of alleged terrorists.[48] The establishment of an advisory board such as the *Grupo Asesor* would be a feasible long-term strategy, particularly with respect to non-state groups that have already been identified as posing a threat, such as Al Qaeda, PKK or FARC.

Due to the often difficult, abstract evaluation of a conflict and its changing nature, state actions must be accompanied by legal supervision. This requires a legal advisor with the authority to restrict the state agents' actions. Today, most modern armed forces already have legal advisors and they are also foreseen in Art. 82 AP I. Hence, the necessary environment should already exist. Strong involvement by the legal branch with public prosecutors and judges is required, particularly where the operation takes place within a law enforcement framework. Finally, legal supervision should be flanked by sufficient post-operational investigation and clarification. States should deploy technical investigation units that are not aligned with the acting agent on the ground, but with the Prosecutor General's office in order to collect evidence and investigate operations performed.

The case of Colonel Klein demonstrates that in extreme cases such investigations are already performed by the involved state.[49] This is not only required to

---

[47] For suggestions to adapt the UN-System's counter-terrorism mechanisms *see* Eric Rosand, *Den Terrorismus weltweit bekämpfen*, 57 Vereinte Nationen 99-103 (2009).

[48] *See* Ian Johnstone, *The UN Security Council, Counterterrorism and Human Rights*, in Counterterrorism: Democracy's Challenge 335, 340 *et seq.* (Andrea Bianchi & Alexis Keller, eds. 2008); International Commission of Jurists, *Assessing Damage, Urging Action: Report of the Eminent Jurist Panel on Terrorism, Counter-terrorism and Human Human Rights*, 113 *et seq.* (2009) online available at http://ejp.icj.org/IMG/EJP-Report.pdf (last visited Mar. 9, 2012); Dominik Schulte, *Der Schutz individueller Rechte gegen Terrorlisten*, 2010.

[49] Einstellungsvermerk des Generalbundesanwalts [Memorandum of the Federal Prosecutor General], 3 BJs 6/10-4 (Apr. 16, 2010), online available at

review the lawfulness of the state's action, but also enables the state to ultimately charge the non-state actors with criminal offenses. In conclusion, with an advisory board, legal advisors in the field, and sufficient post operational investigations, the lawfulness of state action is verified, before, during and after any operation, as is done in the Colombian model by *the Grupo Asesor*, the AJOs and the Office of the Prosecutor General.

d) Applying a Disprovable Assumption

The suggested treatment of controversial cases poses a problem in situations of emergency. On 9/11, for instance, it was not clear from the beginning that Al Qaeda was performing a terrorist attack. Additionally, at that time, it was highly questionable if Al Qaeda would qualify as a party to a NIAC. Nevertheless, their attack caused damage that clearly reached and surpassed the threshold of an armed conflict. The U.S. was therefore in a situation of emergency with no available means to determine the situation. Hence, it would have been impossible for the US to determine whether the immediate response would be governed by an IHL or IHRL regime. In such instances, when a threat occurs and it is unclear who is responsible, or whether the person or group responsible qualifies as a party to a NIAC, a *disprovable assumption* should be applied. This allows states to assume that whenever the violence reaches the threshold of an armed conflict, the responsible non-state group is sufficiently organized to be party to a NIAC. Without further insights into a non-state group, it seems adequate to conclude from a group's capability to cause massive violence that they have sufficient organizational structure.

Past evidence in international terrorism has demonstrated that perpetrators are often very well organized.[50] If Al Qaeda succeeds in performing another violent terror attack, it will be fair to assume that they have regained sufficient organization to once again be considered a party to a NIAC. The state would thus be allowed to treat the conflict as a NIAC and resort to IHL means, although it has not fully verified that Al Qaeda qualifies as a party to a NIAC. This would serve as guidance for state authorities during situations in which a conflict assessment of an advisory board is not available. Once the threat is averted, the assumption must be verified, with subsequent consequences for the treatment of captured

---

www.generalbundesanwalt.de/docs/einstellungsvermerk20100416offen.pdf (last visited Mar. 7, 2012); Constantin von der Groeben, *Criminal Responsibility of German Soldiers in Afghanistan: The Case of Colonel Klein*, 11 German Law Journal No 5, 469-492 (2010).

[50] Heiko F. Schmitz-Elvenich, *Targeted Killing*, 195-6 (2008).

perpetrators. The assumption would be disproved in cases of rampages such as in Colombine,[51] at a German secondary school in Winnenden,[52] or in Norway,[53] where many deaths were caused but perpetrators had no membership to any organization.

The application of a disprovable assumption in situations of emergency leads to the next question of how to determine whether the necessary threshold of violence has been met. As the analysis has shown, a clear-cut threshold is difficult to establish, as every conflict is distinct. Additionally, the threshold of violence was meant to require an overall assessment of factors, including intensity and duration of fighting. The previously mentioned list of factors, applied by the ICTY, is long and contains various elements.[54] For the sake of legal security, during a case of emergency, it is necessary to establish a clearer threshold, which can be assessed within the short amount of time available during a situation of emergency. The two decisive factors suggested here are the use of military means and the expected number of casualties. Therefore, when a threat requires the state to respond with military force and is expected to cause the loss of human lives, it should allow for the assumption that the perpetrator is sufficiently organized to qualify as a party to a NIAC. This evaluation can easily and quickly be made by authorities, thus allowing them to react in a timely and appropriate manner.

---

[51] Gina Lamb, *Columbine High School*, N.Y. Times, Apr. 17, 2008, http://topics.nytimes.com/top/reference/timestopics/organizations/c/columbine_high_school/index.html (last visited May 26, 2012).

[52] *Germany Shocked by Teenager's Killing Spree*, Der Spiegel, Mar. 11, 2009, http://www.spiegel.de/international/germany/0,1518,612612,00.html (last visited May 26, 2012).

[53] *Norway massacre: Anders Behring Breivik 'acted alone'*, BBC News, July 21, 2011, http://www.bbc.co.uk/news/world-europe-14266815 (last visited March 9, 2012); Diana Magnay, *Norwegians value respecting killer's human rights*, CNN, Apr. 17, 2012, http://edition.cnn.com/2012/04/17/world/europe/norway-breivik-court-magnay/ (last visited May 26, 2012).

[54] ICTY, *Prosecutor v. Boskoski et al.*, Case No. IT-04-82-T, Trial Judgement, ¶ 177 (July 10, 2008) (footnotes omitted).

F. Conclusion

It has been shown that there is still room for IHL to regulate transnational conflicts. The current IHL framework is sufficient to do so and the creation of a new category of transnational armed conflicts is not necessary. Instead, the legal regime governing NIACs can be applied. The NIAC regime must be broadly understood as a substitute regime covering all armed conflicts that do not occur between states, whether they are purely internal or transnational.

Even with a transnational understanding of NIACs, the laws of NIACs cannot cover all transnational conflicts. Some conflicts do not have the intensity to reach the threshold of armed conflicts, while in others, the non-state armed groups lack an organizational structure and cannot be regarded as parties to a NIAC. *De lege lata* a number of transnational conflicts, particularly the conflict between the U.S. and Al Qaeda, are not covered by the NIAC regime. Instead, IHRL is applicable to these conflicts. State's actions during these conflicts must be legally qualified as law enforcement, even if performed transnationally.

The IHRL-based law enforcement regime presents an adequate legal framework to regulate transnational conflicts, which falls below the threshold of armed conflicts. The main differences between the two possible legal frameworks pertain to the states' authority to kill and detain non-state actors and to accept collateral damage. Under IHL, the permission to kill depends on an individual's particular status as a member of the non-state group, which is party to the NIAC. Under an IHRL-based law enforcement regime, the use of lethal force is permitted as a rare exception to avert a concrete threat to another person's life. Regarding the regulation of detention, IHL during NIAC does not provide for a comprehensive regulation and many questions, particularly in regards to the duration and applicable procedural rules, remain unclear. IHRL, on the other hand, provides for a more elaborated legal regime with effective judicial review mechanisms in place. The biggest difference exists with respect to collateral damages, which can be legally accepted *ex ante* under an IHL framework. However, under an IHRL based regime, an *ex ante* acceptance of the death of civilians is precluded.

The suggested expansion of the application of the laws of NIACs and the broadening of the understanding of armed conflicts was also addressed. Stronger arguments speak against the further expansion of the laws of NIACs. These arguments include, most importantly, the concern that a further expansion of the concept of NIAC would unduly reduce the protection of innocent civilians. It is imperative to understand that IHL is a regime designed to grant a conflict party the means to annihilate its opponent, whereas an IHRL governed law enforcement regime aims at averting threats to society by bringing down those who pose a threat to justice. Transnational conflicts with non-state groups, such as terrorist organizations, are not wars to be won against an enemy, but rather a challenge to the rule of law. The rule of law is not to win or lose, but rather to endure.[1] It has often been said that freedom must be weighed against security, in the context of the fight against terrorism.[2] In reality, however, it is the weighing of freedom against freedom: the freedom of those who become victims of a terrorist attack and the freedom of those who suffer from the state's preventive measures. A law enforcement regime takes into account both rival freedoms and should be applied as long as possible in order to grant the greatest possible amount of freedom to all. Therefore, an attempt to apply the right to self-defense as a regulatory regime was also refuted. Any approach in this direction is inconsistent with the accepted and necessary differentiation between *jus ad bellum* and *jus in bello*. Instead, an integrated IHL and a law enforcement approach can be applied in practice, with the recent Colombian approach serving as a strong example.

In conclusion, international law provides substantive regulation for transnational conflicts. However, there is not one legal regime that addresses all transnational conflicts. Instead, each conflict must be legally assessed individually, based on the conflict parties and the intensity of violence. The legal analysis to identify and qualify each conflict adequately may be tedious, however, it is the inevitable prerequisite for a state to act lawfully.

---

[1] Helmut Schmidt, *Ich bin in Schuld verstrickt*, Interview in Die Zeit Nr. 36 (Aug.30, 2007) ("Der Rechtsstaat hat nicht zu siegen, er hat auch nicht zu verlieren, sondern er hat zu existieren").

[2] *See* Mathias Bug et al., *Strategien gegen die Unsicherheit. Europäische Sicherheitsmaßnahmen nach 9/11*, 86 Friedenswarte 53, 66 *et seq.* (2011) ("Schließlich ist durch die Einführung und Umsetzung neuer Sicherheitsmaßnahmen stets das sensible Gleichgewicht von Sicherheit und Freiheit berührt – ein Gleichgewicht das es auch im Angesicht neuer Bedrohungen immer wieder sorgsam auszutarieren gilt").

Summary of the Main Findings

An approach that applies the laws of IACs to all transnational conflicts is unconvincing as it disregards the symmetry requirement of IACs. An IAC can only exist where the non-state group is recognized as belligerent or when its actions are attributable to a state.

The laws of NIACs can generally be applied to transnational conflicts, as these laws are not confined to internal conflicts.

The laws of NIACs do not cover all transnational conflicts. Some conflicts do not reach the necessary level of violence and some non-state actors lack the required degree of organization necessary to be a party to a NIAC.

A new legal regime of Extra-State Armed Conflicts or Transnational Armed Conflicts within an IHL framework is unnecessary.

In cases where transnational conflicts are not governed by the laws of NIACs, they are governed by IHRL which is applicable extra-territorially.

An IHRL based transnational law enforcement regime presents as an adequate legal framework to regulate transnational conflicts, which fall below the threshold of armed conflicts.

An IHRL based transnational law enforcement regime is to be preferred over an extended NIAC regime due to the negative effect that the laws of NIACs have with respect to the protection of civilians.

There is no room for a new legal regime based on a state's right to self-defense which conflates the distinction between *jus ad bellum* and *jus in bello*.

The Colombian example offers guidance on how an armed conflict and a law enforcement situation can be differentiated and how, through different legal regulations and certain procedural requirements, the military can be used as a law enforcement agent.

An integrated approach of NIAC and transnational law enforcement is recommended when a transnational conflict oscillates between violence short of and above the armed conflict level.

Bibliography

Abi-Saab, Georges, Non-International Armed Conflicts, in International Dimensions of Humanitarian Law, 217 (UNESCO *ed.* 1988)

Abi-Saab, Georges, Wars of National Liberation in the Geneva Conventions and Protocols, 165 Recueil des Cours de l'Academie de Droit International de la Haye 353 (1979)

Abresch, William, A Human Rights Law of Internal Armed Conflict: the European Court of Human Rights in Chechnya, 16 European Journal of International Law 741 (2005)

Akande, Dapo, Classification of Armed Conflicts: Relevant Legal Concepts, in International Law and the Classification of Conflits 32 (Elizabeth Wilmshurst, ed. 2012)

Alston, Philip, The CIA and Targeted Killings Beyond Borders, 2 Harvard National Security Journal 283 (2011)

Ambos, Kai, Bestätigung der deutschen Strafgewalt für "Kriegsverbrechen" in Bosnien-Herzegowina, 20 Neue Zeitschrift für Strafrecht, 71 (2000)

Anderson, Kenneth, Targeted Killing in US Counterterrorism Strategy and Law (2009), online available at http://www.brookings.edu/~/media/Files/rc/papers/2009/0511_counterterrorism_anderson/0511_counterterrorism_anderson.pdf (last visited Jan. 27, 2011)

Arnold, Roberta, The ICC as a New Instrument for Repressing Terrorism (2004)

Bassiouni, M. Cherif, Legal Control of International Terrorism: A Policy-Oriented Assessment, 43 Harvard International Law Journal 83 (2002)

Bellinger, John, Legal Issues in the War on Terrorism, 8 German Law Journal, 735 (2007)

Ben-Naftali, Orna and Shany, Yuval, Living in Denial: The Application of Human Rights in the Occupied Territories, 37 Israel Law Review 17 (2003-2004)

Bierzanek, Remigiusz, Quelques remarques sur l'applicabilité du droit internaitional humanitaire des conflits armés aux conflits internes internationalisés, *in* Etudes et essais sur le droit international humanitaire et sur les principes de la Croix-Rouge. En l'honneur de Jean Pictet. Genève 281 (Christophe Swinarski and Jean Pictet, eds., Nijhoff Publ. 1984)

Bothe, Michael, Friedenssicherung und Kriegsrecht in Völkerrecht 639 (Wolfgang Graf Vitzthum ed. 2010)

Bothe, Michael, Friedenssicherung und Kriegsrecht in Völkerrecht 589 (Wolfgang Vitzthum and Michael Bothe eds., 2004)

Bothe, Michael, Partsch, Karl J. and *Solf, Waldemar A.*, New Rules for Victims of Armed Conflicts (1982)

Bothe, Michael, Streitkräfte internationaler Organisationen, 103 (1968)

Bothe, Michael, The Status of Captured Fighters, *in* The Right to Life 195 (Christian Tomuschat, Evelyne Lagrange and Stefan Oeter, eds. 2010)

Bradley, Curtis A. and *Goldsmith, Jack L*, The Constitutional Validity of Military Commissions, 5 The Green Bag, 249 (2002)

Bredt, Friederike, Anwendbarkeit des humanitären Völkerrechts im Israel-Palästina-Konflikt (2009)

Brownlie, Ian, International Law (2008).

Bug, Mathias; Enskat, Sebastian; Fischer, Susanne; Klüfers, Philipp; Röllgen; Jasmin and *Wagner, Katrin*, Strategien gegen die Unsicherheit. Europäische Sicherheitsmaßnahmen nach 9/11, 86 Friedenswarte 53 (2011)

Cassel, Douglas, Pretrial and Preventive Detention of Suspected Terrorists: Options and Constraints under International Law, 98 Journal of Criminal Law and Criminology 811 (2008)

Cassese, Antonio, International Law (2005)

Cerone, John, Jurisdiction and Power: The Intersection of Human Rights Law and the Law of Non-International Armed Conflict in an Extraterritorial Context, 40 Israel Law Review, 396 (2007)

Corn, Geoffrey and Jensen, Eric Talbot, Transnational Armed Conflict: A "Principled" Approach to the Regulation of Counter-Terror Combat Operations, 42 Israel Law Review 46 (2009)

Corn, Geoffrey and *Jensen, Eric Talbot*, Untying the Gordian Knot: A Proposal for Determining Applicability of the Laws of War to the War on Terror, 81 Temple Law Review 787 (2008)

Corn, Geoffrey, Making the Case for Conflict Bifurcation in Afghanistan: Transnational Armed Conflict, Al Qaeda, and the Limits of the Associated Militia Concept, 39 Israel Yearbook on Human Rights 27 (2009)

Corn, Geoffrey, What Law Applies to the War on Terror?, in The War on Terror and the Laws of War: A Military Perspective 1 (2009)

Crawford, Emily, The Treatment of Combatants and Insurgents under the Law of Armed Conflict (2010)

Dederer, Hans-Georg, Krieg gegen Terror, 59 Juristen Zeitung 421 (2004)

Delbrück, Jost, Proportionality, in Encyclopedia of Public International Law, Vol. 3, 1140 (1984)

Detter, Ingrid, The Law of War (2000)

Dinstein, Yoram, The Conduct of Hostilities under the Law of International Armed Conflict (2004)

Dinstein, Yoram, The Condunct of Hostilities under the Law of Interantional Armed Conflict (2nd ed. 2010)

Dinstein, Yoram, War, Aggression and Self-Defence (2011)

Dörmann, Knut and *Doswald-Beck, Louise*, Elements of War Crimes under the Rome Statute of the International Criminal Court (2004)

Dörmann, Knut, The Legal Situation of "Unlawful/Unprivileged Combatants", 85 International Review of the Red Cross 45 (March 2003)

Doswald-Beck, Lousie, The Right to Life in Armed Conflict: Does International Humanitarian Law Provide all Answers?, 88 International Review of the Red Cross 881 (2006)

Draper, Gerald I. A. D., The Geneva Conventions of 1949, 114 Recueil des Cours de l'Academie de Droit International de la Haye 59 (1965)

Duffy, Helen, The "War on Terror" and the Framework of International Law (2005)

Fischer, Thomas, Strafgesetzbuch mit Nebengesetzen, § 34 Fn 7 (2012)

Fitzpatrick, Joan, Speaking Law to Power: The War Against Terrorism and Human Rights, 14 European Journal of International Law 241 (2003)

Fleck, Dieter, Non-International Armed Conflict: Legal Qualifications and Parties to the Conflict, in International Humanitarian Law and other Legal Regimes: Interplay in Situations of Violence 27 (International Institute of Humanitarian Law ed. 2003)

Fleck, Dieter, The Law of Non-International Armed Conflict, *in* The Handbook of International Humanitarian Law, 581 (Dieter Fleck ed. 2013);

Frostad, Magne, Jus in Bello after September 11, 2001 (2005)

Frowein, Jochen Abr., Artikel 2 (Recht auf Leben), in Europäische Menschenrechtskonvention – EMRK-Kommentar (Jochen Abr. Frowein and Wolfgang Peukert eds., 3rd ed. 2009)

Frowein, Jochen Abr., Das de-facto-Regime im Völkerrecht. Eine Untersuchung zur Rechtsstellung „nichtanerkannter Staaten" und ähnlicher Gebilde (1968)

Gasser, Hans-Peter and *Melzer, Nils*, Humanitäres Völkerrecht, (2012)

Gasser, Hans-Peter, Internationalized Non-International Armed Conflicts: Case Studies of Afghanistan, Kampuchea and Lebanon, 33 American University Law Review 145 (1983)

Gasser, Hans-Peter and *Dörmann, Knut*, Protection of Civilian Population, in The Handbook of International Humanitarian Law, 231 (Dieter Fleck ed. 2013)

Geiß, Robin, Armed Violence in Fragile States: Low-Intensity Conflicts, Spillover Conflicts, and Sporadic Law Enforcement Operations by Third States, 873 International Review of the Red Cross 127 (2009)

Geiß, Robin, Asymmetric Conflict Structures, 864 International Review of the Red Cross 775 (2006)

Goodman, Ryan, The Detention of Civilians in Armed Conflicts, 103 American Journal of International Law 48 (2009)

Goppel, Anna, Killing Terrorists – A Moral and Legal Analysis (2013)

Grabenwarter, Christoph and *Pabel, Katharina*, Europäische Menschenrechtskonvention (5th ed. 2012)

Greenwood, Christopher, Essays on War in International Law (2006)

Greenwood, Christopher, Historical Development and Legal Basis, in The Handbook of International Humanitarian Law, 1 (Dieter Fleck ed. 2008)

Greenwood, Christopher, International Law and the 'War against Terrorism', 78 International Affair, 301 (2002)

Greenwood, Christopher, Scope of Application of Humanitarian Law, in The Handbook of International Humanitarian Law, 45 (Dieter Fleck ed. 2008)

Grote, Rainer, Between Crime Prevention and the Laws of War, in Terrorism as a Challenge for National and International Law: Security Versus Liberty? 951 (Christian Walter ed., 2004)

Guilfoyle, Douglas, Counter-Piracy Law Enforcement and Human Rights, 59 International and Comparative Law Quarterly 141 (2010)

Hafetz, Jonathan, Habeas Corpus After 9/11: Confronting America's New Global Detention System (2011)

Hakimi, Monica, International Standards for Detaining Terrorism Suspects: Moving Beyond the Armed Conflict-Criminal Divide, 33 Yale Journal of International Law 369 (2008)

Hankel, Gerd, Das Tötungsverbot im Krieg (2011)

Henckaerts, Jean-Marie and Doswald-Beck, Louise, Customary International Humanitarian Law, Vol. I, Rules (2005)

Henkin, Louise, Human Rights, in Encyclopedia of Public International Law, Vol. 2, 886 (1995)

Herdegen, Matthias, Völkerrecht (2013)

Hess, Martin, Die Anwendbarkeit des humanitären Völkerrechts, insbesondere in gemischten Konflikten (1985)

Hoffmann, Bruce, Inside Terrorism (2006)

Hosni, Lori, The ABCs of the Geneva Conventions and Their Applicability to Modern Warfare, 14 New England Journal of International and Comparative Law 135 (2007)

Ipsen, Knut, Combatants and Non-Combatants, in The Handbook of Internatoinal Humanitarian Law, 79 (Dieter Fleck ed. 2013)

Ipsen, Knut, Menzel, Eberhard and *Epping, Volker*, Völkerrecht *(*2004)

Ipsen, Knut, Zum Begriff des "internationalen bewaffneten Konflikts", in Recht im Dienst des Friedens FS für Eberhard Menzel 405 (Jost Delbrück et al. eds. 1975)

Jenks, Chris, Law From Above – Unmanned Aerial Systems, Use of Force, and the Law of Armed Conflict, 85 North Dakota Law Review 649 (2009)

Jinks, Derek, September 11 and the Laws of War, 28 Yale Journal of International Law 1 (2003)

Jochnick, Chris, Confronting the Impunity of Non-State Actors: New Fields for the Promotion of Human Rights, 21 Human Rights Quarterly 56 (1999)

Johann, Christian, Art. 15 -Abweichen im Notstandsfall, in EMRK – Konvention zum Schutz der Menschenrechte und Grundfreiheiten 433 (Ulrich Karpenstein and Franz C. Mayer eds., 2012)

Johnstone, Ian, The UN Security Council, Counterterrorism and Human Rights, in Counterterrorism: Democracy's Challenge 335 (Andrea Bianchi & Alexis Keller, eds. 2008)

Jones, Sarah; Schulz, Jenny and *Castan, Melissa*, The International Covenant on Civil and Political Rights (2004)

Kalshoven, Frits, International Armed Conflict: Legal Qualification and IHL as Lex Specialis, in International Humanitarian Law and Other Legal Regimes: Interplay in Situations of Violence, 63 (International Institute of Humanitarian Law ed. 2003)

Kleffner, Jann K, Operational Detention and the Treatments of Detainees, in The Handbook of the International Law of Military Operations 465 (Terry D. Gill and Dieter Fleck eds., 2010)

Kleffner, Jann K, Section IX of the ICRC Interpretive Guidance on Direct Participation in Hostilities: The end of Jus in Bello Proportionality as We know it? 45 Israel Law Review 35 (2012)

Kleffner, Jann K., Scope of Application of International Humanitarian Law, in The Handbook of International Humanitarian Law, 43 (Dieter Fleck ed. 2013)

Kost, Timo, Mounir El Motassadeq – A missed Chance for Weltinnenpolitik, 8 German Law Journal, 443 (2007)

Kreß, Claus, Friedenssicherungs- und Konfliktvölkerrecht auf der Schwelle zur Postmoderne, 23 Europäische Grundrechte-Zeitschrift 638 (1996)

Kreß, Claus, Gewaltverbot und Selbstverteidigungsrecht nach der Satzung der Vereinten Nationen bei staatlicher Verwicklung in Gewaltakte Privater, 197 (1995)

Kreß, Claus, Some Reflections on the International Legal Framework Governing Transnational Armed Conflicts, 15 Journal of Conflict and Security Law 245 (2010)

Kreß, Claus, Völkerstrafrecht der dritten Generation gegen transnationale Gewalt Privater?, in Die Macht und das Recht, 323 (Gerd Hankel ed., 2008)

Kretzmer, David, Rethinking the Application of IHL in Non-International Armed Conflicts, 42 Israel Law Review 8 (2009)

Lefkowitz, David, Collateral Damage in War – Esssays in Political Philosophy, 145 (Larry May, ed. 2008)

Lombardi, Aldo Virgilio, Bürgerkrieg und Völkerrecht (1976)

Lubell, Noam and *Derejko, Nathan*, A Global Battlefield? Drones and the Geographical Scope of Armed Conflict, 11 Journal of International Criminal Justice 87 (2013)

Lubell, Noam, Extraterritorial Use of Force Against Non-State Actors (2010)

Mammen, Lars, Völkerrechtliche Stellung von internationalen Terrororganisationen (2008)

Melzer, Nils, Targeted Killing in International Law (2008)

Meron, Theodor, The Martens Clause, Principles of Humanity, and Dictates of Public Conscience, 94 American Journal of International Law 78 (2000)

Meyrowitz, Henri, The Law of War in the Vietnamese Conflict, in The Vietnam War and International Law 516 (Richard A. Falk ed., 1969)

Milanovic, Marko and *Hadzi-Vidanovic, Vidan*, A Taxonomy of Armed Conflict, in Research Handbook of International Conflict and Security Law 256 (Nigel White & Christian Henderson, eds. 2013)

Milanovic, Marko, Extraterritorial Application of Human Rights Treaties: Law, Principles and Policy (2011)

Milanovic, Marko, Lesson for Human Rights and Humanitarian Law in the War on Terror: comparing Hamdan and the Israeli Targeted Killings Case, 89 International Review of the Red Cross 373 (June 2007)

Modirzadeh, Naz, The Dark Sides of Convergence: A Pro-Civilian Critique of the Extraterritorial Application of Human Rights Law in Armed Conflict, 86 U.S. Naval War College International Law Studies (Blue Book) Series 349 (2010)

Moir, Lindsay, The Law of Internal Armed Conflict (2002)

Münkler, Herfried, Der Wandel des Krieges (2006)

Münkler, Herfried, The Wars of the 21th Century, 85 International Review of the Red Cross 7 (2003)

Murphy, Sean D., International Law (2006)

Naske, Nina and *Nolte, Georg*, Aerial Security Law, 101 American Journal of International Law 466 (2007)

Nolte, Georg, Preventive Use of Force and Preventive Killings: Moves into a Different Legal Order, 5 Theoretical Inquiries in Law 111 (2004)

Nolte, Georg, The Bundesverfassungsgericht on the German Aerial Security Law: A Sonderweg from Perspective of International Law?, in The Right to Life 83 (Christian Tomuschat, Evelyne Lagrange and Stefan Oeter, eds. 2010)

O'Connell, Daniel Patrick, International Law, Vol. 1 (1970)

O'Connell, Mary Ellen, Defining Armed Conflict, 13 Journal of Conflict and Security Law 393 (2009)

Oeter, Stefan, Terrorismus und Menschenrechte, 40 Archiv des Völkerrechts 422 (2002)

Parks, W. Hays, Air War and the Law of War, 32 Air Force Law Review 1 (1990)

Parks, W. Hays, Memorandum of Law: Executive Order 12333 and Assassination, 1989 Army Lawyer 4 (1989)

Paulus, Andreas and Vashakmadze, Mindia, Asymmetrical War and the Notion of Armed Conflict – A Tentative Conceptualization, 91 International Review of the Red Cross 95 (2009)

Paust, Jordan J, Self-Defense Targetings of Non-State Actors and Permissibility of U.S. Use of Drones in Pakistan, 19 Journal of Transnational Law and Policy 237 (2010)

Paust, Jordan J, War and Enemy Status after 9/11: Attacks on the Laws of War, 28 Yale Journal of International Law 325 (2003)

Paust, Jordan J., There Is No Need to Revise the Laws of War in Light of September 11th, The American Society of International Law Task Force on Terrorism (2002)

Pejic, Jelena, "Unlawful/Enemy Combatants": Interpretations and Consequences", in International Law and Armed Conflict 335 (Michael Schmitt and Jelena Pejic eds., 2007)

Pejic, Jelena, Terrorist Acts and Groups: A Role for International Law? 75 British Yearbook of International Law, 71 (2004)

Pfanner, Toni, Asymmetrical Warfare from the Perspective of Humanitarian Law and Humanitarian Action, 87 International Review of the Red Cross 149 (March 2005)

Pictet, Jean S., Commentary on the Geneva Convention (IV) Relative to the Protection of Civilian Persons in Times of War (1958)

Pictet, Jean S., Commentary on the Geneva Convention for the Amelioration of the Condition of the Wounded and Sick in Armed Forces in the Field (1952)

Pictet, Jean S., Commentary on the Geneva Convention relative to the Treatment of Prisoners of War (1960)

Prill, Florian, Präventivhaft zur Terrorismusbekämpfung (2009)

Provost, René, International Human Rights and Humanitarian Law (2004)

Quénivet, Noelle, The Application of International Humanitarian Law to Situations of a (Counter-)Terrorist Nature, in International Humanitarian Law and the 21st Century's Conflicts 25 (Roberta Arnold and Pierre-Antoine Hildebrand eds. 2005)

Quénivet, Noelle, The Right to Life in International Humanitarian Law and Human Rights Law, in International Humanitarian Law and Human Rights Law 331 (Roberta Arnold and Noelle Quenivet, eds. 2008)

Ratner, Steven R. and *Abrams, Jason S.,* Accountability for Human Rights Atrocities in International Law (2001)

Riedel, Eibe H., Recognition of Belligerency, in Encyclopedia of Public International Law, Vol. 4, 47 (2000)

Roberts, Adam, Transformative Military Occupation: Applying the Laws of War and Human Rights, 100 American Journal of International Law 580 (2006)

Römer, Jan, Killing in a Gray Area between Humanitarian Law and Human Rights Law (2010)

Rona, Gabor, Interesting Times for International Humanitarian Law: Challenges form the "War on Terror", 27/2 Fletcher Forum of World Affairs, 55 (2003)

Rosand, Eric, Den Terrorismus weltweit bekämpfen, 57 Vereinte Nationen 99 (2009)

Safferling, Christoph J.M., Terror and Law – Is the German Legal System able to deal with Terrorism? – The Bundesgerichtshof (Federal Court of Justice) decision in the case against El Motassadeq, 5 German Law Journal, 515 (2004)

Sageman, Marc, Leaderless Jihaad (2008)

Sandoz, Yves, Swinarski, Christophe and *Zimmermann, Bruno* (eds.), Commentary on the Additional Protocols of 8 June 1997 to the Geneva Conventions of 12 August 1949 (1987)

Sassòli, Marco and *Olson, Laura M.*, The Relationship between International Humanitarian and Human Rights Law where it matters: Admissible Killing and Internment of Fighters in Non-International Armed Conflicts, 90 International Review of the Red Cross 599 (2008)

Sassòli, Marco, Terrorism and War, 4 Journal of International Criminal Justice 959 (2006)

Sassòli, Marco, Transnational Armed Groups and International Humanitarian Law, Occasional Paper Series, Program on Humanitarian Policy and Conflict Research, 5 (Harvard University Winter 2006)

Scalabrino, Michelangela, Fighting Against International Terrorism: The Latin American Response, *in* Enforcing International Law Norms Against Terrorism 163 (Andrea Bianchi ed., 2004)

Schabas, William A., Theoretical and International Framework: Punishment of Non-State Actors in Non-international Armed Conflicts, 26 Fordham International Law Journal 907 (2003)

Schäfer, Bernhard, Zum Verhältnis Menschenrechte und humanitäres Völkerrecht, (2006)

Schaller, Christian, Humanitäres Völkerrecht und nichtstaatliche Gewaltakteure (Stiftung Wissenschaft und Politik Studie 2007)

Schindler, Dietrich, The Different Types of Armed Conflicts according to the Geneva Conventions and Protocols, 163 Recueil des Cours de l'Academie de Droit International de la Haye 117 (1979)

Schmitt, Michael N., Targeted Killings in International Law: Law Enforcement, Self-defense, and Armed Conflict, in International Humanitarian Law and Human Rights Law 525, 534 (Roberta Arnold and Noelle Quénivet eds. 2008)

Schmitz-Elvenich, Heiko F., Targeted Killing (2008)

Schöndorf, Roy S., Extra-State Armed Conflicts: Is there a Need for a New Legal Regime?, 37 New York University Journal of Law and Politics 1 (2004)

Schübel-Pfister, Isabel, Art 1 ZP XIII – Abschaffung der Todesstrafe, in EMRK – Konvention zum Schutz der Menschenrechte und Grundfreiheiten 428 (Ulrich Karpenstein and Franz C. Mayer eds., 2012)

Schulte, Dominik, Der Schutz individueller Rechte gegen Terrorlisten (2010)

Silja Vöneky, The Fight against Terrorism and the Rules of International Law – Comment on Papers and Speeches of John B. Bellinger, Chief Legal Advisor to the United States State Department, 8 German Law Journal, 747 (2007)

Sivakumaran, Sandesh, The Law of Non-International Armed Conflict (2012)

Slaughter, Anne-Marie and *Burke-White, William*, An International Constitutional Moment, 43 Harvard International Law Journal, 1 (2002)

Sloane, Robert D., Prologue to a Voluntarist War Convention, 106 Michigan Law Review 443 (2007)

Spieker, Heike, The International Criminal Court and Non-International Armed Conflicts, 13 Leiden Journal of International Law 395 (2000)

Stahn, Carsten, International Law at a Crossroads? 62 Zeitschrift für ausländisches öffentliches Recht und Völkerrecht, 184 (2002)

Stahn, Carsten, Terrorist Acts as "Armed Attack": The Right to Self-Defense, Article 51(1/2) of the UN Charter, and International Terrorism, 27/2 The Fletcher Forum of World Affairs 35 (2003)

Starck, Christian, Anmerkung, 61 Juristenzeitung 417 (2006)

Stephens, Dale, Military Involvement in Law Enforcement, 92 International Review of the Red Cross 453 (2010)

Stewart, James G., Towards a Single Definition of Armed Conflict in International Humanitarian Law: A Critique of Internationalized Armed Conflicts, 85 International Review of the Red Cross 313 (2003)

Tams, Christian J. and Devaney, James G., Applying Necessity and Proportionality to Anti-Terrorist Self-Defence, 45 Israle Law Review 91 (2012)

Tomuschat, Christian, Der Sommerkrieg des Jahres 2006 im Nahen Osten, 81 Friedenswarte 179 (2006)

van Steenberghe, Raphaël, Proportionality under Jus ad Beluum and Jus in Bello: Claryfying their Relationship, 45 Israel Law Review 107 (2012)

Vité, Sylvain, Typology of Armed Conflicts in International Humanitarian Law: Legal Concepts and Actual Situations, 91 International Review of the Red Cross, 69 (2009)

Volz, Markus, Extraterritoriale Terrorismusbekämpfung (2007)

von der Groeben, Constantin, Criminal Responsibility of German Soldiers in Afghanistan: The Case of Colonel Klein, 11 German Law Journal No 5, 469 (2010)

von der Groeben, Constantin, The Conflict in Colombiaand the Relationship between Humanitarian Law and Human Rights Law in Practice, 16 Journal of Conflict and Security Law 141 (2011)

Vöneky, Silja, Die Anwendbarkeit des humanitären Völkerrechts auf terroristische Akte und ihre Bekämpfung, in Rechtsfragen der Terrorismusbekämpfung durch Streitkräfte, 149 (Dieter Fleck and Wolfgang S. Heinz eds. 2004)

Wandscher, Christiane, Internationaler Terrorismus und Selbstverteidigungsrecht (2006)

Warbrick, Colin, The European Response to Terrorism in an Age of Human Rights, 15 European Journal of International Law 989 (2004)

Weissbrodt, David, Immigration, in Max Planck Encyclopedia of Public International Law, Vol 5, 84, (Rudiger Wolfrum, ed., Oxford University Press, 2012)

Zechmeister, David, Die Erosion des humanitären Völkerrechts in den bewaffneten Konflikten der Gegenwart *(*2007)

Zegveld, Liesbeth, Accountability of Armed Opposition Groups in International Law (2003)

Index